The 7 DISCIPLINES OF Breakthrough Results

How to Predictably Achieve High Performance for DGs, CEOs, ESs, PSs, Directors, and Senior Leadership Teams in the Public Sector

Dr. Bolaji Olagunju

lift PUBLISHING

Published by Lift Publishing

Copyright 2024 © Lift Publishing

Disclaimer

All names of persons and organizations used in this book are fictitious and do not represent any actual individuals or entities.

Cover Design: Shayo

Interior Design: meadencreative.com

Hardcover ISBN: 978-1-7339779-2-0

Tradepaper ISBN: 978-1-7339779-3-7

Digital ISBN: 978-1-7339779-0-6

First edition: August 2024

Dedication

In the annals of our history reside heroes unsung.

They are the leaders, past and present, living and dead, who took public leadership to heights never before seen in our country. I would name names, but we all know them. Their results and records are forever etched in time, and they speak even where they no longer have a voice.

They are the men and women who made the vow to serve, not just with words, but with their hearts, souls, and spirits. Their results were different because the fabric of their commitment, competence, and patriotism was different.

They went into service not for glory nor selfish gain, but to make fractured worlds whole; to build the bridge between the hopes and reality of the people they served. They spoke for the voiceless, championed justice, and faced the darkness with unwavering light.

Their leadership competencies were nothing short of extraordinary. They were masters of their fields who understood what needed to be done. They communicated their visions compellingly, dialogued without bias, and diagnosed the deepest needs of the people they were called to serve at a depth that most shy away from. Armed with quality insights, they crafted master strategies and empowered their teams to execute them with maniacal devotion.

The results? They produced breakthrough results that amounted to miracles.

This book is dedicated to these extraordinary leaders.

In remembering them, we celebrate not just their achievements but their enduring legacy—a testament to the power of LEADERSHIP rooted in integrity, driven by purpose, and dedicated to the collective welfare of a nation.

How different would our world be if more of them existed?

May their legacy guide us all to build a brighter future for our beloved country.

Preface

After twenty-eight years of advising senior leaders and board members of private and government entities across Africa on strategic transformations to deliver organizational success, I was inspired to create a public leadership roadmap for achieving solid, quantifiable, and breakthrough results.

The inspiration for *The Seven Disciplines of Breakthrough Results* did not arise from quiet study or a sudden flash of insight. It emerged from the trenches, from witnessing firsthand the daily grind, the daunting challenges, and the incredible weight of responsibility that public leaders carry every single day.

The Call That Changed Everything

About a decade ago, I received a call that would alter my career path and fundamentally change my perspective on public leadership. The caller was a friend, newly appointed as the head of a major public institution. Amidst the celebratory congratulations, a serious tone took over as he shared his apprehensions and ambitions. He did not just want to fill his role; he wanted to redefine it. He aimed to leave a legacy of effective governance and significant public impact.

His call was not just a plea for help; it was a challenge to immerse myself in the underestimated complexities of public sector leadership. With my background in private sector consulting, where efficiency and results are paramount, my transition to the public sector's unique landscape was profound and eye-opening. This experience marked the beginning of a journey into understanding and redefining public leadership.

The Realities of Public Sector Challenges

Working closely with my friend, it quickly became apparent why many public leaders struggle to translate their vision into reality. The public sector's intricacies are manifold: bureaucratic inertia, political pressures, public scrutiny, and the colossal task of managing resources efficiently. Each day brought new insights into how these factors can stifle innovation and hinder effective leadership.

The challenges were not just organizational but deeply personal. Public leaders often face loneliness in their roles, compounded by the weight of public expectations and the constant balancing act between various stakeholder interests. This environment can be unforgiving, and the cost of failure is not just a personal setback but a public one, affecting lives and communities.

A Resolve to Forge a New Path

Determined not to let these challenges be an endpoint but a beginning, I committed to developing a deeper understanding of what constitutes effective leadership in the public sector. This commitment led to years of study, observation, and interaction with numerous public leaders who had either excelled or faltered in their roles.

My exploration was guided by three key questions:

- What distinguishes successful public leaders from those who fail?
- How can effective leadership practices be standardized and taught within the public sector?
- Is there a scalable model that can consistently promote high performance and ethical governance?

These questions demanded rigorous investigation and thoughtful reflection. They required dissecting successful leadership cases and understanding failures not as mere setbacks but as learning opportunities.

Building the Framework: Research and Collaboration

The development of the model presented in this book was neither quick nor easy. It involved extensive research, including academic studies, leadership theories, and direct consultations with successful leaders. Each discipline of the proposed model was tested and refined through real-world application and feedback.

Collaboration was key. Engaging with academics, experienced public administrators, and emerging leaders provided diverse perspectives that enriched the model. This collaborative approach ensured that the model was robust, versatile, and applicable across various contexts within the public sector.

Lessons from the Field

Throughout this journey, several key lessons emerged that shaped the final model:

- The importance of context: Effective public leadership is highly contextual. Strategies that work in one setting may not work in another due to cultural, economic, and social differences.

- The need for adaptability: Public sector environments are dynamic. Leaders who succeed are those who can adapt their strategies to changing circumstances without losing sight of their core objectives.

- The power of ethical leadership: More than in any other sector, public leadership must be grounded in ethics and transparency. The public's trust is both fragile and essential.

The Model Comes to Life

The culmination of this journey is the Seven-Discipline Model that forms the core of this book. Each discipline has been crafted to address specific aspects of public leadership, from establishing effective communication (dialogue) to ensuring that plans are executed and objectives met (drive). The model is designed not only to improve individual leaders' effectiveness but also to enhance the institutional performance of public sector organizations.

Sharing the Vision: The Book as a Beacon

Writing this book became the next logical step in sharing the knowledge and strategies that I had developed and honed. It is intended as both a manual and a manifesto, a guide for current and future leaders who face the evolving challenges of public sector leadership.

The Seven Disciplines of Breakthrough Results is more than just another book on public leadership; it is a goal, a commitment, and a journey. It reflects a belief in the potential of good leadership to transform public institutions and, by extension, the societies they serve.

This book is an invitation to all public sector leaders to join in this transformative journey; to learn, apply, and lead with excellence, guided by a model that was both forged in the complexities of real-world challenges and has been proven in practice.

Within these pages, I trust that you will discover a wealth of valuable insights. May you then translate that knowledge into actions that deliver breakthrough results for the people and communities you have pledged to serve.

Dr. Bolaji Olagunju
Director General
National Leadership Organization
dg@nlonigeria.org
nlonigeria.org/breakthroughresults
Abuja, Nigeria
August 2024

Contents

Introduction

Public service is not just a job. It is a calling to go beyond doing what is necessary to what is possible.

– Barbara Jordan

Do leaders shape the future? Can a handful of individuals truly transform the lives of millions? Perhaps a better way to ask this question is: Have past leaders, in any way or form, shaped the present we now live in? The answer is obvious: Absolutely.

Leaders are undeniably vital to the outcomes of our world. Their decisions, actions, and vision not only influence immediate outcomes but echo through generations. Behind most institutional failures, and most problems in the world today, lies a leadership deficiency challenge. Leadership is almost always the cause, and all the problems we see are merely effects.

When leaders get things right, the spheres within their influence—whether state, organization, or nation—prosper. Conversely, when institutions or nations fail to deliver on their mandates, it is often because their leaders have failed to foresee, adapt to, or effectively manage the challenges they face. History is rife with the consequences of effective and ineffective leadership, and our world bears the mark to this day. It is therefore not an overstatement to say that everything rises and falls on leadership.

This principle holds particular weight in Africa, where many countries face persistent issues like corruption and poverty despite their immense economic potential.

For decades, there have been numerous calls for a more transformative approach to leadership that will elevate African economies mired in underdevelopment. They all convey one message: **The future of Africa hinges on achieving breakthrough results in the public sector.**

In this context, breakthrough results refer to substantial and transformative changes achieved through high-performance leadership practices that significantly enhance the efficiency, effectiveness, and impact of public services. Breakthrough results go beyond incremental improvements; they address the root causes of systemic issues, leading to profound and lasting positive outcomes for communities and society as a whole.

The development of every nation hinges on the quality of the public institutions that run the country. Therefore, if a nation is to develop, the responsibility rests on the leaders within those public institutions to deliver breakthrough results that tackle the core issues impeding progress.

However, as critical as breakthrough results are to the survival and success of public institutions and the nations they serve, such results never happen by chance. They are achieved through strict adherence to firm principles and disciplined practices. Without adherence to these disciplines, any results a leader produces will be by happenstance and, at best, unpredictable and unrepeatable.

Peter F. Drucker, renowned as the father of modern management, emphasized this clearly when he said, "**Only three things happen naturally in organizations: friction, confusion, and underperformance. Everything else requires leadership.**"

The fundamental job of the best leaders, therefore, is not just to ensure that performance occurs sporadically; it is to transform the very DNA of their organizations and alter how they work to deliver long-term results.

This is the purpose of this book. It was written to support public leaders in delivering transformative outcomes, and it is premised on the belief that the time is now for a new mindset and a fresh approach to leadership in the African public sector. It is founded on the belief that Africans have the solutions to Africa's challenges. By achieving breakthrough results within their institutions, public leaders can catalyze a renaissance and unlock the continent's immense potential.

The Imperative of Effective Leadership and Breakthrough Results in the African Public Sector

In the African public sector, the need for breakthrough results has never been more pressing. As the continent grapples with a myriad of challenges ranging from poverty and inequality to inadequate infrastructure and governance issues, the demand for transformative leadership has reached a critical juncture. With Africa's population projected to double by 2050, unprecedented pressure will be placed on public services, infrastructure, and resources. Persistent issues such as poverty, corruption, unemployment, and inadequate healthcare and education systems cannot be effectively addressed through business-as-usual approaches. Breakthrough results are needed to tackle these problems head-on and create sustainable solutions that uplift communities and drive progress.

Without significant changes in healthcare, education, and urban planning, the continent risks being overwhelmed by the demands of its rapidly expanding population. Public leaders must rise to this challenge by implementing visionary strategies that anticipate and meet the needs of future generations.

However, as urgent and undeniable as this need is, breakthrough results will never materialize if leaders remain entrenched in outdated paradigms and cling to familiar routines. Replicating past strategies in the face of evolving challenges stifles innovation and limits growth potential. Traditional methods, hierarchical structures, and bureaucratic processes constrain creativity and hamper progress.

To deliver breakthrough results, leaders must boldly challenge the status quo, question established norms, and venture into uncharted territory.

They must embrace new ideas, cultivate a culture of experimentation where failure is seen as a stepping stone to success, and leverage emerging technologies.

This is crucial because at the heart of every successful public sector organization lies strong and visionary leadership. The importance of effective leadership in the public sector extends far beyond individual organizations. It directly impacts the well-being and prosperity of entire communities and nations. When public sector leaders are effective, they can drive positive change, improve service delivery, and foster economic growth. Conversely, when leadership falters, the consequences can be severe, leading to inefficiency, mismanagement, and a loss of public trust.

Moreover, effective leadership sets the tone for organizational culture and values. Leaders who prioritize transparency, accountability, and integrity create an environment where employees feel empowered and motivated to perform at their best. This, in turn, leads to higher levels of engagement, productivity, and job satisfaction.

As we look to a future that will be fraught with rapid technological advancements, demographic shifts, and global challenges, the need for visionary, ethical, and highly effective African public leaders has never been greater. These leaders will only emerge by investing in context-driven leadership education that equips them with the capabilities and knowledge to navigate the complexities of the African public sector.

This context-driven leadership education, crucial for driving breakthrough results, begins with and hinges upon a comprehensive understanding of the environment in which public sector leaders operate.

Understanding the Public Sector Landscape

Just how challenging public leadership is remains one of the most underappreciated realities of our world today.

While leadership in other sectors plays a crucial role in the proper functioning of society, each contributing to various aspects of our collective well-being, public sector leadership stands out because it impacts the lives of millions of people daily. Business leaders might influence a company or industry, but public leaders shape businesses, industries and entire communities and nations. The sheer number of individuals and entities impacted by public sector decisions elevates the importance of public leadership and makes it inherently more demanding and challenging.

All across the globe, public sector leaders face vastly different and more challenging conditions than their private sector counterparts. They must deftly navigate a web of diverse stakeholders, including government officials, elected representatives, regulatory bodies, civil servants, advocacy groups, and the general public, each with unique priorities and expectations.

Moreover, they are bound by stringent regulations that curtail flexibility, demanding expertise and patience to implement changes or innovative solutions within a bureaucratic framework. Public leaders also operate under constant scrutiny and political influence. They must withstand media attention, public debate, and intense external pressure. All of this necessitates adeptness at transparency, effective communication, and fostering public trust.

In addition to these challenges, they must constantly adapt to a changing external environment, which makes leadership in the public sector exceptionally demanding yet indispensable.

This ongoing need to navigate a landscape filled with bureaucratic red tape, political pressures, public accountability, and resource constraints significantly complicates decision-making and strategic planning. These factors profoundly impact a public leader's ability to effectively execute organizational agendas and deliver substantial societal value.

A Leadership Gap in Critical Competencies

To navigate the complexities of public sector management, leaders require a unique blend of capabilities. Specifically, they need to master seven critical disciplines that, if well-engineered, can enable leaders to create breakthrough results for their organizations.

Mastery of these disciplines will achieve three key outcomes for leaders: First, they will enable leaders to envision a brighter future for their communities and equip them to translate those visions into actionable plans. Second, the disciplines will strengthen their role as visionary and strategic leaders, equipping them with the innovative capabilities needed to challenge the status quo and find creative solutions within established regulations. Third, mastery of these disciplines will empower public leaders to effectively balance wielding authority to guide their teams and inspire action while fostering collaboration through the consideration of diverse perspectives.

Yet, for the most part, leadership development programs in the public sector focus predominantly on administrative competencies without providing sufficient opportunities for leaders to master the vital capabilities required for strategic vision, adaptability, and the capacity to innovate, inspire, and execute their strategies. Few leadership development curricula offer leaders a thorough education in the disciplines that create transformative results for organizations. As a result, the pervasive influence of public leaders often falls short of its potential, leading to inconsistencies, gaps, and missteps that affect millions.

Our societies are desperate for competent leaders—individuals who aspire not just to lead but to transform; leaders who envision better communities and robust institutions. However, the complexity of public sector leadership, with its unique demands and high stakes, requires more than just good intentions. It demands a practical framework that addresses the specific challenges of public governance—a framework that effectively enables leaders to master the seven disciplines that produce breakthrough results for organizations.

This framework is precisely what *The Seven Disciplines of Breakthrough Results* offers.

What to Expect from This Book

To truly grasp the value within these pages, it is necessary to define the concept of "breakthrough results."

The term "breakthrough" is often used casually, but at its core, what does it truly mean? "Breakthrough" conveys a sense of significant progress or achievement. It implies a substantial leap forward, not just incremental improvement. A true breakthrough has a lasting impact. It is not a fleeting success but a substantial change that creates a ripple effect of positive consequences.

In the context of leadership, a leader who achieves breakthrough results goes beyond what has been accomplished before, reaching an unprecedented level of success or progress that represents a major leap forward.

Breakthrough results are not just about being competent or achieving basic goals; they are about pushing boundaries and reaching levels of success that were previously thought impossible. It is about exceeding expectations and creating lasting positive change.

How different would our world be if more public leaders aimed for and achieved breakthrough results?

With these definitions in mind, the promise of *The Seven Disciplines of Breakthrough Results* is clear: It offers any public leader who sincerely yearns to make a difference a disciplined approach to consistently achieve exceptional results.

Some may question the feasibility of such a promise. They may doubt the possibility of consistently achieving high performance in the public sector.

Public leadership is intricate, demanding, and often unpredictable. Is consistent high performance feasible in this ever-evolving landscape?

Overwhelmingly, evidence from extensive research papers, reports, and datasets focusing on governance and leadership within both developing and developed countries suggests that it absolutely is.

Research has proven that disciplined public leaders substantially enhance their chances of success by:

1. Utilizing frameworks and roadmaps to establish structure amidst chaos, navigate complexity, facilitate informed decision-making, and cultivate high-performing teams while adhering to core leadership principles.

2. Basing critical decisions on data, not guesswork; letting evidence guide their path rather than relying on intuition, thus ensuring effective problem-solving.

Think of it as constructing a house: A blueprint (a disciplined approach) does not guarantee perfection, but it vastly improves outcomes compared to improvisation.

Regrettably, most leaders, sworn into office with great expectations, are woefully unprepared for the demanding task ahead.

Yet history has repeatedly shown that exceptional leaders do not achieve their results by going in blind or winging it. They do not bank on random luck or individual brilliance. Instead, they become students of high performance, studying and leveraging replicable strategies that can be learned and applied, ultimately delivering exceptional results that earn them recognition and acclaim.

This book offers an accessible and practical blueprint to support public leaders in establishing structure amidst chaos, navigating complexity, and executing well-informed strategies that enable them to deliver exceptionally on their mandates.

A Proven Model for High-Performance Leadership

Built on extensive research, personal experience, and the synthesis of best practices from highly effective public sector leaders worldwide, *The Seven Disciplines of Breakthrough Results* has been designed as an indispensable resource for public sector leaders who aspire to drive significant change and achieve high standards of performance in their organizations.

The core objective of this book is to transform the practice of public leadership by providing a comprehensive, proven model that enhances both individual leadership capabilities and organizational effectiveness.

This book addresses the critical need for a specialized approach to public sector leadership—a need underscored by the unique challenges of governance and public accountability. Through a blend of theoretical insights and practical strategies, it aims to equip leaders with the tools and knowledge necessary to excel in their roles.

The Unique Value Proposition of This Book

The unique value of this book lies in its integration of empirical research with real-world applications, making it both a scholarly and a practical guide. Unlike other leadership books that may offer generic advice, *The Seven Disciplines of Breakthrough Results* probes deep into the specificities of the public sector, providing tailored advice that considers the complexities of governmental operations, public policy, and community engagement.

A Brief Exploration of the Model

This book hinges on a groundbreaking Seven-Discipline Model, meticulously crafted to guide public leaders toward exceptional achievements. These disciplines were not randomly chosen or mere theoretical constructs; they are the culmination of extensive research and have been proven to be effective in real-world public sector applications.

Each chapter within the book is dedicated to a discipline, providing a comprehensive exploration of the importance, applications, and real-life examples of successful implementation of each discipline.

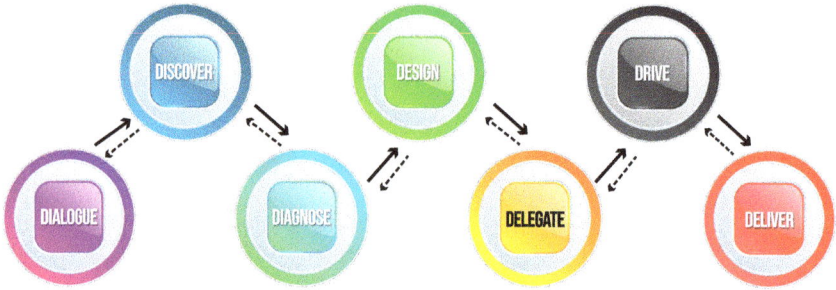

Figure 1. The Seven Disciplines of Breakthrough Results

The following is a glimpse into the seven disciplines that constitute the model:

1. **Dialogue:** Building trust through effective communication.

2. **Discover:** Identifying key opportunities for success.

3. **Diagnose:** Uncovering the root causes of organizational issues to facilitate data-driven decisions for maximum impact.

4. **Design:** Moving from vision to actionable strategies.

5. **Delegate:** Empowering teams to implement strategies and achieve peak performance.

6. **Drive:** Converting ideas and strategies into measurable results.

7. **Deliver:** Setting up systems and infrastructures to institutionalize high performance within organizations.

Each of these disciplines is accompanied by actionable steps, tools, and techniques that leaders can immediately apply. The discussions include challenges that leaders may face when implementing these disciplines and provide strategies for overcoming such obstacles.

Anticipated Outcomes

By following the model presented in this book, public sector leaders can expect to achieve several key outcomes:

- Enhanced leadership effectiveness: Leaders will develop stronger leadership skills that are specifically tailored to the needs and challenges of the public sector.

- Improved organizational performance: Organizations will benefit from strategies that improve efficiency, responsiveness, and service delivery.

- Increased public trust and engagement: Through effective leadership practices, leaders will be able to build trust and foster greater engagement with the communities they serve.

- Sustainable impact: The strategies and practices outlined in the book are designed to promote long-term improvements and sustainable success in public sector organizations.

How This Book is Structured

The Seven Disciplines of Breakthrough Results is more than just a collection of chapters, it is a meticulously crafted roadmap designed to guide public sector leaders on a progressive journey toward leadership excellence. This journey builds upon each step, seamlessly transforming theoretical knowledge into actionable practice.

Having established the foundation of the model's necessity, we can now turn our attention to the book's organizational framework, exploring the unique features and layout that facilitate a deep understanding and application of the Seven-Discipline Model.

Part 1: As the Journey Begins

Chapter 1: The Call to Leadership – This chapter sets the stage by exploring the fundamental role of leadership in the public sector. It addresses the intrinsic challenges and rewards, providing an inspiring call to action for current and aspiring leaders. The chapter discusses the profound impact of effective leadership on organizational success and public trust, emphasizing the high stakes involved in public sector leadership roles.

Chapter 2: Discipline 1: Dialogue – Dialogue is the first of the seven disciplines and is critical for establishing a foundation of trust and clear communication. This chapter focuses on strategies for effective communication that engage both internal team members and external stakeholders. Techniques for navigating complex political landscapes and managing public expectations are also covered, providing leaders with tools to foster transparency and inclusivity.

Part 2: Understanding the Situation

Chapter 3: Discipline 2: Discover – Discovery involves gathering and analyzing information that informs leadership decisions. This chapter teaches leaders how to implement systematic methods for understanding the environments in which they operate, including analyzing stakeholders, environmental scanning, and leveraging data for strategic insights.

Chapter 4: Discipline 3: Diagnose – Following discovery, diagnosis helps leaders identify not just problems but opportunities. This chapter delves into methodologies for assessing organizational health and performance, guiding leaders in using analytical tools to pinpoint areas for improvement and innovation.

Part 3: Execute

Chapter 5: Discipline 4: Design – Designing effective strategies and structures is essential for achieving organizational goals. This chapter focuses on translating insights gained from the discovery and diagnosis phases into actionable strategies that align with both organizational capacities and external demands.

Chapter 6: Discipline 5: Delegate – Delegation is crucial for operational efficiency and empowering teams. This chapter provides a framework for identifying which tasks to delegate and to whom, discussing how to ensure accountability and foster skill development within teams.

Chapter 7: Discipline 6: Drive – Drive encompasses the techniques and leadership behaviors required to maintain momentum and ensure the implementation of strategies. This chapter covers motivational techniques, overcoming resistance to change, and sustaining drive within oneself and one's team.

Part 4: Excel

Chapter 8: Discipline 7: Deliver – The final discipline is about leaving a lasting impact. It discusses how leaders can extend their influence beyond their immediate organizational roles, contributing to broader societal outcomes and setting the stage for sustainable success and ongoing improvement.

Chapter 9: Conclusion: Putting It All Together – This chapter wraps up the journey through *The Seven Disciplines of Breakthrough Results*, highlighting the crucial role of disciplined leadership in achieving high performance in the public sector. It recaps the challenges faced by public leaders and reemphasizes the need for a clear roadmap to navigate these obstacles.

Unique Features and Learning Tools in This Book

Each chapter is enhanced with specific learning tools designed to deepen understanding and facilitate the application of the concepts discussed:

- Case studies: True-to-life examples from public sector settings illustrate the practical application of each discipline.

- Facilitator manuals and checklists: In the book's appendix, you will find comprehensive manuals and checklists summarizing actionable steps for leaders and facilitators to implement the discussed disciplines.

- Online Support Resources: The book's appendix also includes a link to online supplementary materials, such as video tutorials, webinars, and upcoming workshops.

Who Should Read This Book?

The Seven Disciplines of Breakthrough Results is designed to serve a broad spectrum of readers within the public sector, each of whom plays a critical role in shaping the landscape of public services. From directors-general, CEOs, executive secretaries, and permanent secretaries to senior leadership teams, the book equips leaders with a practical framework to achieve exceptional outcomes in the public sector.

Essentially, the book caters to the following audiences:

- **Newly appointed public sector leaders** – New leaders often face a steep learning curve, and this book provides them with a structured pathway to understanding the complexities of public sector leadership. It equips them with essential skills and strategies to navigate their new roles effectively.

  Key benefits: New leaders will develop a strong foundation in public sector leadership dynamics, acquire critical skills for managing teams and projects, and learn how to implement strategies and changes that promote organizational improvement.

- **Experienced public sector leaders** – This book offers valuable insights and strategies for experienced leaders looking to refresh their skill set or gain fresh perspectives on advanced leadership challenges.

  Key benefits: Seasoned leaders will develop advanced leadership techniques to elevate their public organizations to new heights.

- **Aspiring leaders** – Individuals aspiring to step into leadership roles in the future will find this book an invaluable resource to prepare themselves for the challenges and opportunities of public sector leadership.

  Key benefits: Aspiring leaders will gain a head start by understanding the demands of effective public sector leadership and cultivating the necessary skills and leadership approaches for future success.

- **Strategic Leadership Support:** Chiefs of Staff, Special Advisers, Executive Assistants, Technical Assistants, and Heads of Strategy can use this book to gain leverage and enhance their strategic execution support, helping leaders achieve desired results.

- **Policy makers and government officials:** Those involved in shaping policies that affect leadership structures and practices in the public sector can gain insights into fostering leadership qualities that enhance organizational effectiveness and public trust.

- **Academics and students in public administration:** Educators and students specializing in public administration or related fields can use this book as a resource to understand the practical aspects of leadership beyond theoretical concepts.

- **Human resources professionals in the public sector:** HR professionals can use this book to help devise training programs and development plans that align with proven leadership models, enhancing the overall capability of their organizations.

- **Consultants specializing in organizational development:** Consultants who provide advisory services to public sector organizations can utilize the strategies and models discussed in this book to enhance their service offerings and support their clients more effectively.

Go from reading to leading powerfully

This book can transform your results as a public leader. Let it!

When most people buy a book like this, their intention is usually to extract knowledge and apply it to get quality results in their roles. Unfortunately, somewhere along the line, many readers become passive consumers of information.

Let this book be different. It is not designed to be a passive read; it is designed as a catalyst for real change. While the content has been painstakingly developed for maximum impact, the true power lies in your commitment to its implementation.

By actively engaging with the content and embracing its implementation, you have the potential to make a significant and lasting impact on the organization you serve.

Remember, *The Seven Disciplines of Breakthrough Results* is NOT just a guide for ideation; it is a call to action, to concrete execution.

If your desire is indeed to be a public leader who delivers breakthrough results, you have in your hands the tools to actualize that desire powerfully. In doing so, you will find that there is no higher calling than the opportunity to make a difference in people's lives and improve the world.

PART 1
AS THE JOURNEY BEGINS

Chapter 1
The Call to Public Leadership

Congratulations!

You have just been elected or re-elected to public office. If this is your first time, what do you imagine awaits you? If you imagine that your call to public leadership is a call to fame, prestige, and access to unlimited resources and power, you have imagined it wrong. If you imagine that it is a call to serve the common good and that the path will be smooth and easy, again, you have imagined it only half correctly.

What then is your call?

The call to public leadership is a call to responsibility. It is a call to be a change-maker. It is a call to be the bridge between the dreams of people and the reality on the ground. It is a summons to shoulder the weight of the hopes and aspirations of the people you serve, to be their voice in the corridors of power and to advocate tirelessly on their behalf for a more just and equitable society.

The call to public leadership is a relentless pursuit of progress, a constant wrestling with complex issues, and a commitment to leaving the organization, constituent, state, or nation better than you found it. It is a commitment to serve effectively, and sometimes at great expense to your person. The call to leadership is a tough call.

As with all things complex and tough to put into words, an anecdote that captures the true essence of the difficulties of public leadership is necessary.

The Burden of Command: The Case of Toka Peterson

Toka Peterson had always aspired to make a difference in the world, a desire that led him to pursue a career in public service. His journey began with promise and passion, fueled by his commitment to serving his country. With years of hard work, Toka climbed the ranks to eventually become the head of the National Health Services Department, a position that placed him at the helm of public health initiatives across the nation. It was a role he had dreamt of, one that offered the chance to effect significant change—but it was also a role that would test him beyond his expectations.

The Glittering Start

Toka's tenure began under promising circumstances. The media lauded his innovative approach and his mandate to reform the healthcare system. He was celebrated at conferences and featured on magazine covers, portrayed as the face of progressive change in a sector fraught with challenges. The external glamour of his position was undeniable. He received invitations to speak at international events and was often recognized by grateful citizens in public.

Yet, as the months passed, the sheen of his new role began to dim under the harsh realities of public sector leadership. The weight of his responsibilities became a daily burden, and the complexities of his position soon overshadowed the initial excitement.

The Weight of Reality

Toka's first major initiative was a comprehensive healthcare reform intended to increase accessibility and reduce costs. However, he quickly encountered a web of bureaucratic red tape and conflicting interests from various stakeholders. Each decision required navigating a maze of regulations, with constant pushback from powerful interest groups and government officials resistant to change.

The criticism was unrelenting. Media outlets, once supportive, scrutinized every minor setback, amplifying them to the public. What most people didn't see was the brutal nature of Toka's daily grind—the late nights, the weekends spent working instead of being with his family, and the strain on his health.

The Crisis Unfolds

The defining moment of Toka's career came with the outbreak of a disease of unknown origin. The situation required swift, decisive action and transparent communication, qualities expected of a leader in his position. Initially, Toka handled the crisis with aplomb, managing resources and coordinating responses across departments. But as the outbreak worsened, so did the public and political pressures.

Toka found himself caught between the demands of the government, which wanted quick fixes, and the reality of medical and logistical limitations. The media frenzy intensified, with every new death adding to a narrative of failure on his part. Public confidence waned, and with it, the support from his political superiors.

Exhausted, stressed, and feeling isolated, Toka's health began to falter. The relentless pressure led to high blood pressure and severe anxiety, which he kept hidden from his team and family. The fear of appearing weak or incapable in the eyes of the public and his peers kept him from seeking the help he desperately needed.

The Fall

The situation reached a breaking point when, during a crucial national briefing, Toka was publicly berated by a high-ranking government official for his perceived incompetence. The official's harsh words, delivered in front of his peers and subordinates, struck a deep blow to Toka's confidence and morale. This humiliating experience, coupled with the relentless pressure and criticism he faced, shattered his resolve. Feeling demoralized and disheartened, Toka began to question his ability to lead effectively.

The incident became a turning point in Toka's career, marking the beginning of his downward spiral. His once unwavering commitment to public service was overshadowed by self-doubt and uncertainty. He struggled to regain his footing amidst the mounting challenges and setbacks, but the damage to his reputation and confidence proved to be irreversible.

As news of the incident spread, rumors and speculation about Toka's competence began to circulate within the corridors of power. His credibility as a leader was called into question, and doubts were cast on his capacity to handle the responsibilities of his position. The fallout from the incident further eroded Toka's standing within the organization and undermined his ability to garner support for his initiatives.

Unable to bear the weight of the scrutiny and criticism, Toka resigned. As he grappled with the fallout from the incident, Toka was forced to confront the harsh realities of public leadership and the toll it can take on even the most dedicated and capable individuals.

This case study vividly illustrates the immense challenges and responsibilities inherent in public leadership. Even with the best intentions, leading in the public sector demands deep resilience, adaptability, and a proven roadmap to navigate the complexities and uncertainties ahead.

The rest of this chapter delves deeply into the essence of public leadership, offering a comprehensive exploration of its true significance. We will examine the core meaning of leadership, distinguishing between what it truly is and what it is not. The harsh realities of serving as a public leader will be discussed, along with the intrinsic rewards of public service. We will also address the high stakes of public leadership by examining both the short- and long-term consequences of ineffective leadership and highlighting common reasons why public leaders often miss the mark.

The chapter will conclude by identifying the essential qualities of the public leaders that Africa needs. By the end, you will have a nuanced understanding of public leadership and be better equipped with insights to guide your journey as a leader committed to making a profound impact.

Dissecting the Real Meaning of Public Leadership

At its heart, the sole purpose of public leadership is to **SERVE THE COMMON GOOD.** It is to advocate for the interests of society and ensure the equitable distribution of resources and opportunities.

It's about setting a vision, fostering collaboration, and making decisions that benefit the collective. Public leaders are entrusted with the responsibility of guiding communities, addressing societal challenges, and fostering inclusive and sustainable development. Public leadership is vital for the survival of society because it ensures effective governance, facilitates positive change, empowers communities, and tackles pressing issues.

Without effective public leadership, societies would struggle to function, progress, and adapt to a constantly changing world. In its absence, progress would stall, challenges would fester, and the very fabric of communities would unravel.

What Public Leadership is:

- **A commitment to the collective good:** True public leadership is about selfless service to the public. It is a call to prioritize the collective well-being of citizens over personal gain, special interests, or political ambitions. It is a call to courage, a call to confront entrenched interests, to challenge the status quo, and to stand up for what is right, even in the face of adversity. All too often, the fear of reprisal and political pressure can silence even the most well-intentioned leaders. But true leadership requires the courage to speak truth to power, to champion justice and equality, and to defend the rights of the marginalized and vulnerable. The decisions of public leaders must be driven by a deep desire to create a more just, equitable, and prosperous society for all.

True leaders prioritize the welfare of their constituents over personal gain, demonstrating humility, empathy, and a genuine commitment to improving society. They are the architects of a better future, not just for themselves, but for generations to come.

- **A commitment to be adaptive and resilient:** If public leaders are to succeed in the call to labor for the common good, then they must navigate complex and dynamic environments, adapt their approaches to changing circumstances, and overcome obstacles with resilience and determination. They are called to embrace innovation, learn from setbacks, and leverage adversity as an opportunity for growth.

- **A call to transparency and accountability:** Public trust is the oxygen of effective leadership. The call to public leadership is therefore a call to integrity. It is a commitment to uphold the highest ethical standards and to act with honesty and transparency. True public leaders hold themselves accountable to the people they serve. In a continent plagued by corruption and nepotism, maintaining integrity is perhaps the greatest challenge facing African public leaders. But it is also the most essential. Without integrity, trust in government will continue to erode, and the social contract between leaders and citizens will stay broken.

- **A call to effective collaboration:** Africa's most pressing challenges demand solutions bigger than any one person. The call to public leadership is therefore a compulsory call to collaboration. It is a call to recognize that no one person has all the answers, and that progress can only be achieved through collective effort. The most effective leaders build coalitions, forge partnerships, and harness the collective wisdom of diverse stakeholders to address complex challenges. Public leaders see collaboration not as a sign of weakness but of strength—a recognition that we are stronger together than we are apart.

What Public Leadership is Not

- **Self-promotion masquerading as service:** Public leadership is not about self-aggrandizement or using one's position for personal gain. It's about service, sacrifice, and a commitment to leaving a positive legacy, not accumulating wealth or influence. The spotlight is a tool to illuminate the path forward, not a stage for personal glorification.

- **The tyranny of the status quo:** The world is constantly evolving, and public leaders must be agents of positive change. True public leaders understand that clinging to the status quo serves no one. Therefore, they challenge outdated practices, embrace innovation, and champion solutions that meet the needs of the present and prepare for the future rather than succumbing to inertia or stagnation.

- **Authoritarianism or micromanagement:** True public leadership rejects authoritarian models, emphasizing participatory governance and respect for individual rights and dignity. Effective public leaders inspire and empower others. They create environments where creativity flourishes and diverse voices are heard because they understand that command-and-control tactics stifle progress and leave potential untapped.

- **Political expediency over long-term vision:** Public leadership requires a long-term perspective focused on sustainable solutions and enduring impact rather than short-term gains or popularity. True public leaders therefore make decisions based on principles and a vision for the future, not simply to appease short-term political pressures. They understand that the path to a better tomorrow may not always be popular but is the right course to take.

- **Isolationism:** Public leadership is not a solitary pursuit. When leaders operate in isolation, they disconnect from the public they serve and surround themselves with yes-men and like-minded individuals who reinforce their biases and hinder critical thinking. Isolation creates an echo chamber where flawed ideas go unchallenged, leading to poor decision-making.

In essence, public leadership is not about wielding power for power's sake but harnessing it for the common good. It's a demanding path, requiring dedication, resilience, and a willingness to make a difference, no matter the cost. Just how complex and challenging public leadership is will be the subject of our next exploration.

Unmasking the Realities of Public Leadership

Every public leader who has ever made a significant difference, the kind of impact that reverberates in the lives of people in their hundreds, thousands, and millions, can attest that the pathway to that achievement was fraught with difficulties. The late Dora Akunyili, former director-general of Nigeria's National Agency for Food and Drug Administration and Control (NAFDAC), spoke of the relentless pressure and personal toll such leadership demands. She famously faced death threats and intimidation tactics from powerful criminal organizations while combating the counterfeit drug trade. Yet, her unwavering commitment to public health, despite immense opposition, ultimately led to a significant reduction in the availability of counterfeit drugs in Nigeria, saving countless lives.

As the case of the former director-general of NAFDAC shows, while the trappings of public office may project an image of power and privilege, the day-to-day reality of these roles involves navigating a minefield of challenges that can have severe personal and professional repercussions.

A Deeper Exploration of the Complexities and Challenges of Leading in the Public Sector

Unlike the private sector, where profit margins and shareholder value reign supreme, public sector leaders confront a uniquely challenging landscape marked by intricate complexities, uncertainty, ambiguity, and volatility. These leaders face a relentless test of their capabilities and resilience, dealing with a broad spectrum of issues that test the mettle of even the most seasoned leader.

The following is an in-depth look at the dimensions of complexities and challenges public leaders navigate, highlighting the unique pressures that shape their daily lives as they operate in volatile, uncertain, complex, and ambiguous environments.

1. Systemic Complexities Public Leaders Must Navigate to Create Public Value

Public sector leaders encounter a myriad of inherent fundamental challenges and issues that are more structural and institutional in nature than isolated and occasional. Their deep-rooted nature poses great complexity for public leaders to tackle. In this aspect, some of the key challenges they contend with include:

- **Regulatory and compliance challenges**: Public sector leaders operate within environments that are highly regulated. They are constantly navigating a web of constantly changing laws, regulations, and mandates that govern public institutions. Failure to comply can lead to legal repercussions and operational inefficiencies.

- **Fiscal constraints**: Public sector leaders often face limited resources and budgetary restrictions. Maximizing output and efficiency becomes paramount, requiring them to be resourceful and make tough decisions about where to allocate scarce funds.

- **Changing political climates**: The public sector is subject to frequent shifts in policies and priorities, especially with changes in political leadership. Leaders face the challenge of adapting to new administrations or shifts in political agendas that overturn existing policies. This creates an environment of uncertainty where long-term planning becomes challenging. Leaders need to be flexible and resilient to navigate these changes, realign and build consensus for their own priorities, and manage the effect of changes on their institutions, plans, and programs.

- **Unclear policies**: Legislative mandates and policy directives are not always crystal clear. Ambiguity in legislative mandates and policy directives can complicate the ability of leaders to make decisive and effective decisions. Leaders must be able to resolve the challenges caused by ambiguities, vagueness, or conflicts in policies, legislation, and directives, consult with stakeholders, and make sound decisions within the boundaries of the law.

- **Bureaucratic and operational inefficiencies**: Excessive red tape, mandate overlaps, and outdated processes are experienced across the public service. Public leaders must learn to navigate the intricacies and complexities of intra-governmental relations and inter-agency coordination to steer their organizations to sustainable success.

2. Challenges of Managing Delicate Stakeholder Dynamics and Environmental Complexities

Today's public sector leaders face an unprecedented interplay of global complexities overlaid by escalating local intricacies and complications. The public sector is volatile not only due to the nature of the environmental landscape but also because of the diverse and often conflicting interests of various stakeholders. Leaders must adeptly manage these dynamics while striving to fulfill both the explicit needs (outlined in legislation) and implicit expectations (unsaid desires of the community) of these groups. The challenges they face in these areas include:

- **Constant crisis management**: The public sector is on the front lines when unforeseen crises strike both at the local and global levels. Leaders must be prepared to respond to public health emergencies, economic downturns, environmental issues, and the effect of international and local unrests on the supply chains under their purview with immediate and effective action. This requires resilience, a strong sense of urgency, clear decision-making abilities, and the capacity to inspire and lead during challenging times.

- **Political pressures**: Public leaders are not immune to political interference or expectations from political figures and parties. These pressures can influence decision-making and strategic priorities, sometimes compromising long-term goals for short-term political gains.

- **Opposition from vested interests**: Public sector initiatives often encounter resistance from powerful groups or individuals who may benefit from the status quo. Leaders must develop strategies to overcome opposition, build coalitions, and gain public support for their agendas.

- **Increasing public scrutiny**: Public sector leaders are under constant scrutiny of the public and media, who demand accountability. Meeting the direct needs of communities is crucial. These needs may vary widely across different regions, demographics, and socioeconomic backgrounds. Navigating media scrutiny requires transparency, effective communication strategies, and the ability to explain complex issues in clear and concise language. They must constantly balance the demands of good governance with the needs of the communities they serve, build public trust and ensure transparency and accountability in all their actions. This requires meticulous record-keeping, clear communication strategies, and a willingness to engage with the public openly and honestly. Finding common ground and balancing the needs and desires of multiple and diverse stakeholders is a constant balancing act. Public sector leaders must effectively engage with government officials, private sector partners, non-governmental organizations, and the public.

3. The Complexities of Adapting to Constant Change and Transitions in Public Service

Public sector leaders are likely to encounter a variety of changes throughout their tenure, demanding adaptability and a willingness to embrace continuous learning. Some key areas of change include:

- **Policy reforms**: The needs of society are constantly evolving. Public leaders must be prepared to implement new policies or reform existing ones in response to these changes. This requires a deep understanding of current issues, the ability to anticipate future needs, and the courage to make tough decisions that may not be universally popular.

- **Organizational restructuring**: Public institutions are not immune to mergers, splits, or reorganizations. Leaders must effectively manage these changes to minimize disruption, ensure a smooth transition, and maintain employee morale during periods of uncertainty.

- **Technological advancements**: Technology is rapidly transforming the way we live and work. Public sector leaders must be open to integrating new technologies to improve service delivery, enhance operational efficiency, and streamline processes.

- **Workforce dynamics**: The public sector workforce is changing. Leaders need to address changes in workforce demographics, expectations, and the evolving nature of work. This may involve developing new training programs, fostering a culture of innovation, and creating a work environment that attracts and retains top talent.

- **Global influences**: The world is interconnected. Public sector leaders must be aware of international events or global pressures that affect domestic policies and practices. Understanding these influences allows them to anticipate potential challenges, collaborate with international partners, and adapt their strategies accordingly.

Leading effectively in the public sector is undeniably intricate. It's not for the faint of heart. It's a crucible that will test your resolve, your ingenuity, and your capacity for compassion. There will be setbacks, moments of frustration, and days that feel like an uphill battle against an insurmountable tide. It will demand exceptional skills, unwavering resilience, and a deep commitment to serving the greater good. Yet, for those who are passionate about making a positive difference in the lives of others, the rewards are profound.

The Intrinsic Rewards of Public Service

The opportunity to shape public policy, improve public services, and leave a lasting legacy on society is a powerful motivator. Public sector leadership may be a thankless task at times, but for the dedicated leader, the satisfaction of knowing their work has a meaningful impact makes the journey worthwhile. Here are some of the key intrinsic rewards that attract and sustain passionate individuals in these roles:

- **Serving a cause greater than oneself:** Public service allows individuals to transcend personal ambitions and contribute to a cause far grander. Leaders and bureaucrats alike can find immense satisfaction in knowing their work directly benefits the collective good. From crafting policies that promote social justice to developing programs that improve public health, the very essence of public service is anchored in making a positive difference in the lives of others.

- **Witnessing the ripple effect of one's efforts:** The impact of public service often extends beyond immediate results. Policies enacted today can have a lasting ripple effect on future generations. Imagine a leader spearheading a campaign for early childhood education. Witnessing countless children benefit from improved learning opportunities decades later is a testament to the enduring impact of public service. Even seemingly small contributions can snowball into positive change, fostering a sense of pride and accomplishment.

- **The power to inspire and shape a better future:** Public leaders serve as role models, inspiring others to get involved and contribute to their communities. Effective public service leadership can spark a wave of positive change, encouraging citizens to become active participants in shaping their own destinies. For those driven by a desire to leave the world a better place, the opportunity to inspire others to work towards a common good is a deeply rewarding experience.

- **The constant pursuit of knowledge and growth:** Public service is a continuous learning journey. Navigating complex challenges, forging partnerships, and developing innovative solutions require a constant acquisition of new skills and knowledge. Leaders must stay abreast of current trends, immerse themselves in diverse perspectives, and adapt to an ever-changing landscape. This dynamic environment fosters intellectual growth and keeps leaders at the forefront of their fields.

- **The satisfaction of building a more just and equitable society:** Public service empowers individuals to tackle societal issues like poverty, inequality, and human rights abuses. The act of advocating for the vulnerable, crafting policies that promote fairness, and striving to create a level playing field can be immensely rewarding. Witnessing the positive transformation of communities and the increased well-being of citizens serves as powerful validation of the importance of public service.

- **Leaving a legacy of positive change:** Public service allows individuals to leave a lasting legacy. Crafting policies or implementing programs that shape the future of a community, a nation, or even the world is an unparalleled privilege. The knowledge that one's work has a positive impact on generations to come provides a profound sense of purpose and fulfillment.

Over the centuries, thousands of public leaders have learned firsthand that, while few challenges are as demanding as leading in the public sector, there are few honors greater than the privilege of improving the lives of thousands and millions through public service. As echoed by Woodrow Wilson, the twenty-eighth president of the United States, *"There is no higher religion than human service. To work for the common good is the greatest creed."*

The next section delves into the high stakes of public leadership, exploring common reasons for leadership failures and the short- and long-term consequences of ineffective leadership. By understanding these pitfalls, both seasoned and aspiring leaders can navigate the complexities of public service more effectively, striving to become the breakthrough leaders that Africa needs.

The High Stakes of Public Leadership

Considering the vast number of people affected by the decisions and actions of public leaders, along with the far-reaching consequences of their performance, the implication is clear: Leading in the public sector is more than just a job; it is a grave responsibility that carries immense importance. The consequences of ineffective leadership carry both short- and long-term implications as shown below.

The Short- and Long-term Consequences of Ineffective Leadership

Short-term consequences may manifest as inefficiencies within government agencies and departments, inevitably leading to frustration for citizens and businesses alike as essential services are delivered slowly or poorly.

Long-term consequences can be even more damaging and may include:

- **Institutional decay and democratic erosion**: Sustained weak leadership will weaken democratic institutions and erode the public's faith in government. This will eventually lead to corruption and a decline in civic engagement.

- **Economic decline and opportunity loss**: Ineffective leadership will inevitably stifle economic growth, leading to job losses, decreased investment, and a decline in living standards.

- **Social polarization and fragmentation**: When leaders fail to address societal needs or prioritize the interests of a select few, it often culminates in exacerbated social divisions and creates a climate of distrust.

- **Loss of global standing and influence**: On the international stage, ineffective leadership will ultimately damage a country's reputation and diminish its ability to influence global affairs.

While most public leaders understand these consequences and few enter office with a deliberate plan to underperform, the critical question we must explore and address is: Why, then, do public leaders underperform?

Common Reasons for Public Leadership Failures

Public leadership underperformance can stem from a variety of factors, ranging from individual shortcomings to systemic issues within the governance framework. Here are some common reasons why public leaders fail:

1. The Complexities and Pressures of Public Leadership

Public leadership underperformance often stems from the intricate complexities of the public sector and the intense pressures leaders face. Leaders must navigate a web of competing priorities and stakeholder demands within bureaucratic processes, often with insufficient resources due to chronic budget constraints. The constantly evolving political landscape, with shifting priorities and policy uncertainty, requires leaders to be highly adaptable. Political interference from actors, interest groups, or powerful elites can pressure leaders to prioritize partisan interests over the public good, compromising their effectiveness and integrity.

Additionally, the political cycle incentivizes short-term thinking, with leaders prioritizing immediate gains and re-election prospects over long-term strategic planning and sustainable solutions. This can result in the neglect of crucial infrastructure projects and underfunding of essential services. Public leaders also face relentless media scrutiny, where every word and action is dissected and judged. This can be emotionally draining, stifle creativity, and lead to isolation. Leaders unable to manage this pressure may struggle to make sound decisions or clearly communicate their vision.

2. The Challenges of Leading Change and Innovation

Public sector leaders face significant hurdles in driving change and fostering innovation. Bureaucratic inertia and resistance to change often stifle innovation, slow decision-making, and hinder the implementation of effective solutions. Leaders who cannot navigate this complex regulatory and procedural landscape may struggle to deliver on their promises. Additionally, the rapid pace of technological disruption demands that leaders embrace new technologies to enhance service delivery and operational efficiency. Those who fail to adapt risk falling behind and impeding progress.

Protracted national emergencies like unchecked inflation and economic downturns require immediate, innovative and effective action. Leaders must be prepared to manage both inherited and unforeseen crises, make sound decisions under pressure, and effectively communicate with the public during times of uncertainty. Leaders who are caught unprepared for crises, fail to communicate effectively, or make poor decisions under pressure can exacerbate the situation and erode public confidence.

3. Personal Shortcomings and Leadership Pitfalls

All too often, leaders falter due to a lack of clear vision and strategic thinking, which are essential for inspiring progress and guiding policy decisions. Poor decision-making, often driven by personal interests or political expediency rather than informed judgment, further complicates matters, potentially exacerbating existing issues or creating new ones. Effective leadership also relies heavily on adept communication and robust stakeholder engagement to build trust and achieve consensus among diverse constituencies. Leaders who fall short in these areas risk alienating the public and hindering meaningful progress.

Another factor that significantly inhibits a leader's ability to deliver impactful results is the influence of echo chambers and confirmation bias. When leaders surround themselves with like-minded advisors, they may struggle to consider alternative perspectives, leading to flawed decision-making and resistance to adapting to changing circumstances. Additionally, the pervasive issue of corruption poses a serious threat, eroding public trust and diverting resources away from vital services. Combating corruption demands an unwavering commitment to transparency and accountability, crucial for upholding the integrity of public institutions and ensuring fair service delivery.

Furthermore, the temptation of populism is another cause of underperformance. While appealing to the emotions and frustrations of the electorate can be a powerful political tool, leaders who resort to scapegoating and simplistic solutions over evidence-based policy risk disastrous outcomes. Public leaders who succumb to the allure of populism jeopardize public trust, undermine democratic institutions, and neglect the genuine needs of their constituents.

4. The External Environment: Broader Societal Challenges

Public leaders face formidable challenges in the broader societal context. Deep-seated issues like socioeconomic inequality and social unrest demand multifaceted approaches and long-term commitments. Failing to address poverty and inequality effectively can lead to instability and erode public confidence in leadership. Additionally, global challenges such as wars, pandemics, and economic recessions require leaders to collaborate with international partners. The inability to address these interconnected issues can have dire consequences for the well-being of citizens, emphasizing the need for robust, proactive leadership.

It is clear from the foregoing that public leadership failures are rarely the result of a single misstep, but rather an accumulation of avoidable errors. The consequences of these failures, especially when prolonged, can be devastating. They ripple outward, affecting both the immediate and long-term well-being of a nation. This underscores the critical importance of addressing broader societal challenges with strategic foresight and effective collaboration.

Public sector leadership is no trivial matter and certainly not something to be left to chance. The consequences of failure in this domain are profound, as evidenced by the economic stagnation, social unrest, and widespread poverty plaguing many underdeveloped and developing African countries today. Inflation, public debt, and food insecurity are at record highs, creating a critical situation.

As African nations grapple with these complex challenges, the time is ripe for a new generation of leaders to emerge—leaders who are both equipped and committed to delivering breakthrough results.

The Hallmarks of the Breakthrough Public Leaders that Africa Needs

For decades, we have recognized that our biggest challenge as a continent is leadership. We need leaders who are not just competent but who are single-mindedly committed to achieving significant positive change and progress for Africa. Individuals who are passionately driven to go beyond the ordinary to make a real difference in translating Africa's wealth in natural and human capital resources into prosperity for Africans. We need breakthrough leaders who possess the following unique set of attributes and qualities that are essential for addressing the complex challenges we face today:

- **Visionary leadership**: Breakthrough public leaders in Africa must exhibit visionary leadership, with a clear and inspiring vision for the future of their organizations and nations. They envision progress, prosperity, and social cohesion, rallying citizens and stakeholders behind transformative goals and initiatives. By articulating a compelling vision, these leaders inspire hope and mobilize collective action toward shared objectives.

- **Integrity and ethics:** Leaders who deliver breakthrough results are fierce about their integrity and are ethical to the core. They uphold the highest standards of honesty, transparency, and accountability in their governance practices. By fostering a culture of integrity, these leaders earn the trust and confidence of citizens, promote good governance, and combat corruption, which is a major impediment to development in many African countries.

- **Inclusive governance:** Breakthrough public leaders prioritize inclusive governance, ensuring that all segments of society have a voice in decision-making processes. They embrace diversity, respect human rights, and promote social justice and equality. By fostering inclusive governance, these leaders harness the collective wisdom and talents of diverse communities, driving innovation, and fostering social cohesion.

- **Courageous action:** Courage is one attribute an African leader must possess in hefty doses. They must demonstrate courage in confronting vested interests, challenging the status quo, and advocating for meaningful reforms, even in the face of adversity. By taking bold and principled action, these leaders will inspire confidence, instigate positive change, and overcome entrenched barriers to progress.

- **Agile and adaptable:** The world is constantly changing, and the leaders that Africa needs are adaptable. They are lifelong learners, continuously seeking out new information and fresh perspectives. They are comfortable navigating uncertainty and making adjustments to their strategies when necessary. They demonstrate flexibility, resilience, and agility in responding to emerging challenges and opportunities. By embracing change and innovation, these leaders effectively navigate complexities, seize opportunities, and steer their nations toward sustainable development.

- **Collaborative partnerships**: Collaboration is a key trademark that breakthrough public leaders possess. They forge strategic partnerships with diverse stakeholders, including governments, civil society, the private sector, and international organizations. By leveraging collective expertise and resources, these leaders amplify impact, drive innovation, and advance shared development priorities.

- **Tech-savvy and resourceful**: Breakthrough leaders leverage technology to improve governance, enhance service delivery, and bridge the digital divide. They are resourceful and adept at identifying and maximizing opportunities within limited resources.

- **Pan-African vision:** While recognizing the unique needs of their own nations, these leaders understand the interconnectedness of Africa. They foster collaboration and partnerships with other African nations to address regional challenges and promote continental development.

What Would It Take to Raise an Army of Breakthrough Leaders for Africa?

As millions of Africans grapple with poverty, limited resources, and social unrest, the need for breakthrough public leaders has never been greater. The leaders we need are those who possess the degree of patriotism, vision, integrity, and innovative thinking required to navigate complex socioeconomic and political landscapes and drive meaningful change that translates to improved services and a brighter future for all. But leaders like this don't arise by happenstance. We can only cultivate them through a highly efficient system for leadership development, built on a proven model for driving high-performance leadership.

This book, *The Seven Disciplines of Breakthrough Results*, provides existing and incoming leaders with exactly that.

Imagine it as a compass and roadmap for public leadership—a tool so integrated with the principles of exceptional leadership that it transforms the daunting task of public management into a structured, controllable process. This model is not just a theoretical framework but a practical guide that equips leaders to address the day-to-day challenges they face.

One of the most significant features of the model presented in this book is its capacity to create buy-in and engage stakeholders at every level. By learning how to involve stakeholders in the dialogue process, leaders can make decisions that reflect a wide range of perspectives and are more likely to be supported. This engagement fosters a sense of ownership across the organization, enhancing motivation and commitment to achieving shared goals.

Another equally important feature is its capacity to transform how leaders review and track performance. The model enables leaders to monitor progress, evaluate the effectiveness of their strategies, and make informed adjustments. This continuous loop of assessment and adaptation is essential for navigating the ever-changing landscape of the public sector and for meeting the high standards of accountability and transparency required in public administration.

Call to Action

Become a Leader Who Drives Breakthrough Results

The call to public leadership is a call to be a transformational force. It is a call not only to manage the present but also to fundamentally reshape the future of your organization, your community, your nation, and perhaps even the continent. It's a call to be a leader who:

- **Breaks cycles of poverty and inequality:** You are tasked with crafting policies and programs that empower individuals and communities to rise above their circumstances.

- **Ignites innovation and entrepreneurship:** Africa is a breeding ground for creativity and resourcefulness. Your role is to foster an environment where these qualities can flourish, leading to sustainable development and economic growth.

- **Upholds transparency and accountability:** Earning and maintaining public trust is paramount. You must be a champion for good governance, ensuring that resources are used effectively and decisions are made with integrity.

- **Embraces collaboration:** The challenges we face are complex and multifaceted. True progress requires collaboration across sectors, with governments, civil society, the private sector, and the international community working together towards shared goals.

This is the essence of the call to public leadership in Africa. It is a call to be a trailblazer, a champion for progress, and a tireless advocate for the people you serve.

It is a demanding yet incredibly rewarding path, offering the opportunity to leave a lasting legacy and contribute to a brighter future for generations to come. It is a chance to etch your name not only in the halls of power but also in the hearts and minds of the people you serve.

This is the call. Are you ready to answer?

Your journey to high performance and breakthrough results begins in Chapter 2.

Chapter 2
Discipline 1 - Dialogue

Imagine stepping into the role of director-general of a government agency renowned more for its failures than its successes. The initial flurry of congratulations has waned, leaving behind the stark reality: You face the daunting challenge of revitalizing an institution plagued by years of instability and scandal. This was the exact predicament Dr. Ahmed Soyab found himself in upon assuming leadership.

The Challenging Dilemma of Dr. Ahmed Soyab

Before Dr. Soyab's arrival, the agency had cycled through three directors-general in just five years, each departure leaving behind a trail of demoralization and ineffectiveness. The workforce, once vibrant and engaged, was now cynical and dispirited. Public opinion was at an all-time low, with recent leaders under investigation for corruption and nepotism.

Dr. Soyab faces a colossal task. He must not only steer the agency back to its original mandate but also restore trust and inspire a demoralized workforce. How can he introduce himself in a way that affirms his competence and dedication while also mobilizing widespread support? How can he instill a renewed sense of hope and rally the troops for the arduous journey ahead?

His challenge extends beyond making a memorable first impression. Dr. Soyab must foster an environment of openness and transparency. He needs to encourage his constituents to voice their challenges openly, share their perspectives, and suggest necessary changes. The path to transforming the agency into a high-performance organization requires full participation and engagement from every quarter.

A Leader at an Inflection Point

So, what steps should Dr. Soyab take to achieve these goals? How should he engage with his audience to secure their trust and lead the transformation of the agency? What strategies can he employ to ensure that the stakeholders are not just on board but are active participants in this transformation journey?

Consider the gravity of Dr. Soyab's situation: A leader at an inflection point, tasked with turning around the fortunes of an ailing public agency under the watchful eyes of a skeptical public and a wary workforce. How should he navigate these turbulent waters to foster a culture of excellence and integrity?

These are the dilemmas and challenges that Dr. Soyab—and many leaders like him—face as they step into roles of significant public and organizational responsibility. The obstacles delineated above are not exclusive to newly minted public institution leaders. Regrettably, those already entrenched in the public sector encounter similar intricate challenges when endeavoring to elevate agency performance, instigate change, foster transformation, enhance efficiency, and fulfill their mandates.

Whether new to the role or seasoned veterans, public sector leaders confront some of the most formidable hurdles in driving institutional effectiveness and performance. In light of these complexities, it becomes evident that the starting point for resolving the challenges confronting both new and established public sector leaders is **DIALOGUE.**

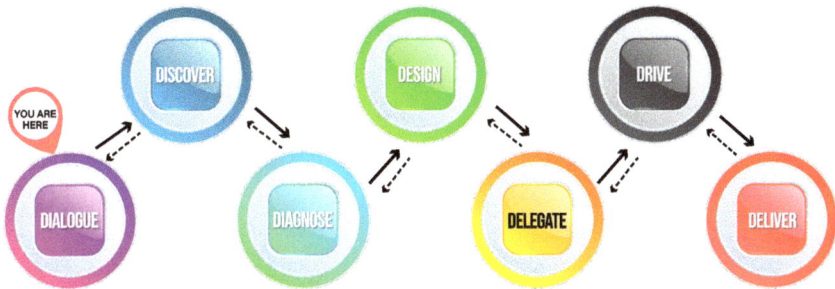

Figure 2. The Seven Disciplines of Breakthrough Results: Dialogue

Introduction to Dialogue: The Keystone of Public Sector Leadership

Many leaders mistakenly believe that leadership is about barking orders and telling people what to do. There is simply more to it than that. True leadership extends far beyond mere authority. As Colin Powell, a respected public leader, once said, "A leader is someone unafraid to take charge, someone people respond to and are willing to follow." The key here **lies in the willingness to follow.**

The foundation of effective leadership is rooted in establishing meaningful relationships that inspire others to follow willingly. Essential to forming these relationships is the ability to engage in effective dialogue.

While it is true that leaders must possess a variety of skills to be effective, the ability to engage others in dialogue is perhaps the most crucial skill, especially for leaders seeking to deliver breakthrough results. Dialogue serves as the very foundation for building relationships, establishing trust, and aligning visions. When done right, it fosters a safe space for open and honest conversation, leading to a more cohesive team with increased trust, understanding, and shared purpose.

Effective dialogue is therefore the first discipline that every leader must master, regardless of whether they are new or seasoned leaders in the public sector.

What is Dialogue in Public Leadership?

Dialogue, in the context of public sector leadership, transcends ordinary conversations. It is a deliberate, structured exchange that seeks to bridge the gap between leaders and their constituents, weaving together diverse threads of opinions, insights, and aspirations.

For a new leader, dialogue serves as a pivotal platform for introduction—an opportunity not only to impart their vision but also to absorb the cultural and operational ethos of the organization. For the established leader, it is a chance to reaffirm connections, reevaluate the path, and realign the organization's objectives with the needs of those it serves.

Dialogue must be approached from both internal and external perspectives. Internally, leaders must engage with their teams to foster an inclusive environment where every voice matters. This means actively listening to employees, understanding their concerns, and incorporating their feedback into decision-making processes. Externally, dialogue involves a deep engagement with the broader community, stakeholders, government entities, and private sector partners that the organization serves. This type of dialogue is essential for understanding and responding to the needs and expectations of the public.

Why is Dialogue Vital to Setting the Stage for Strong Performance?

The importance of dialogue cannot be overstated. It is the foundation upon which trust is built and leadership is legitimized. In the public sector, where the stakes include the welfare of communities and the efficiency of institutions, effective dialogue determines a leader's success in navigating the complexities of public administration. Dialogue is the leader's tool for unveiling the unspoken, understanding undercurrents, and unearthing organizational potential.

The Benefits of Well-Structured Dialogue

- **Setting new directions:** Through internal dialogue, leaders can introduce new ideas, assess readiness for change, and lay the groundwork for transformation. It allows them to articulate a fresh vision and set the direction for the organization's future.

- **Alignment and buy-in:** Strategic dialogue ensures that all stakeholders understand and align with the organization's goals. It builds consensus and fosters cooperative engagement, securing collective commitment.

- **Detecting and resolving issues**: Regular dialogue serves as an early diagnostic tool to identify and address issues before they escalate, keeping the organization proactive.

- **Observation and insight gathering**: Dialogue allows leaders to read verbal and non-verbal cues, revealing true sentiments and attitudes within the organization.

- **Understanding community needs:** By engaging with community members and other stakeholders, leaders can gain valuable insights into the issues and concerns that matter most to the public. This understanding allows for more targeted and effective policy-making.

- **Building public trust:** Transparent and consistent communication with external stakeholders builds public trust. When the community sees that their input is valued and acted upon, it enhances the credibility and legitimacy of the leadership.

- **Fostering partnerships:** External dialogue can lead to the development of strategic partnerships with other organizations. These collaborations can bring additional resources, expertise, and support, amplifying the impact of the agency's initiatives.

- **Unburdening hearts and renewing hope**: Open dialogue provides a therapeutic release, allowing team members to express concerns and frustrations constructively, renewing their hope and commitment.

- **Identifying change agents and insights**: Leaders can identify potential change agents and gather valuable insights that shape better policies and practices.

Embracing the Power of Dialogue

In an era of fragile public trust, effective dialogue with stakeholders is crucial for successful public service. It transforms challenges into opportunities, skepticism into support, and plans into actions. Leaders who excel in fostering open dialogue succeed in implementing sustainable changes, achieving goals, and maintaining high morale. These structured conversations allow leaders to take ownership, control complex situations, and guide their organizations toward exceptional performance.

Igniting transformation, setting new agendas, and rallying the troops all start with engaging in dialogue. This practice reflects a leader's commitment to transparency, inclusiveness, and responsiveness. As a leader, your ability to conduct effective dialogue will define your legacy and determine how well your organization responds to challenges, adapts to change, and fulfills its mandate.

In the rest of this chapter, we will explore how leaders can effectively master this discipline, ensuring that every dialogue contributes to moving their organization closer to its goals.

Mastering the Discipline of Dialogue in Public Sector Leadership

The ability to conduct effective dialogue is a fundamental skill for leaders across all sectors. However, in the public sector, it takes on paramount importance. Here, the quality of dialogue directly influences governance success and community well-being. This heightened significance prompts critical questions:

- How can effective and successful dialogue sessions be cultivated in this crucial context?

- What are the critical success factors for dialogue sessions in the public sector?

- What key elements must be present to ensure each dialogue session fulfills its purpose?

To establish a strong foundation for mastering the execution of effective public sector dialogue, we will start by exploring the core principles of productive dialogue.

Key Tenets of Productive Dialogue

Public sector dialogues require a purposeful structure and strategic direction. This structured approach ensures focused discussion, maximizes productivity, and achieves the desired outcomes. The key components of an effective public sector dialogue are:

- **Openness:** Leaders must approach dialogue with an open mind, actively listening to and considering diverse viewpoints without judgment or preconceived biases. This fosters a safe space for honest exchanges and fosters creative solutions.

- **Respect:** All participants, regardless of background or position, must feel respected and valued. Leaders should create an environment where everyone feels comfortable contributing and sharing their perspectives. This inclusivity leads to a wider range of ideas and fosters a sense of shared ownership.

- **Clarity:** Communication should be clear, concise, and jargon-free. Leaders should explain complex issues in understandable terms and actively encourage participants to ask questions. This ensures everyone is on the same page and can fully engage in the discussion.

- **Purpose:** Every dialogue session should have a clearly defined objective. Examples of such objectives are:

- Gather input: Leaders aim to understand citizen needs and priorities to inform policy development or program design.

- Communicate a policy change: Leaders explain a new policy direction and address potential concerns.

- Resolve a conflict: Stakeholders with differing viewpoints come together to find common ground and solutions.

- Build relationships: Leaders foster trust and collaboration between the public sector and the community.

With the key tenets of productive dialogue established, we will now demonstrate how leaders can effectively execute dialogue sessions to maximize productivity.

Executing Dialogue: A Stage-by-Stage Guide

Effective dialogue hinges on three fundamental stages, outlined below:

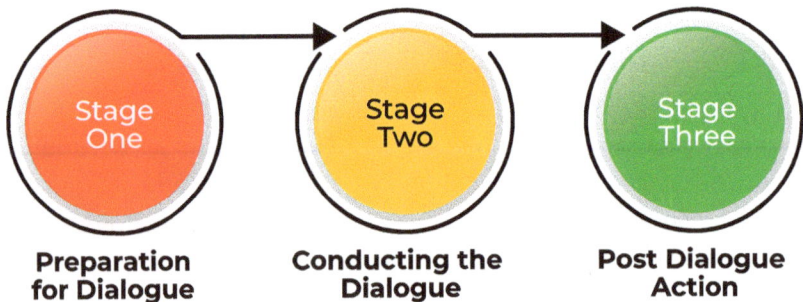

Stage One

Preparation for Dialogue

Stage Two

Conducting the Dialogue

Stage Three

Post Dialogue Action

Figure 3. The Three Stages of Dialogue

Stage 1: Preparing for Dialogue

An effective dialogue does not happen by accident; it requires careful preparation. Leaders must be clear about the purpose of the dialogue, the outcomes they expect, and the stakeholders they need to engage.

The following are the steps for preparing for dialogue:

- **Define the purpose**: Clearly identify the intended outcome of the dialogue session. Is it to introduce a new initiative, solve a problem, or gather specific information to inform decision-making? State this objective beforehand to ensure a focused discussion that facilitates achieving desired results. Specifying the information you hope to gather or the decisions that need to be made further clarifies the purpose and helps guide the dialogue.

- **Identify stakeholders**: Determine who needs to be involved in the conversation. This may include team members, other department heads, community leaders, or the general public.

- **Choose the right setting**: The setting can influence the tone and success of the dialogue. Choose a neutral and accessible location to encourage open and honest communication. The setting should also reflect the type of dialogue planned. Town halls might benefit from larger auditoriums, while focus groups might be better suited for smaller conference rooms.

- **Set the agenda:** Develop a clear agenda that outlines the topics to be discussed. It is helpful to outline the topics in a logical sequence, allocate sufficient time for each discussion point, and include opportunities for various participation methods (presentations, brainstorming sessions, Q&A sessions). Share this agenda with participants beforehand. This allows them to prepare their thoughts and questions, leading to a more productive dialogue.

- **Establish ground rules for respectful communication:** Begin by setting clear expectations for participation, ensuring that everyone has an opportunity to voice their opinions and perspectives in a respectful manner. Encourage participants to focus on constructive solutions and collaborative problem-solving rather than engaging in personal attacks or unproductive conflicts. Additionally, outline the decision-making process or method for reaching conclusions following the dialogue. Will it be a consensus-based approach, or will leader input be considered after the discussion?

Stage 2: Conducting the Dialogue

With a solid foundation laid through preparation, the focus shifts to effectively leading the dialogue session. This stage is critical and requires active, mindful engagement from the leader or facilitator to ensure a productive and inclusive discussion.

Here are the key techniques for facilitating an effective dialogue:

- **Active listening:** Leaders must demonstrate active listening, which goes beyond simply hearing the words spoken. This involves:

  - Nonverbal cues: Maintain eye contact, use body language that conveys attentiveness, and avoid distractions like checking phones.

  - Verbal acknowledgements: Nod your head, use phrases like "I understand" or "That's a good point" to show you're engaged.

  - Clarifying questions: Ask thoughtful questions to probe deeper and ensure you grasp the speaker's perspective fully.

- **Foster participation:** Encourage a safe space for all voices to be heard. Techniques to do this include:

  - Open-ended questions: Use questions that begin with "how," "why," or "what" to spark detailed responses and encourage participants to elaborate on their ideas.

  - Inviting quiet voices: Directly address individuals who haven't spoken, encouraging them to share their perspectives.

- **Manage disagreements constructively:** Disagreements are natural, but they can be channeled into productive discussions. Here's how:

  - Acknowledgement: Acknowledge differing viewpoints and validate the emotions behind them.

  - Find common ground: Seek areas of agreement and use them as a foundation for building towards solutions.

  - Focus on solutions: Encourage participants to move beyond identifying problems and brainstorm solutions together.

- **Capture key points:** Don't let valuable insights slip away. Capture key ideas, concerns, and suggestions through:

  o Visible note-taking: Write down key points on a whiteboard or flipchart for everyone to follow the discussion flow.

  o Designated recorder: Assign someone to document the dialogue electronically or with detailed notes for future reference.

- **Summarizing and reflecting:** Conclude by summarizing the key points discussed, decisions made, and any action items identified. This ensures everyone leaves with a clear understanding of the dialogue's outcomes and next steps.

Stage 3: Post-dialogue Actions

The success of a dialogue session extends beyond the closing remarks. Effective leaders capitalize on the momentum and insights gained by taking concrete steps to ensure meaningful action.

Below are some key follow-up strategies to maximize the impact of your dialogue:

1. Documenting and Sharing Key Outcomes

- **Formalize the discussion:** Create a clear and concise document summarizing the key points discussed, decisions made, and any action items identified.

- **Ensure accessibility and transparency:** Make this document readily available to all participants and relevant stakeholders. This ensures everyone is on the same page and fosters a sense of transparency.

- **Communicate broader impact:** Share the results of the dialogue with the wider organization or community, even those who were not present. This builds trust and demonstrates the value placed on citizen input or employee feedback.

2. Implementing Decisions and Fostering Accountability

- **Action planning:** Develop a concrete action plan that outlines the steps needed to implement the decisions made during the dialogue.

- **Assigning ownership:** Clearly assign responsibilities for each action item, ensuring everyone is accountable for their contribution.

- **Setting timelines:** Establish clear and achievable timelines for completing action items. This keeps the momentum going and ensures progress is made.

3. Evaluating the Process

- **Gather feedback:** Gather feedback from participants about their experience in the dialogue session. This can be done through surveys or focus groups.

- **Refine the process:** Reflect on the effectiveness of the dialogue session. What worked well? What could be improved in terms of format, participation, or facilitation techniques? Use this evaluation to refine the process for future dialogues, ensuring continuous improvement in your approach.

4. Continuous Improvement

Mastering the art of dialogue is an ongoing process. Public sector leaders can consistently enhance their skills through dedicated effort and a commitment to learning. The following are strategies to elevate your dialogue facilitation abilities:

- **Seek and act on feedback:** After each dialogue session, actively solicit constructive feedback from participants on both the process and your performance as a facilitator. Use this feedback to identify areas for improvement and implement changes in future sessions.

- **Invest in training:** Participate in workshops and seminars focused on effective communication, conflict resolution, and fostering inclusive dialogue. These programs can equip you with valuable tools and techniques to navigate complex conversations and guide productive discussions.

- **Embrace reflective practice:** Regularly reflect on your dialogue experiences. Consider keeping a dedicated journal to record key takeaways, insights you gained from participants, and lessons learned. Use this self-reflection to continuously refine your approach.

- **Learn from exemplary leaders:** Study how successful leaders handle dialogue situations. Observe their communication styles, how they manage disagreements, and how they build consensus. These insights can inspire your own leadership approach.

The three stages outlined above provide a roadmap for leaders to effectively execute dialogue sessions. By following these steps, leaders can set the stage for success, especially early in their terms. However, regardless of a leader's best intentions, executing effective dialogue in an organizational context, especially in the public sector, is fraught with challenges and obstacles. Identifying and overcoming these challenges is crucial for leaders to foster trust, engagement, and transformative results.

Navigating Challenges in Dialogue: Overcoming Common Obstacles

The following is a detailed examination of the common obstacles that often arise during dialogue and the strategies to overcome them:

1. **Lack of trust:** Distrust between leaders and employees or stakeholders can significantly hinder open communication. This often results in superficial dialogue where underlying issues remain unaddressed and true sentiments are concealed. To build trust, leaders must consistently demonstrate integrity and transparency by following through on promises and commitments. Building personal relationships with employees at all levels and prioritizing openness and honesty are also essential. Addressing past issues and mistakes openly shows a commitment to improvement and honesty.

2. **Communication barriers:** Differences in language, jargon, and communication styles can create misunderstandings. Simplifying communication by using clear, concise, and jargon-free language

ensures messages are easily understood by all participants. Practicing active listening and showing genuine interest in employees' opinions by reflecting on what you hear helps demonstrate that their input is valued. Creating an environment where participants feel comfortable asking questions to ensure clarity and prevent miscommunication is also crucial.

3. **Power dynamics:** Hierarchical structures can inhibit open dialogue, as employees may fear repercussions for speaking honestly. To mitigate this, leaders should create more egalitarian meeting structures where all voices are given equal weight. Allowing for anonymous input ensures candid feedback without fear of retribution, and encouraging managers to empower their teams to speak up and participate actively in decision-making processes can help flatten hierarchies.

4. **Inadequate facilitation skills:** Leaders may lack the skills necessary to facilitate effective dialogue. Investing in facilitation training for leaders helps develop their skills in managing discussions and conflicts. Bringing in external facilitators to guide critical dialogue sessions and encouraging continuous learning and development can enhance leaders' facilitation capabilities.

5. **Lack of clear objectives:** Dialogue sessions without clear goals can become unfocused and unproductive. Defining the purpose and goals of each dialogue session beforehand, creating and sharing structured agendas, and tracking outcomes and action items from dialogue sessions ensure objectives are met and discussions remain focused on key topics.

6. **Insufficient follow-up:** Failure to follow up on dialogue outcomes can lead to cynicism and disengagement in future dialogues. Developing detailed action plans post-dialogue, providing regular updates on the progress of agreed-upon actions, and establishing feedback loops to gather input on the effectiveness of follow-up actions demonstrate that input is making a real difference, reinforcing trust and encouraging ongoing participation.

7. **Limited participation**: Incomplete perspectives and solutions can arise when not all relevant stakeholders participate. Ensuring all relevant stakeholders are invited and encouraged to participate, scheduling sessions at convenient times for all participants, and utilizing hybrid models (in-person and virtual) to accommodate those who cannot attend physically can maximize attendance and broaden perspectives.

8. **Emotional and psychological barriers**: Personal biases, emotions, and psychological safety concerns can hinder open dialogue. Creating a psychologically safe environment where participants feel comfortable expressing their true thoughts and feelings is crucial. Training leaders in emotional intelligence to manage and navigate emotional dynamics effectively and implementing conflict resolution mechanisms to address interpersonal conflicts that arise during dialogue are also important strategies.

By proactively addressing these obstacles, leaders can create a conducive environment for effective dialogue, paving the way for improved organizational performance, enhanced trust, and successful transformation initiatives.

The Power of Embedding Dialogue in Everyday Leadership

Given the emphasis on the importance of dialogue at the beginning of a leader's tenure, public sector leaders might be inclined to view it as a one-time kickoff event or merely as a tool for occasional problem-solving or conflict resolution. However, the real power of dialogue lies in making it a cornerstone of everyday leadership. This continuous approach fosters ongoing engagement, sparks innovation, and enables leaders to adapt to evolving community needs, ultimately leading to more effective and responsive governance.

Here's why incorporating dialogue as a staple in daily leadership activities can revolutionize public sector organizations:

- **Enhances decision-making**: Regular dialogue ensures that decisions are informed by a diversity of viewpoints, leading to more robust, inclusive, and effective outcomes.

- **Builds and sustains trust**: Consistent and open communication fosters trust both within the organization and with the public, a crucial asset for any public sector entity.

- **Drives organizational learning**: Continuous dialogue facilitates a learning culture where feedback is actively sought and valued, leading to constant improvement and innovation.

- **Encourages employee engagement**: When staff feel their voices are heard and their contributions matter, their engagement and commitment to organizational goals increase significantly.

Strategies for Embedding Dialogue in Leadership Practices

To make dialogue a core aspect of leadership, certain strategies can be particularly effective:

- **Leading by example:** Leaders must be active champions of dialogue. Regular participation in dialogue sessions demonstrates their commitment to open communication and sets the cultural tone for the organization. When leaders actively listen, engage respectfully, and value diverse perspectives, they inspire others to do the same.

- **Dialogue as the norm, not the exception:** Don't relegate dialogue to occasional events. Integrate dialogue principles into routine operations. Schedule regular check-ins, team meetings, and feedback sessions that prioritize open exchange and active listening. By making dialogue a predictable and valued part of the work routine, leaders foster a culture of continuous communication.

- **Strategic planning through inclusive dialogue:** Strategic planning sessions should not be isolated exercises. Involve a broad range of stakeholders in structured dialogue sessions. This inclusivity not only leverages the collective wisdom of the community but also fosters a sense of ownership and buy-in for the strategies developed. When people feel heard and their perspectives valued, they're more likely to actively support the implementation of a plan.

- **Building bridges with continuous feedback systems:** Dialogue shouldn't end after a single meeting. Implement systems that encourage ongoing communication between leadership, staff, and stakeholders. This could include digital platforms for anonymous feedback, suggestion boxes strategically placed throughout the workplace, or hosting regular open forums where anyone can voice their ideas or concerns. By creating multiple channels for continuous feedback, leaders demonstrate their commitment to open communication and gather valuable insights that can inform future decisions.

After thoroughly examining the principles and mechanics of effective dialogue, we will now illustrate how dialogue works through practical examples using two case studies: One showcasing successful dialogue and the other highlighting failures in dialogue execution.

Case Study 1
Dialogue Done Right

Background

Dr. Chinedu Okonkwo, the newly appointed director of public health, encountered a pressing challenge upon assuming his role. The public health department had come under scrutiny due to recent inefficiencies, leading to widespread dissatisfaction with health services.

Recognizing the urgency of the situation, Dr. Okonkwo knew that immediate action was required to rebuild trust and enhance service delivery.

Consequently, he made the strategic decision to launch a comprehensive dialogue intervention. The primary objectives of this intervention were to realign the department's goals, foster deeper stakeholder engagement, and pinpoint actionable solutions to address existing issues.

Key Players

- **Dr. Chinedu Okonkwo (newly appointed director of public health):** Led the dialogue to address inefficiencies and rebuild trust in the public health department.

- **Department staff:** Employees at various levels within the public health department who were involved in daily operations and management.

- **Local government representatives:** Officials from the local government who provided policy support and governance oversight.

- **Healthcare providers:** Medical professionals and organizations who delivered health services and care.

- **Community leaders**: Influential figures within the local community who advocated for community interests and needs.

- **Professional facilitator:** An expert who was hired to guide and manage the dialogue session, ensuring productive and focused discussions.

- **Emergency department staff:** Stakeholders who advocated for investment in preventive health measures, highlighting the strain on emergency services.

The Dialogue Process

Stage 1: Preparing for Dialogue

Dr. Okonkwo scheduled a full-day dialogue session at the local community center, inviting a diverse group of stakeholders, including department staff at various levels, representatives from the local government, healthcare providers, and community leaders. He and his team took the following steps to meticulously prepare for the dialogue session:

Agenda development: The group created a detailed agenda that included time for open discussions, breakout sessions, and action planning.

Participant briefing: Before the meeting, all participants received a briefing package that included the agenda, key topics for discussion, and background information on the department's current challenges and opportunities.

Stage 2: Conducting the Dialogue

Opening remarks: Dr. Okonkwo opened the session by clearly stating the objectives of the session and emphasizing the importance of every participant's contribution. He expressed his commitment to transparency and collaborative problem-solving.

Facilitation: To facilitate the discussions, Dr. Okonkwo employed the services of a professional facilitator who helped ensure that the dialogue remained focused and productive. The facilitator managed time effectively, handled conflicts with neutrality, and encouraged participants to share their thoughts openly.

Active listening and engagement: Throughout the session, Dr. Okonkwo actively listened to the feedback and concerns raised by participants. He took notes and asked clarifying questions to delve deeper into the issues discussed.

Breakout sessions: Participants were divided into smaller groups to discuss specific issues such as patient wait times, staff training needs, and community outreach programs. Each group included a mix of department staff and external stakeholders to ensure diverse perspectives were considered.

Critical Moments and Turning Points

Tension over resource allocation: A key point of contention emerged during the discussions: Resource allocation between emergency services and preventative care. The emergency department staff passionately advocated for increased funding, citing the recent surge in critical cases that strained their capabilities. They emphasized the need to be well-equipped to handle immediate life-or-death situations.

On the other hand, preventative care advocates presented a compelling argument for long-term community health benefits. They argued that investing in preventative measures, such as health education and wellness programs, could ultimately reduce the overall burden on emergency services and improve the health of the community as a whole.

Resolution: The skilled facilitator recognized the importance of addressing both immediate needs and long-term goals. The facilitator skillfully guided the discussion toward exploring potential solutions that could bridge the gap between the two perspectives.

Dr. Okonkwo played a key role in fostering this collaborative spirit. He proposed a pilot project that would integrate certain preventive measures within existing emergency care protocols. This innovative approach addressed the emergency department's concerns about immediate patient needs while also laying the groundwork for preventative care initiatives. The pilot project was well-received by both sides, offering a path forward that balanced immediate response with a focus on long-term community health.

Near miss on community outreach program: During a breakout session, the community leaders expressed concerns that the proposed outreach program was top-down and did not adequately address local cultural nuances.

Recovery and alignment: Dr. Okonkwo acknowledged the oversight and invited two community leaders to join the planning committee. This move ensured that the program development was more inclusive and community-focused.

Achieving Outcomes

By the end of the session, the dialogue had successfully achieved several key outcomes:

New direction and renewed hope: Dr. Okonkwo's openness and responsive leadership inspired confidence among stakeholders, setting a new direction for the department.

Alignment and buy-in: The collaborative approach to discussing and resolving issues led to broad consensus on the department's priorities and strategies.

Identification of change agents: Several participants emerged as potential leaders during the discussions, particularly in breakout sessions, and were invited to take on roles in new initiatives.

Actionable insights and quick wins: The session produced several actionable insights, including the immediate improvement of patient triage procedures, which was identified as a quick win that could be rapidly implemented.

The dialogue session ended on a high note, with stakeholders feeling energized and committed to the new path forward. Dr. Okonkwo scheduled follow-up sessions to review progress and made it clear that dialogue would remain a central component of his leadership approach.

Stage 3: Post-dialogue Actions

Dr. Okonkwo and his team understood that the success of the dialogue session depended on concrete actions taken afterward. They promptly took the following steps to implement decisions and sustain momentum:

Documenting and sharing key outcomes: Immediately following the session, he and his team compiled a comprehensive summary of the dialogue. This document outlined the key points discussed, decisions made, and specific action items identified. The summary was promptly shared with all participants and relevant stakeholders to ensure transparency and alignment.

Implementing decisions and fostering accountability: Dr. Okonkwo developed a detailed action plan that specified the steps needed to implement the decisions made during the dialogue. Responsibilities for each action item were clearly assigned to team members, with specific timelines set for completion. Regular progress reviews were scheduled to maintain accountability and address any obstacles promptly.

Evaluating the process: A few weeks after the session, Dr. Okonkwo conducted a follow-up survey to gather feedback from participants on their experience. The feedback highlighted session strengths and areas for improvement, aiding in refining the approach for future dialogues.

Continuous improvement: Dr. Okonkwo also committed to continuous improvement by seeking feedback after each dialogue session, investing in further training for himself and his team, and reflecting on each dialogue's outcomes and processes. He encouraged his team to learn from exemplary leaders and regularly participated in workshops focused on effective communication and conflict resolution.

Conclusion and Lessons Learned

The entire process concluded with participants feeling heard and valued, with many expressing newfound optimism about the direction of the public health department under Dr. Okonkwo's leadership.

This case study exemplifies how effective dialogue can transform public sector leadership and governance, fostering a collaborative environment that not only addresses immediate challenges but also paves the way for sustained improvements and stakeholder engagement.

Case Study 2
Dialogue Gone Wrong

Background

Mr. Ali Johnson, the recently appointed head of the Agency for Urban Roads Management, found himself confronted with mounting challenges concerning urban road transit and infrastructure deficiencies. Eager to take decisive action and effect meaningful changes, Mr. Johnson orchestrated a comprehensive dialogue session involving stakeholders from various sectors across the city. Recognizing the complexity of the issues at hand, he sought to foster collaboration and gather diverse perspectives to devise holistic solutions to enhance the city's road systems and infrastructure.

Key Players

- **Mr. Ali Johnson (head of the Agency for Urban Roads Management):** The newly appointed leader who initiated the dialogue session.

- **City planners (urban development and infrastructure experts):** Provided technical insights and urban planning perspectives.

- **Local business leaders (representatives from the business community):** Advocated for economic considerations and impacts on business operations.

- **Community activists (advocates for local community interests and concerns):** Represented public sentiment and community needs.

- **Department employees (staff members from the Agency for Urban Roads Management):** Frontline workers and operational staff involved in roads maintenance and management.

- **Senior planner (high-ranking planner):** Challenged Mr. Johnson's approach from a strategic planning standpoint.

- **Other stakeholders (various participants invited to provide input on road infrastructure issues):** Included representatives from unions, civic groups, and other relevant bodies.

The Dialogue Process

Stage 1: Preparing for Dialogue

Agenda development: Despite the complexity and scale of the issues at hand, the preparation for the stakeholder dialogue session fell short. The agenda, overly ambitious in scope, attempted to cram too many complex topics into a single day. This left insufficient time for in-depth discussions on each crucial issue, potentially limiting the opportunity for valuable insights to emerge.

Participants briefing: Participants received minimal background information and only received the agenda a few days before the meeting. This lack of preparation time potentially stifled meaningful participation and hampered their ability to come to the table with well-considered ideas.

Stage 2: Conducting the Dialogue

Opening remarks: Mr. Johnson opened the session with a long speech detailing his vision and planned reforms, but he failed to clearly articulate the session's objectives or how input from stakeholders would be integrated.

Facilitation: The session lacked a professional facilitator. Mr. Johnson attempted to manage the dialogue himself but struggled to keep discussions on track and manage time effectively.

Engagement and interaction: As the day progressed, frustration grew. Mr. Johnson's top-down communication style and lack of receptiveness to feedback stifled meaningful exchange and collaboration.

Critical Moments and Turning Points

Escalating tensions over policy changes: The discussion on budget allocation turned into a heated exchange when the topic of reallocating funds from road repairs to expand bike lanes arose. Long-standing department staff, with their wealth of experience in maintaining the city's infrastructure, felt their voices were unheard. They expressed frustration that their practical concerns about the feasibility and potential consequences of reduced road maintenance were being sidelined in favor of what they perceived as untested ideas.

Conflict eruption: The simmering tensions surrounding budget allocation reached a boiling point when a senior planner publicly challenged Mr. Johnson's approach. The planner, highlighting the logistical complexities of the bike lane proposal, directly criticized Mr. Johnson for overlooking these ground realities. This accusation of being "out of touch" was a blow to Mr. Johnson's authority and ultimately derailed the constructive dialogue.

The public confrontation fractured the group's focus, making it difficult to find common ground and move forward productively.

Mismanagement of conflict: Unfortunately, the opportunity to address the department staff's concerns and engage in constructive dialogue was missed. Instead of actively mediating the situation or acknowledging the raised points, Mr. Johnson reacted defensively. This defensive response further alienated the department staff and potentially discouraged other stakeholders from voicing their opinions. A more measured approach, focused on acknowledging concerns and finding common ground, could have prevented the situation from escalating and fostered a more productive dialogue.

Breakdown of the Dialogue

The public dialogue session, initially intended to address pressing road management issues in the city, ultimately fell short of its goals. The session deteriorated rapidly as tensions over budget allocation escalated. The senior planner's public criticism of Mr. Johnson's approach, coupled with a perceived lack of responsiveness to staff concerns, resulted in a breakdown of constructive dialogue.

Several key stakeholders, dissatisfied with the session's conduct and skeptical about the future under Mr. Johnson's leadership, chose to withdraw their participation. This not only left the session without a sense of resolution but also fostered a general feeling of discontent and disillusionment.

Stage 3: Post-dialogue Actions

Mr. Johnson and his team failed to take concrete actions after the dialogue. They failed to take the necessary steps to implement decisions and sustain momentum:

Documenting and sharing key outcomes: After the dialogue process ended, no comprehensive summary was created or shared, further eroding trust and alignment.

Implementing decisions and fostering accountability: No detailed action plan was developed, and responsibilities were not clearly assigned. The lack of progress reviews allowed obstacles to go unaddressed.

Evaluating the process: Further compounding the issue, there was no apparent effort made by Mr. Johnson or his team in the days following the dialogue to reach out to disgruntled stakeholders or address the concerns raised. There was no follow-up survey, leading to a missed opportunity to gather feedback and identify areas for improvement.

Continuous improvement: Without feedback or reflection, opportunities for improvement were lost. The absence of commitment to continuous learning further hindered future dialogue efforts. This lack of follow-up further eroded trust and effectively shut down potential avenues for future collaboration.

Outcomes of the Failed Dialogue

The poorly managed dialogue session had significant negative consequences for the Agency for Urban Roads Management and its efforts to address the city's road challenges.

Shattered trust: Mr. Johnson's inability to effectively manage the dialogue severely damaged relationships with department staff and crucial external stakeholders. This eroded trust in his leadership and his ability to navigate complex situations.

Stalled progress: The public backlash that followed the contentious dialogue session effectively stalled his proposed road initiatives. Without the necessary support and collaboration from key stakeholders, moving forward with these initiatives became an uphill battle.

Demoralized workforce: The department's morale took a significant hit. Disgruntled staff members felt unheard, demoralized, and uncertain about their roles and the future direction of the department under Mr. Johnson's leadership.

Conclusion and Lessons Learned

This case study of a failed dialogue session serves as a core lesson in the importance of careful planning and execution in public leadership communication. Here are some key takeaways:

The power of preparation: Thorough preparation is crucial for a successful dialogue session. This includes defining clear objectives, developing a focused agenda, and providing participants with adequate background information beforehand. This ensures everyone arrives informed and ready to engage productively.

The value of skilled facilitation: A skilled facilitator plays a vital role in guiding the conversation, ensuring all voices are heard, and managing any disagreements constructively. Their expertise can help keep the dialogue focused on solutions and prevent it from derailing due to emotional outbursts or unresolved conflicts.

Fostering a culture of respectful dialogue: Creating an environment where diverse perspectives are valued and participants feel comfortable expressing their opinions is essential. Leaders must prioritize active listening, acknowledge concerns, and demonstrate a commitment to open and transparent communication.

By following these principles, public leaders can leverage the power of dialogue to build trust, address complex challenges, and achieve positive outcomes for their communities.

Call to Action
Embrace Dialogue for Breakthrough Results

Leadership is often associated with decisiveness and providing answers. However, the most effective leaders understand that their true strength lies in cultivating an environment where questions are encouraged and powerful solutions are co-created through dialogue. By actively engaging with diverse perspectives, leaders can foster:

- **Adaptability:** Open communication allows your organization to respond effectively to changing needs and seize new opportunities.

- **Transparency:** Dialogue builds trust by ensuring all voices are heard and valued.

- **Community alignment:** Through open dialogue, you gain a deeper understanding of the needs and aspirations of the people you serve.

As a leader, your journey to breakthrough results begins with effective dialogues. Assess your current dialogue practices. Are you creating spaces for open exchange? Are diverse perspectives truly valued? Identify areas for improvement. Next, take action. Gradually integrate the strategies outlined in this chapter into your routine. Schedule regular dialogue sessions, actively solicit feedback from your team and stakeholders, and demonstrate a commitment to active listening. Remember, dialogue is a continuous process. Embrace continuous learning, refine your approach as you go, and explore new ways to expand the conversation.

As you integrate these practices, monitor the positive impact. Track how enhanced dialogue strengthens your organization's culture, effectiveness, and public perception. This dedication to open communication will foster a vibrant and responsive organization, one that truly reflects the values and needs of the community it serves.

Master the discipline of dialogue and lead the transformation of your organization's results.

The Discipline of Dialogue at a Glance

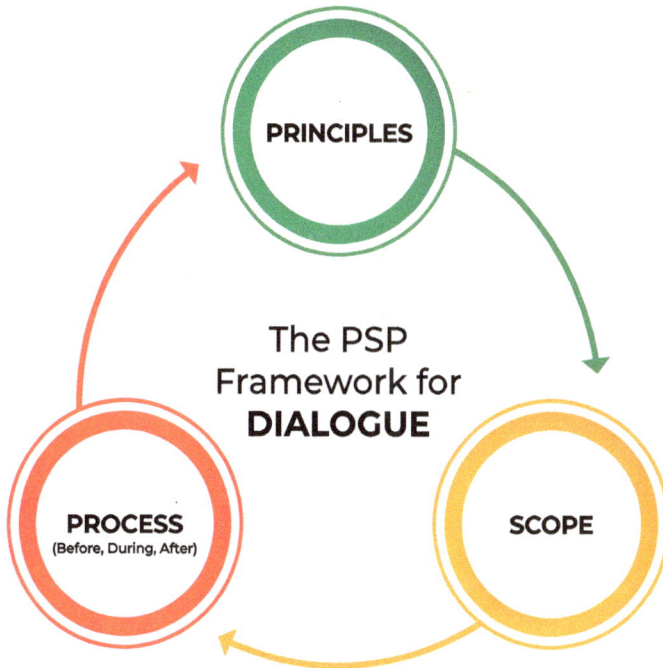

Figure 4. Framework for Mastering DIALOGUE: PSP

⚡ WHY IS DIALOGUE IMPORTANT FOR PUBLIC LEADERS?

- Dialogue is essential for building trust, establishing legitimacy, and fostering meaningful relationships, which are crucial for effective leadership.

- In the public sector, dialogue helps leaders navigate complexities, understand undercurrents, and unlock the potential within their organizations.

- Effective dialogue transforms challenges into opportunities, aligns stakeholders with organizational goals, and enhances public trust and morale.

⚙ WHAT ARE THE BIG IDEAS?

- Effective dialogue is the cornerstone of public leadership, crucial for setting new directions, aligning stakeholders, and securing buy-in.

- Well-structured dialogue sessions enable leaders to detect and resolve issues early, gather insights, and identify change agents, thus driving proactive and informed decision-making.

- To effectively execute dialogue, leaders must be careful to understand the principles, scope, and steps governing the process.

- Engaging in dialogue reflects a leader's commitment to transparency and inclusiveness, essential for rallying support, igniting transformation, and ensuring long-term success in public service.

- By fostering a culture of continuous dialogue, leaders can stimulate innovation, adapt to changing circumstances, and stay ahead of emerging challenges, ensuring organizational resilience and relevance.

🔧 HOW DO I MAKE IT HAPPEN?

Follow a three-stage process to execute an effective dialogue session:

Stage 1: Preparation for Dialogue

Stage 2: Conducting the Dialogue

Stage 3: Post-dialogue Actions

PART 2
UNDERSTANDING THE SITUATION

Chapter 3
Discipline 2 - Discover

From the very beginning of their tenure, the best public leaders prioritize creating environments where everyone feels comfortable sharing their pressing concerns, problems, and ideas. This embodies the essence of the discipline of dialogue. When conducted effectively with both internal and external stakeholders, dialogue provides leaders with a wealth of information about their organization, as it did for Dr. Ruth Obiedo, the newly appointed director-general of a respected public agency.

Dealing with the Aftermath of Dialogue: The Case of Dr. Ruth Obiedo

After conducting a series of successful dialogue sessions upon taking office, Dr. Ruth Obiedo gained a deeper understanding of her institution's condition. The feedback revealed significant challenges and troubling issues, providing a clear picture of the institution's hurdles and operational weaknesses that required immediate attention.

Employees expressed feelings of stagnation, having experienced minimal career progression for over a decade. External stakeholders voiced frustrations with poor service delivery, a sense of marginalization, and suspected pervasive corruption. Allegations of a "pay-to-play" culture pointed to deeper problems in procurement and operations. Complaints of career manipulation, victimization, and unfair treatment indicated a larger systemic issue. Vendors reported waiting years for payments, highlighting a breakdown of trust and financial integrity. Industry associations labeled the institution a failed entity, unable to fulfill its mandate.

This flood of feedback, while daunting, provided Dr. Obiedo with invaluable direction. Now she—and every public leader in her position—faces the question: How should I use this information?

After Dialogue: What Comes Next?

After intensive and extensive dialogue sessions leave you with a mountain of feedback, what should be your next step?

As a leader tasked with steering an institution out of its present difficulties, it is essential to build your strategy rooted in the principle of discovery. True change begins with a thorough and honest evaluation of the current state of affairs. Understanding these issues in depth is crucial for developing effective solutions that are not only responsive but also sustainable. Thus, the next critical step in your leadership journey is engaging deeply with the discipline of discovery.

Discovery involves systematically analyzing each identified issue and understanding its origins, impact on the organization, and the stakeholders it affects. By adopting a methodical approach to unraveling these complexities, leaders can begin to craft comprehensive strategies to address the existing challenges.

The discipline of discovery will not only shed light on the underlying causes of these issues but also pave the way for a transformative agenda that seeks to realign the institution's objectives with its capabilities and societal expectations.

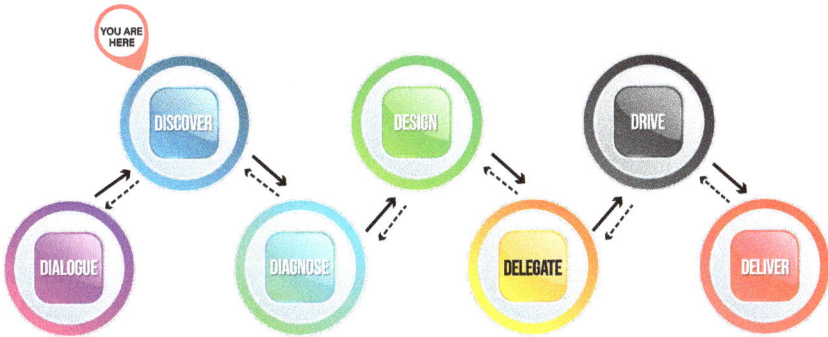

Figure 5. The Seven Disciplines of Breakthrough Results: Discover

Introduction to Discovery: Unveiling Organizational Realities

Public institutions are incredibly complex entities, with numerous layers and elements that make reshaping them and driving them toward strong performance a daunting task. This is why **DISCOVERY**, the second discipline in breakthrough leadership, stands as a crucial step that shapes the direction of leadership and organizational success.

Discovery is a dynamic, interactive process that requires leaders to engage actively with the diverse elements that constitute their organization. At its heart, discovery is about peeling back layers to reveal the underlying structures, processes, and cultures that drive an organization. It is about discerning not just what people are doing, but why they are doing it, how effectively they are doing it, and what could be improved.

For new leaders, this discipline is their first deep introduction to the organization's inner workings, beyond what board reports and briefings can convey. For seasoned leaders, it is an opportunity to realign their perceptions and strategies with the evolving realities of their environment. In either case, a successful discovery process can illuminate the path forward with insights that are critical for informed decision-making and strategic planning.

The benefits of a well-conducted discovery process extend beyond the leader to the entire organization. It establishes a foundation of transparency and trust, signaling to employees at all levels that their insights and experiences are valued. This inclusive approach not only enhances morale but also encourages a culture of openness that can lead to more innovative solutions to entrenched problems.

In addition, the data gathered during discovery can help identify strengths to build upon and weaknesses that need attention, providing a clear direction for future initiatives. It can highlight emerging opportunities that might be capitalized on and pinpoint looming threats that need to be mitigated.

In a nutshell, discovery sets the stage for a deep dive into the inner workings of the organization. It is not just about gathering information—it is about uncovering truths that will shape the leader's ability to make tangible changes.

The rest of this chapter equips public sector leaders with the understanding and tools they need to navigate this complex but rewarding phase with confidence and clarity. It delves deeper into the essence of discovery, exploring why thorough engagement in this process with internal teams and external stakeholders is crucial for both new and existing leaders.

The Imperative of Discovery: Why is this Discipline so Vital to Effective Leadership?

Imagine stepping into a gigantic library with hundreds of rows of books stretching out before you. Leading a public organization without a profound understanding of its internal mechanics and external influences is akin to navigating this library blindfolded. Discovery is that critical phase where public sector leaders remove the blindfold, illuminating the path ahead with the light of knowledge and insight.

At its core, the discovery phase is about connection and clarity. It provides leaders with a direct line to the pulse of their departments, the voices of their stakeholders, and a deeper understanding of the organization's inner workings. This process is not just about finding out what exists but understanding how it affects the broader vision and mission of the organization. It is about uncovering the realities that lie beneath the surface—the hidden currents that propel the organization forward or the warning signs that need attention.

How Strategic Discovery Empowers Leaders

Strategic discovery goes beyond passive observation; it is an active, purpose-driven engagement that aims to uncover the complex essence of an organization and translate it into actionable insights. For both new and seasoned leaders, strategic discovery provides a foundation for informed decisions, culturally aligned strategies, and rejuvenated organizational focus.

Strategic discovery is crucial because it prevents leaders from operating in an isolated environment, a known cause of leadership failure. It ensures they are constantly informed about internal dynamics and external expectations. To be effective, leaders need to immerse themselves in their organizational ecosystem, engaging with everything from frontline employee insights to feedback from community stakeholders. This comprehensive approach helps them anticipate challenges and seize emerging opportunities that might otherwise be overlooked.

Benefits of a Well-structured Discovery Session

If leaders want to avoid leading blindly, firing blanks, or making unnecessary and costly mistakes, if they want every decision to feel certain and every step to be free of needless risks, then they will need a well-structured discovery session to help them achieve clarity. A well-structured discovery session acts as a leader's roadmap, illuminating the path forward with clarity and direction. It offers several key advantages:

- **Gaining clarity and direction:** Discovery sessions reveal the current state of your organization, highlighting strengths to build on and areas for improvement.

- **Fostering transparency and trust:** By involving various stakeholders in the process, leaders build a culture of openness and trust, demonstrating a commitment to inclusivity and collaboration.

- **Empowering decision-making:** Discovery sessions equip leaders with comprehensive insights, enabling them to make data-driven decisions that enhance the effectiveness and relevance of strategic initiatives.

- **Igniting transformation:** Discovery often uncovers gaps and opportunities for innovation, serving as a catalyst for transformative changes that propel the organization forward.

For leaders poised at the helm of public sector organizations, the discovery phase is a strategic imperative that can define the trajectory of their leadership and the future of their organization. By embracing this deep dive into the operational and cultural fabric of their institutions, leaders are better equipped to steer their ships through turbulent waters and into thriving futures.

Having established a firm understanding of the meaning and necessity of the discipline of discovery, the following sections will explore how leaders can systematically discover their organizations.

Mastering the Discipline of Discovery in Public Sector Leadership

The discovery phase is a critical juncture for any leader in the public sector. It serves not only as the initial step in understanding the intricate workings of your organization but also as the cornerstone for every strategic decision you will make throughout your tenure.

Without access to accurate information, leaders risk basing their entire tenure on flawed assumptions. To mitigate this risk, leaders must first undertake a thorough mapping of the areas within their organizations that need to be discovered. They must then master the tools and techniques to effectively uncover insights about their organizations, followed by mastering the systematic process of discovery.

We will start by examining the crucial first step leaders must take: mapping out the discovery landscape.

Mapping the Discovery Landscape: What Leaders Need to Know

To conduct an effective discovery, public sector leaders need a comprehensive understanding of the landscape within which their organization operates. This landscape is vast and varied, encompassing every aspect of the organization, from its daily operations to its cultural dynamics. Leaders venturing into this terrain need a map to guide them.

The following are the key territories they must explore:

- **Organizational structure and hierarchy:** Understanding how the organization is structured is crucial. This includes knowledge of reporting lines, departmental interdependencies, and the flow of information.

- **Operational processes:** A deep dive into the processes that drive daily operations helps identify efficiency gaps and areas for improvement.

- **Cultural norms and employee sentiment:** Organizational culture significantly influences employee behavior and organizational efficacy. Leaders need to grasp the prevailing norms, values, and sentiments that permeate their teams.

- **External environment:** This involves understanding the regulatory, economic, and competitive landscape in which the organization operates, as well as the public perception and expectations.

- **Technological infrastructure:** Assessing the organization's technology stack and its ability to support current and future needs ensures leaders leverage technology effectively.

- **Financial health:** Insight into the organization's financial status, including budget allocations, revenue streams, and expenditure, is critical for making informed strategic decisions.

Now equipped with a map of the discovery landscape, leaders must master the tools and techniques necessary to explore and understand their organizations.

The Tools and Techniques Required for Effective Discovery

The following is a breakdown of the essential tools and techniques you will need to learn to conduct an effective discovery process.

1. Surveys and questionnaires: Gauging the pulse of your organization

- **Purpose:** To gather quantitative and qualitative data from a broad employee base and external stakeholders.

- **How to implement**: Develop clear, concise questions that cover a wide range of topics from job satisfaction to operational challenges. Use digital platforms for ease of distribution and data compilation.

- **Benefits:** Provides you with a snapshot of employee sentiment, allowing you to identify specific areas for improvement across departments, leadership styles, and overall work culture.

2. Interviews and focus groups: unveiling deep-dive insights

- **Purpose:** To obtain detailed, qualitative insights from key individuals or groups within and outside the organization.

- **How to implement:** Prepare semi-structured interview guides that allow for flexibility and depth in responses. Focus groups should be diverse to ensure a range of perspectives are represented.

- **Benefits:** Uncover root causes of challenges, gain fresh ideas for innovation, and understand the perspectives of those most impacted by organizational decisions.

3. Document reviews: Unearthing the organizational story

- **Purpose**: To analyze existing documents and records for historical insights and current practices.

- **How to implement**: Review strategic plans, annual reports, operational manuals, and past audits. Use content analysis techniques to identify trends and recurring issues.

- **Benefits:** Gain a historical perspective on the organization's journey, identify areas where practices may have become outdated, and track progress toward past goals.

4. Observation: Witnessing the workplace in action

- **Purpose:** To understand the real-time dynamics of workplace interactions and operational workflows.

- **How to implement**: Conduct site visits and shadowing sessions to observe processes and employee interactions in their natural settings.

- **Benefits:** Gain a deeper understanding of how work actually gets done, identify potential bottlenecks in processes, and observe communication dynamics between employees.

5. SWOT analysis: Charting your course forward

- **Purpose:** To structure the qualitative and quantitative data into a framework that assesses strengths, weaknesses, opportunities, and threats.

- **How to implement**: Organize findings from all other tools into the SWOT framework to visualize where the organization stands and where it needs to go.

- **Benefits:** Identify areas for improvement, leverage existing strengths to exploit new opportunities, and develop strategies to mitigate potential risks.

Having identified the essential tools and techniques for organizational discovery, leaders must take one final preparatory step: Building a strong foundation for their efforts. This involves putting in place critical infrastructure to ensure a smooth and unhindered discovery process.

Essential Practices to Optimize the Discovery Process

To ensure the effectiveness of the discovery process, leaders must be proactive in implementing these practices:

- **Equipping their team for success through training and capacity building:** Equip team members with the skills they need to utilize discovery tools effectively. Training sessions and workshops can empower them to gather and analyze data with confidence.

- **Prioritizing Thoroughness by Scheduling and Planning:** Allocate sufficient time for each stage of the discovery process. This meticulous planning avoids rushed work and ensures thorough data collection and analysis.

- **Maintaining Ethical Standards by Upholding Transparency and Trust:** Maintain high ethical standards throughout data collection and analysis. This includes respecting privacy and confidentiality and ensuring transparency in how data will be used. By prioritizing ethical conduct, you foster trust and cooperation within the organization.

With the preparatory steps mentioned above in place, we can now proceed to the blueprint for executing discovery.

Executing Discovery: A Stage-by-Stage Guide

Embarking on a journey of organizational discovery involves systematic steps that lay the groundwork for informed decision-making and strategic alignment. The process unfolds in four essential stages, each building upon the previous to ensure comprehensive exploration and insightful outcomes.

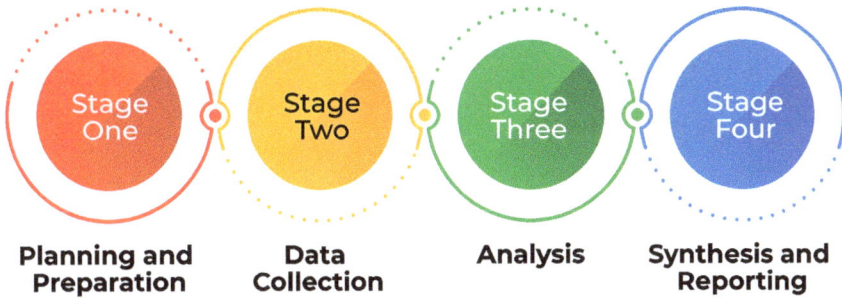

Figure 6. The Four Stages of Discovery

Stage 1: Planning and Preparation

Before diving into data collection and analysis, meticulous planning sets the stage for a successful discovery process. The following are the critical steps in this stage:

- **Set clear objectives:** Define precise goals for the discovery process. Whether aimed at understanding past failures, identifying new opportunities, or evaluating the impact of strategic decisions, clarity of purpose is key.

- **Identify key stakeholders:** Compile a list of all internal and external stakeholders essential to the process. Their perspectives and inputs will shape the outcomes of the discovery effort.

- **Develop a timeline:** Establish a realistic timeline that outlines milestones and deadlines for each stage of the discovery journey. This structured approach ensures efficient progress and timely completion.

Stage 2: Data Collection

With the groundwork laid, the focus shifts to gathering comprehensive data from diverse sources within and outside of the organization.

- **Internal reviews:** Conduct thorough reviews of internal documents such as financial statements, HR reports, past audits, and strategic plans. These documents provide insights into operational performance and organizational health.

- **Surveys and questionnaires:** Deploy surveys designed to capture feedback from employees at all levels. Use anonymous surveys where necessary. Anonymity fosters candid responses, offering valuable perspectives on organizational dynamics and challenges.

- **Interviews:** Schedule in-depth interviews with department heads, key personnel, and external stakeholders. These conversations delve into nuanced insights and personal experiences, enriching the understanding of organizational strengths and weaknesses.

Stage 3: Analysis

Armed with a wealth of data, the focus now turns to meticulous analysis to uncover meaningful patterns and insights.

- **Data analysis:** Utilize statistical tools and methods to analyze the data collected. Identify trends, anomalies, and correlations that shed light on operational efficiencies and areas needing improvement.

- **SWOT analysis:** Conduct a SWOT analysis to assess internal strengths, weaknesses, external opportunities, and threats. This structured evaluation provides a strategic framework for decision-making.

- **Gap analysis:** Evaluate the gaps between the current organizational state and desired future outcomes. This process highlights areas requiring immediate attention and strategic intervention.

Stage 4: Synthesis and Reporting

The final stage consolidates findings into actionable insights and communicates them effectively to key stakeholders.

- **Compile findings:** Synthesize all data and insights into a cohesive report. This document serves as a comprehensive overview of the organization's current state, challenges, and opportunities.

- **Feedback sessions:** Present the findings to senior management and stakeholders for validation and further insights. Open dialogue during these sessions fosters collective understanding and agreement on priorities.

- **Develop actionable insights:** Translate data-driven insights into actionable strategies and initiatives. These recommendations guide strategic decisions aimed at enhancing organizational effectiveness and achieving long-term goals.

As a leader focused on achieving breakthrough results, mastering and effectively executing the four stages of discovery outlined above will pave the way for informed decision-making and strategic alignment within your organization. However, after uncovering a wealth of valuable insights, you will need effective techniques to extract the maximum value from them and ensure that the information is complete.

Techniques for Maximizing Discovery Outcomes

In this crucial section, we delve into strategies public sector leaders can employ to maximize the value extracted from the discovery process. Remember, the goal is to uncover accurate and comprehensive information that fuels well-informed decisions, ultimately leading to your organization's success. Here, we explore three key techniques:

1. Data Triangulation: Building a Strong Foundation of Evidence

Data triangulation is a powerful technique for strengthening the validity of your discoveries. Imagine building a case—the more evidence you have from various sources, the stronger the case becomes. In discovery, triangulation involves verifying the information you gather through one method by comparing it with data obtained from other sources. This can involve:

- **Surveys:** Structured surveys provide quantitative data that can be statistically analyzed.

- **Interviews:** In-depth interviews offer qualitative insights and allow for probing deeper into specific themes.

- **Document reviews:** Analyzing existing reports, policies, and data sets can reveal historical trends and patterns.

- **Observations:** Direct observation of work processes or stakeholder interactions can provide valuable context.

By combining data from these diverse sources, you can reduce bias inherent in any single method and gain a more complete picture of the situation.

2. Stakeholder Mapping and Engagement: Capturing the Full Spectrum of Voices

Bearing in mind that public organizations are complex ecosystems with diverse stakeholders, each with a unique perspective, effective discovery requires ensuring that all relevant voices are heard and their inputs integrated into the process. Here's how stakeholder mapping and engagement can be implemented:

- **Stakeholder mapping:** Create a visual representation that identifies key stakeholder groups and individuals. This map should categorize stakeholders based on their influence and interest in your organization's outcomes.

- **Tailored engagement strategies:** Develop specific strategies to gather diverse perspectives from each stakeholder group. Surveys, focus groups, town hall meetings, or targeted interviews can all be valuable tools. By engaging stakeholders meaningfully, you ensure a richer understanding of your organization's strengths, weaknesses, opportunities, and threats.

3. Iterative Feedback Loops: Refining Insights through Continuous Dialogue

The discovery process should not be a one-shot deal. To ensure the accuracy and completeness of your findings, incorporate iterative feedback loops. This works as follows:

- **Present preliminary findings:** Do not wait until the discovery process is complete to share your insights. Present preliminary findings to different stakeholder groups throughout various phases.

- **Gather feedback:** Encourage stakeholders to provide feedback on your initial observations and conclusions. This allows you to course-correct and refine your understanding based on their valuable perspectives.

- **Refine the report:** Integrate stakeholder feedback into your final report. This iterative approach ensures the accuracy and completeness of your discoveries, leading to more impactful recommendations.

By employing these techniques, you can maximize the return on your discovery investment, transforming raw information into actionable insights that drive positive change within your organization.

In the next section, we explore a vital aspect of the discipline of discovery: Ensuring that the process unveils the complete picture of the organization. This includes both internal and external perspectives.

Unveiling the Whole Picture: Balancing Internal and External Discovery

To gain a thorough understanding of your organization, a multifaceted discovery approach is essential. This involves integrating both internal and external perspectives. While distinct, these perspectives are intricately linked, each playing a crucial role in constructing a comprehensive picture of your organization's ecosystem.

Understanding Internal Discovery

Internal discovery delves deep into the organization's inner workings, focusing on its processes, culture, and the perceptions of internal stakeholders. This dimension is essential for uncovering inefficiencies, identifying strengths, and understanding the morale and engagement levels of the workforce. To achieve this, several tools and techniques are employed.

1. Employee Surveys and Interviews

Surveys and interviews play a pivotal role in gathering insights. By conducting anonymous surveys and confidential interviews, leaders can obtain honest feedback regarding workplace satisfaction, operational challenges, and suggestions for improvement. This approach allows for a nuanced understanding of employee sentiments and concerns, helping to pinpoint areas needing attention.

2. Process Mapping

This involves detailed analyses of workflow processes across different departments. This method aims to identify bottlenecks, redundancies, and opportunities for streamlining operations. By mapping out how tasks flow within the organization, leaders can visualize and address inefficiencies that may hinder productivity or quality.

3. Presentations

Presentations by key internal stakeholders provide a comprehensive view of their respective areas within the organization. These sessions offer insights into the organization's current state, past performance, and future potential, facilitating a holistic understanding of operational dynamics and strategic alignment.

4. Reviewing Performance Data

Reviewing metrics is another critical component of internal discovery. Analyzing performance trends and historical data enables leaders to assess productivity levels, the quality of outputs, and the organization's alignment with strategic goals. This data-driven approach helps in identifying successes and areas needing improvement, guiding informed decision-making.

Together, these approaches create a robust framework for internal discovery, ensuring that leaders gain a comprehensive understanding of their organization's internal landscape. This holistic insight enables targeted interventions and strategic initiatives that enhance organizational effectiveness and drive positive change.

The Benefits of Conducting an Internal Discovery

Conducting an internal discovery offers several key benefits. First, it provides a deeper understanding of the organization's dynamics and employee morale. By gathering insights through surveys, interviews, and process mapping, leaders can uncover hidden strengths, identify areas for improvement, and anticipate potential challenges that could hinder success.

Second, internal discovery enhances efficiency and effectiveness within the organization. Through detailed analysis of workflow processes, performance data review, and stakeholder presentations, leaders can identify inefficiencies, streamline operations, and optimize resource allocation. This structured approach facilitates smoother execution of strategic goals and initiatives, leading to more efficient outcomes.

A final significant outcome of internal discovery is fostering a culture of transparency and continuous improvement. By involving stakeholders in the discovery process and encouraging open communication, organizations empower their employees. This empowerment not only enhances morale but also cultivates a proactive environment where innovation thrives and challenges are tackled collaboratively. Ultimately, these practices position the organization for long-term success by adapting to changes, improving performance, and sustaining growth.

Exploring External Discovery

Exploring external discovery involves examining an organization's interactions and positioning within its broader external environment. This encompasses relationships with stakeholders, compliance with regulatory frameworks, and its public image and reputation. An external perspective is crucial for understanding how external factors impact organizational performance and for aligning strategies with external expectations and requirements. To conduct external discovery, several tools and techniques are employed.

1. Stakeholder Meetings and Forums

Stakeholder meetings and forums play a central role, enabling organizations to engage with external stakeholders such as customers, partners, local communities, and regulatory bodies. These interactions provide valuable feedback and insights into external perceptions and expectations.

2. Market Analysis

Market analysis is another essential component of external discovery. This involves conducting comprehensive analyses of market trends, competitive benchmarks, and regulatory changes. By assessing these factors, organizations can gauge their external standing and strategically position themselves within their industry and market environment.

3. Public Sentiment Analysis

Utilizing tools like social media analytics and public surveys, leaders can monitor and gain an understanding of public perceptions of the organization's effectiveness and responsiveness. This feedback is crucial for managing reputation and ensuring alignment with public expectations.

Benefits of Conducting an External Discovery

Conducting an external discovery offers several significant benefits for public sector organizations. It provides insights into how external factors influence organizational performance, helping leaders make informed decisions about strategic directions and resource allocation. Understanding external factors allows public sector entities to better anticipate policy changes, regulatory developments, and socio-economic trends, which is crucial for developing resilient and adaptive strategies. This proactive approach to gathering data and insights ensures more effective use of resources, better program planning, and improved service delivery.

Moreover, external discovery facilitates the alignment of organizational strategies with public expectations, enhancing stakeholder relations and fostering trust within the community. By understanding the expectations of external stakeholders, such as citizens, regulators, and community groups, public sector organizations can adjust their strategies and operations to build stronger relationships and enhance their reputation. This alignment can lead to increased support from key stakeholders, helping to ensure continuity of services and mitigate the impact of external challenges.

Ultimately, public sector organizations that engage in regular external discovery are better positioned to identify new opportunities for innovation and adaptability. Staying attuned to external changes allows these organizations to navigate challenges effectively and seize new opportunities, contributing to long-term success and sustainable community development. By proactively managing risks and fostering innovation, public sector entities can achieve continuous improvement and remain responsive to the needs of the public they serve.

Synthesizing Internal and External Insights

The true power of discovery lies in the integration of internal and external insights. By integrating these insights, leaders can make informed decisions that optimize internal processes while aligning them with external expectations and market realities.

To achieve effective integration, leaders employ various strategies:

- **Cross-functional workshops:** Bringing together representatives from different internal departments and external stakeholders facilitates a comprehensive discussion of discovery findings and invites collaborative solutions. This collaborative approach ensures that diverse perspectives are considered, fostering innovative solutions and alignment across the organization.

- **SWOT analysis:** A SWOT analysis can further enhance integration efforts by systematically evaluating internal strengths and weaknesses alongside external opportunities and threats. This strategic framework guides comprehensive organizational planning, enabling leaders to capitalize on strengths, mitigate weaknesses, and seize opportunities while navigating potential threats.

- **Continuous feedback loops:** Establishing continuous feedback loops is essential for maintaining alignment with both internal and external environments. These mechanisms enable ongoing input from stakeholders, ensuring that strategies and operations remain responsive to evolving insights and changing circumstances. By prioritizing continuous improvement and adaptation, organizations can sustain their competitive edge and effectively navigate complexities in their operating environment.

In conclusion, synthesizing internal and external insights through effective integration strategies empowers leaders to make informed decisions that drive sustainable growth and success. By leveraging the strengths of both perspectives, leaders can foster resilience, innovation, and strategic alignment, positioning their organizations for long-term excellence and relevance in a dynamic and competitive landscape.

Navigating Challenges in Discovery: Overcoming Common Obstacles

While the discipline of discovery is pivotal for enhancing public service delivery, public sector leaders often face significant challenges that can impede its execution and effectiveness.

Here, we outline common barriers encountered during this critical process and strategies to overcome them.

1. **Silos and resistance to change:** This manifests through departmental reluctance to share information openly, driven by competition for resources or fear of losing autonomy. Employee concerns about job security and resistance from executives further hinder collaboration and transparency. This barrier results in incomplete data and difficulty identifying organizational inefficiencies and opportunities for collaboration. Strategies to overcome this include promoting transparency and collaboration, emphasizing the benefits of the discovery process, and encouraging inclusive participation across all levels and departments.

2. **Information overload:** The flood of data from diverse sources such as surveys, interviews, and public records can overwhelm decision-makers, leading to analysis paralysis and hindering timely decision-making. It can also result in wasted resources and difficulty extracting meaningful insights. To address this, organizations should prioritize data collection based on specific objectives, leverage data management tools to streamline analysis, and focus on quality data that provides actionable insights.

3. **A lack of clearly defined objectives:** When discovery goals are ambiguous, it becomes challenging to collect relevant data that address organizational challenges effectively. This barrier also complicates measuring the success of the discovery process and translating findings into actionable recommendations. Strategies to mitigate this include establishing clear objectives from the outset, effectively communicating these goals to stakeholders, and developing a detailed discovery roadmap outlining each step and expected outcomes.

4. **Limited resources and skill gaps:** These include inadequate budgets for essential tools and technology, as well as insufficient training in stakeholder engagement, data collection methodologies, and analytical techniques. This leads to capacity constraints in gathering and interpreting data accurately, and difficulty translating findings into actionable strategies. Overcoming this barrier involves allocating adequate resources, investing in training programs to enhance team capabilities, and considering partnerships with external consultants to supplement expertise.

In conclusion, addressing these common barriers through proactive strategies will enable public sector leaders to conduct effective discovery processes. By promoting collaboration, managing data effectively, setting clear objectives, and investing in resources and skills development, organizations can maximize the value of discovery efforts, foster innovation, and drive meaningful improvements in public service delivery.

After thoroughly examining the principles and mechanics of effective discovery, we will now illustrate how the discipline works through practical examples using two case studies, one showcasing a successful discovery and the other highlighting failures in the execution of the discovery process.

Case Study 1
Discovery Done Right

Background

After serving as Executive Secretary of the National Gas Supply Stabilization Fund (NGSS) for over a year, Mrs. Adaobi Nwosu reached a critical realization: Her conservative approaches were no longer yielding the desired results for the organization. Faced with declining efficiency and persistent failures to meet the organization's objectives, Mrs. Nwosu embarked on a journey of discovery and transformation.

Supported by a committed team, she delved deeply into the inner workings of the organization, attentively listening to the feedback of both internal and external stakeholders. Her objective was to uncover the underlying issues hindering the organization's performance and strategically reposition the NGSS for sustained success in the future.

Key Players

- **Mrs. Adaobi Nwosu (ES):** Champion of the discovery process, guiding the organization towards transformation.

- **Mr. Ziola Tomuro (CFO):** Led internal reviews, providing critical financial insights.

- **Mr. Labaran Dankoko (VP, Technical Operations)**: Led reviews relating to technical operations

- **Mrs. Paibi Pere (HR director):** Managed employee surveys, capturing internal feedback.

- **Mr. Ahmadu Abdullahi (COO):** Conducted interviews, gathering external stakeholder perspectives.

- **Mr. Kunle Ogunleye (data analyst):** Analyzed data to identify trends and anomalies.

- **Ms. Inaya Dawari (communications director):** Compiled findings into a comprehensive report.

- **Stakeholders:** Employees, union representatives, city officials, commuters, and external partners.

The Discovery Process

Stage 1: Planning and Preparation

The objective: Mrs. Nwosu, along with her executive team, defined clear objectives for the discovery phase: To understand past failures, identify new opportunities for growth, and evaluate the impact of strategic decisions.

Stakeholder identification: The team compiled a list of key stakeholders, including NGSS employees, energy sector stakeholders including gas producers, pipeline operators, energy traders, the regulator, union representatives, and leaders of host communities. They recognized that each group's input was crucial for a holistic understanding of the organization's challenges and opportunities.

Timeline development: A realistic timeline was established, outlining milestones and deadlines for each phase of the discovery journey. This structured approach ensured efficient progress and timely completion, with specific checkpoints for reviewing progress and making necessary adjustments.

Stage 2: Data Collection

Internal reviews: The discovery team, led by CFO Mr. Ziola Tomuro and Vice President, Technical Operations, Mr. Labaran Dankoko conducted thorough reviews of internal documents such as financial statements, fund disbursement schedules, gas supply contracts, sector performance reports, memoranda of understanding with operators and partners, HR reports, past audits, and strategic plans. These documents provided insights into NGSS' operational performance and sector impact.

Surveys and questionnaires: HR Director Mrs. Paibi Pere deployed surveys to capture feedback from employees at all levels. Anonymous surveys were used to foster candid responses, revealing valuable perspectives on organizational dynamics and challenges.

Interviews: COO Mr. Ahmadu Abdullahi scheduled in-depth interviews with department heads, key personnel, and external stakeholders, including gas operators and sector stakeholders. These conversations provided nuanced insights and personal experiences, enriching the understanding of NGSS' strengths and weaknesses.

Stage 3: Analysis

Data analysis: Using statistical tools, the data team, led by Data Analyst Mr. Kunle Ogunleye, analyzed the collected data to identify trends, anomalies, and correlations. This analysis shed light on operational efficiencies and areas needing improvement.

SWOT analysis: A SWOT analysis was conducted to assess internal strengths and weaknesses, and external opportunities and threats. This structured evaluation provided a strategic framework for decision-making.

Gap analysis: The team evaluated the gaps between NGSS' current state and desired future outcomes. This process highlighted areas requiring immediate attention and strategic intervention.

Stage 4: Synthesis and Reporting

Compile findings: All data and insights were synthesized into a cohesive report by Communications Director Ms. Inaya Dawari. This document served as a comprehensive overview of NGSS' current state, challenges, and opportunities.

Feedback sessions: The findings were presented to senior management and stakeholders for validation and further insights. Open dialogue during these sessions fostered collective understanding and agreement on priorities.

Develop actionable insights: Data-driven insights were translated into actionable strategies and initiatives. These recommendations guided strategic decisions aimed at enhancing NGSS' effectiveness and achieving long-term goals.

Maximizing Discovery Outcomes

The discovery team employed data triangulation to strengthen the validity of their findings. They compared survey results with interview insights, document reviews, and direct observations. This comprehensive approach reduced bias and provided a complete picture of the situation.

Stakeholder mapping was used to identify key groups and individuals, categorizing them based on their influence and interest in NGSS' outcomes. Tailored engagement strategies, including focus groups and town hall meetings, ensured that diverse perspectives were captured.

Preliminary findings were shared with different stakeholder groups throughout the discovery process. Feedback was gathered and integrated into the final report, refining the understanding and ensuring the accuracy and completeness of the discoveries.

Tensions and Critical Moments

As the discovery process unfolded, initial surveys revealed deep-seated frustrations among employees, particularly regarding communication and decision-making transparency. Anonymous feedback highlighted a disconnect between frontline staff and senior management.

During interviews, key personnel and external stakeholders expressed concerns about the organization's strategic direction and operational inefficiencies. Operators and the regulator emphasized the need for NGSS to align more closely with broader gas sector development goals, understand practical realities and improve their turnaround time.

Data analysis uncovered unexpected anomalies, such as discrepancies in financial reporting, fund statements and third-party sector reports. These findings prompted a deeper investigation into NGSS internal processes and systems.

Turning Challenges into Opportunities

Despite these challenges, iterative feedback loops ensured continuous improvement. Preliminary findings were shared with stakeholder groups, allowing for real-time adjustments and refinements. This approach fostered a culture of transparency and collaboration, with all voices being heard and valued.

The discovery team's use of data triangulation provided a robust foundation of evidence. By comparing survey results with interview insights, document reviews, and direct observations, the team built a comprehensive understanding of NGSS' current state and areas for improvement.

The Outcome

The discovery process culminated in a detailed report, presented to senior management and stakeholders. The report highlighted key findings, including the need for improved response time, financial data accuracy, streamlined operational processes, and better understanding and alignment with gas sector goals and new developments.

Based on these insights, NGSS developed actionable strategies to address identified issues. Initiatives included enhanced stakeholder engagement programs including stronger inter-agency coordination with the regulator, revamped financial management and reconciliation systems, improved decision-making process, and strengthened internal capacity to efficiently manage operator contracts and fund applications.

A New Direction

As NGSS embarked on this new strategic direction, the organization experienced a renewed sense of purpose and alignment. Employees felt more engaged and valued, knowing that their voices had been heard. External stakeholders recognized NGSS' commitment to transparency and collaboration.

By mastering and effectively executing the four stages of discovery, NGSS successfully navigated its challenges and positioned itself for sustained success. The organization's journey of introspection and transformation, guided by Mrs. Nwosu's leadership and the discovery team's efforts, became a blueprint for effective organizational discovery and strategic realignment.

Conclusion and Lesson Learned

The NGSS case study demonstrates the critical success factors in executing a discovery process. By setting clear objectives, engaging stakeholders, employing data triangulation, and incorporating iterative feedback loops, organizations can uncover valuable insights and drive positive change. Through meticulous planning, comprehensive data collection, and strategic analysis, public sector leaders can ensure informed decision-making and alignment with long-term goals, ultimately leading to organizational success.

Case Study 2
Discovery Gone Wrong

Background

Following his appointment as the new Chief Technology Officer (CTO) for the Alpha State Technology Authority (ASTA), Mr. Adango Afini initiated a discovery process. ASTA, responsible for overseeing and enhancing technology infrastructure and services in Alpha State, faced growing concerns about inefficiencies and alleged mismanagement, particularly highlighted during a recent cybersecurity incident. The objective of the discovery process was to uncover internal operational challenges and enhance technology service delivery.

Key Players

- **Mr. Adango Afini (CTO):** Initially championed the discovery process but struggled with execution.

- **Ms. Evelyn Ruko (CFO):** Responsible for internal reviews but faced significant data inaccuracies.

- **Mr. Samuel Udo (HR Director):** Managed employee surveys, which yielded limited responses.

- **Mrs. Tina Mohammed (COO):** Conducted interviews but failed to gather comprehensive insights.

- **Mr. Tunde Ayeni (Data Analyst):** Analyzed data but missed critical trends.

- **Ms. Linda Eku (Communications Director):** Compiled findings into a report that lacked coherence.

- **Stakeholders:** Employees, technology operators, city officials, tech users, and external partners.

The Discovery Process

Stage 1: Planning and Preparation

Objective: Mr. Afini and his executive team attempted to define clear objectives for the discovery phase but struggled to align on priorities. They aimed to improve service delivery and enhance stakeholder satisfaction but failed to clearly articulate these goals.

Stakeholder Identification: The team compiled a list of stakeholders, but significant groups were overlooked. The inclusion of some influential voices was missed, leading to a lack of comprehensive input.

Timeline Development: A timeline was established but proved unrealistic, with overly ambitious milestones and insufficient buffer time for adjustments. This rushed approach set the stage for further complications.

Stage 2: Data Collection

Internal Reviews: Led by Ms. Evelyn Ruko, the team conducted reviews of internal documents. However, many documents were outdated or incomplete. Technical reviews of technological infrastructure – central servers, data repositories, and cybersecurity monitoring systems - were not conducted, resulting in a flawed understanding of the organization's current state.

Surveys and Questionnaires: Mr. Samuel Udo deployed surveys to capture employee feedback. However, the response rate was low due to poor communication and a lack of anonymity, leading to skewed and unrepresentative data.

Interviews: Mrs. Tina Mohammed scheduled interviews with key personnel and stakeholders, but many sessions were poorly prepared and unfocused. Important insights were missed, and the data collected was fragmented.

Stage 3: Analysis

Data Analysis: Mr. Tunde Ayeni used statistical tools to analyze the collected data but failed to identify key trends and correlations. The absence of technical infrastructure assessment data was a major gap. Critical issues went unnoticed, and the analysis lacked depth.

SWOT Analysis: A SWOT analysis was conducted, but due to the poor quality of the initial data, the results were unreliable. The team could not accurately assess the organization's strengths, weaknesses, opportunities, and threats.

Gap Analysis: The team attempted a gap analysis but failed to clearly define the desired future state. This resulted in vague recommendations that lacked actionable insights.

Stage 4: Synthesis and Reporting

Compile Findings: Ms. Linda Eku synthesized the data into a report, but it lacked coherence and clarity. The report was filled with contradictions and failed to provide a clear overview of the organization's challenges and opportunities.

Feedback Sessions: During feedback sessions, stakeholders expressed confusion and frustration over the findings. The lack of clear, actionable insights led to disengagement and skepticism about the process.

Develop Actionable Insights: Due to the flawed data and analysis, the recommendations were broad and non-specific. Strategic initiatives lacked a clear direction, and the proposed actions were not aligned with the organization's needs.

Tensions and Critical Moments

Employee Frustration: Initial surveys revealed deep-seated frustrations among employees regarding communication and transparency. However, these issues were not addressed adequately, leading to further discontent.

Stakeholder Concerns: During interviews, key personnel and external stakeholders expressed concerns about the organization's strategic direction, industry leadership and operational inefficiencies. Allegations were raised about the recent data breach and associated losses to the businesses of external partners. These concerns were not effectively integrated into the final analysis.

Challenges that Turned into Misses

Despite identifying several issues, the team failed to turn challenges into opportunities. The lack of iterative feedback loops meant that preliminary findings were not adequately shared or refined. The continuous improvement culture was absent, leading to stagnation.

The Outcome

The discovery process culminated in a report that was presented to senior management and stakeholders. However, the report was met with disappointment and criticism. The key findings were ambiguous, and the proposed strategies lacked substance.

As the organization attempted to move forward, it became clear that the discovery process had failed to address core issues. Employees felt disengaged and undervalued, knowing that their voices had not been heard. External stakeholders viewed the organization as disorganized and unresponsive.

Conclusion and Lesson Learned

The case study of the failed discovery at Alpha State Technology Authority highlights the critical pitfalls in executing a discovery process. By setting unclear objectives, overlooking key stakeholders, employing flawed data collection methods, and failing to integrate iterative feedback, the organization was unable to uncover valuable insights or drive positive change. The result was a demotivated workforce, dissatisfied stakeholders, and missed opportunities for improvement.

This scenario underscores the importance of meticulous planning, comprehensive data collection, strategic analysis, and continuous stakeholder engagement in achieving successful outcomes. Without these elements, the discovery process is doomed to fail, leaving the organization struggling to find its way.

Call to Action
Master Discovery and Set the Stage for Breakthrough Results

This chapter has explored the discipline of discovery, not just as data collection, but as a strategic roadmap for your success as a public sector leader. Implemented effectively, discovery will empower you to navigate the complexities of your organization, regardless of your experience level. This, in turn, will pave the way for exceptional service delivery and operational excellence.

By adhering to the key principles outlined here—a comprehensive approach, the right tools and techniques, and most importantly, active stakeholder engagement—you will gain a comprehensive understanding of your internal operations and external influences. This knowledge will equip you to make informed decisions that will lead to significant improvements in service delivery, operational efficiency, and ultimately, the betterment of the public good.

However, the discovery process will not be without its challenges. The strategies provided in this chapter will help you anticipate and mitigate these potential roadblocks.

As the saying goes, effective leaders must know their mission, understand their people and organization, and lead from the front. Mastering the discipline of discovery empowers you to do exactly that.

Implement the strategies outlined in this chapter and you will foster a culture of open communication and inclusivity within your organization. This will translate into concrete actions that drive positive change.

Embrace the discipline of discovery to actively shape the future of your organization, paving the way for positive, lasting change.

The Discipline of Discovery at a Glance

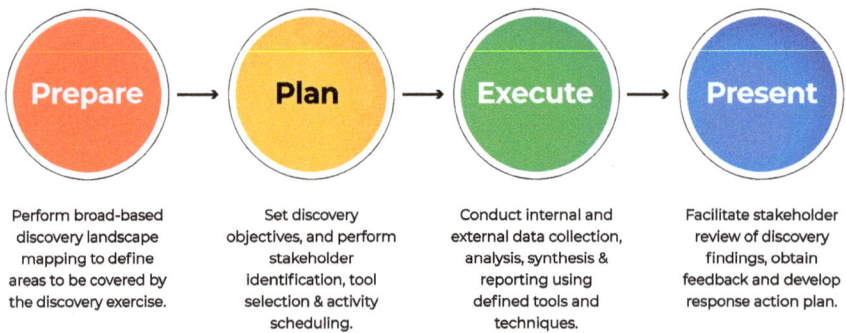

Prepare	Plan	Execute	Present
Perform broad-based discovery landscape mapping to define areas to be covered by the discovery exercise.	Set discovery objectives, and perform stakeholder identification, tool selection & activity scheduling.	Conduct internal and external data collection, analysis, synthesis & reporting using defined tools and techniques.	Facilitate stakeholder review of discovery findings, obtain feedback and develop response action plan.

Figure 7. Framework for Mastering DISCOVERY: PPEP

⚡ WHY IS DISCOVERY IMPORTANT FOR PUBLIC LEADERS?

- **Informed decision-making**: Discovery equips leaders with comprehensive insights into internal operations and external influences, enabling data-driven and effective strategic decisions.

- **Transparency and trust**: It fosters a culture of openness and trust, demonstrating a commitment to inclusivity and collaboration, which enhances morale and stakeholder engagement.

- **Identification of challenges and opportunities**: Discovery helps uncover hidden inefficiencies, systemic issues, and potential areas for innovation, providing a clear path for transformative changes.

- **Alignment with stakeholder expectations**: By integrating internal and external perspectives, leaders can align organizational strategies with market realities and stakeholder needs, ensuring long-term relevance and success.

☀ WHAT ARE THE BIG IDEAS?

- Effective dialogue with internal and external stakeholders forms the foundation of a robust discovery process, providing a wealth of actionable information about the organization.

- Leaders need to explore the organizational structure, operational processes, cultural norms, external environment, technological infrastructure, and financial health to fully understand their organizations.

- Employing tools such as surveys, interviews, document reviews, observations, and SWOT analysis helps systematically unravel organizational complexities and generate actionable insights.

- Addressing challenges such as siloed mindsets, information overload, unclear objectives, and limited resources through proactive strategies is crucial for the success of the discovery process and subsequent organizational improvements.

⚒ HOW DO I MAKE IT HAPPEN?

Follow a four-stage process to effectively discover your organization.

Stage 1: Planning and Preparation

Stage 2: Data Collection

Stage 3: Analysis

Stage 4: Synthesis and Reporting

Chapter 4
Discipline 3 - Diagnose

When leaders embark on the discovery process, they do so with the intention of uncovering the unvarnished reality of their organization. However, they often find themselves unprepared for the full spectrum of truths that emerge. Discovery serves as a critical X-ray for any organization, laying bare its strengths and weaknesses in stark detail. The clarity it provides can be both enlightening and unsettling. While leaders may hope for positive revelations, the process inevitably exposes deeply rooted problems and harsh realities that are challenging to address.

In all the years that I have worked with leaders in both the private and public sectors to discover their organizations, I have observed recurring themes and issues that arise in the aftermath of these sessions.

One of the most common outcomes is the identification of hidden assets, both human and non-human, that were previously obscured by a lack of awareness, siloed information, or outdated structures. These valuable resources often include talented individuals who have been flying under the radar—individuals possessing unique skills, exceptional work ethic, or innovative ideas that have not been fully recognized within the current structure.

Another frequent positive outcome is the discovery of underutilized equipment, forgotten intellectual property, or hidden data insights that can fuel innovation and organizational progress. The process can also bring to light unexpected connections and synergies between departments or teams that, when developed, can foster collaboration and unlock the organization's untapped potential.

On the other side of the spectrum are the negative revelations that leaders may encounter post-discovery. An all-too-frequent outcome is the presence of presentations with hidden agendas or politically motivated motives. In some cases, stakeholders attempt to manipulate or skew the findings of the discovery session to serve their own interests or agendas rather than the best interests of the organization as a whole.

Despite efforts to promote transparency and open communication, some individuals within the organization may be tempted to conceal or downplay poor performance due to concerns related to job security. It is common to discover that departmental heads and team leads have manipulated data, omitted crucial information, or provided misleading narratives during interviews. Often, leaders of siloed departments or teams may attempt to distort information to protect themselves and their teams. This could involve underreporting resources or exaggerating challenges to justify their continued control. Individuals fearing repercussions for past mistakes might try to deflect blame by misrepresenting information or pointing fingers at others. They might fabricate evidence or downplay their role in problems identified during discovery.

Given this, leaders embarking on the discovery process must remain vigilant for instances of outright deception. When done effectively, the discovery phase will reveal a range of issues, the volume of which can prove overwhelming for leaders and their teams. Sorting through mountains of data to identify key insights and actionable recommendations requires careful analysis and prioritization to ensure that valuable insights are not lost in the deluge of information.

Some issues uncovered will be more severe and deeply ingrained than others. Yet, regardless of the severity of these issues, the most pressing question is: **What actions should leaders take post-discovery to propel the institution forward?**

This is where the next discipline, **<u>DIAGNOSIS</u>**, comes into play.

Diagnosis involves delving deep into the findings from the discovery phase to unearth the root causes of the challenges hindering the organization from achieving its objectives. Prioritizing these findings and conducting a thorough diagnosis is crucial for leaders aiming to transform their organization into a high-performing and effective entity. The importance of this step cannot be overstated.

With this in mind, let's now explore what it takes to conduct an effective and successful diagnosis of an organization.

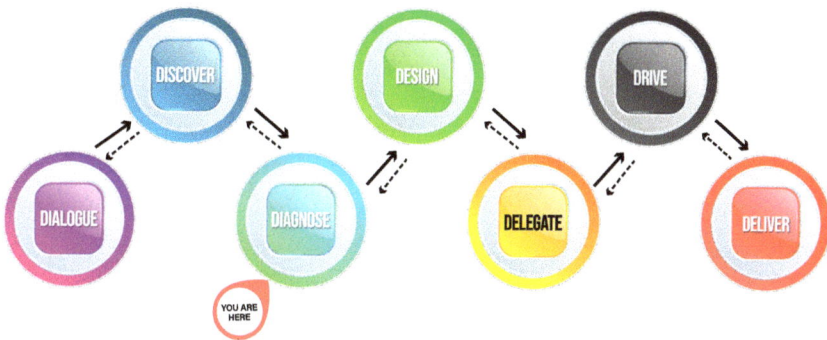

Figure 8. The Seven Disciplines of Breakthrough Results: Diagnose

Introduction to Diagnosis: Unraveling the Fabric of Organizational Challenges

In the complex ecosystem of public sector management, the ability to not just identify but deeply understand organizational challenges is what separates transformative leaders from mere administrators. This is where the critical process of diagnosis comes into play—a meticulous exploration into the undercurrents that define an organization's current state and its obstacles to success.

Just as a medical doctor would not prescribe treatment without a thorough diagnosis, a public sector leader must not attempt to implement solutions without a precise understanding of the underlying issues.

The Essence of Diagnosis in Public Leadership

Diagnosis in the context of public sector leadership goes beyond surface-level observation; it is an investigative process aimed at uncovering the root causes of organizational challenges. It is about peeling back the layers of daily operations and strategic decisions to reveal the deeper truths that may be hindering progress. For new leaders, it offers the first real insight into the heart of the organization's issues. For seasoned leaders, it is a chance to recalibrate and realign their strategies to address evolving challenges effectively.

The significance of the discipline of diagnosis lies in its capacity to provide leaders with a clear, detailed map of organizational health and dysfunction. Without this clarity, efforts to drive change are often misguided, addressing symptoms rather than causes, and are doomed to yield only temporary relief or, worse, exacerbate existing problems.

Benefits of a Well-executed Diagnosis

Borrowing again from the analogy of a medical practitioner, when diagnosis is well done, it provides a clear roadmap for effective treatment. Similarly, in organizational settings, a thorough diagnosis lays the foundation for targeted interventions that address core challenges and propel the institution toward its goals with precision and efficacy.

The following are the core benefits of a well-executed diagnosis process:

- **Accurate problem identification:** While the discovery process reveals a plethora of symptoms—declining performance metrics, low employee morale, or disjointed processes—a well-structured diagnosis digs deeper, moving beyond the surface symptoms to identify the root causes. It asks for the "why" behind the "what" uncovered during discovery. A well-conducted diagnosis ensures that problems are not just identified but are understood in their entirety. This prevents the common pitfalls of addressing the wrong issues or overlooking hidden factors that could later surface as major challenges. A thorough diagnosis ensures that leaders are not simply treating symptoms, but that they are addressing the core problems that threaten organizational health.

- **Strategic insight:** Discovery sessions can provide valuable insights, but they can also be siloed, focusing on specific departments or functions. Diagnosis takes a holistic approach. It gathers data from diverse sources, analyzes trends, and identifies interdependencies between seemingly disparate issues. This comprehensive analysis provides leaders with a 360-degree view of the organization, revealing hidden connections and external influences that might otherwise be overlooked. This broader perspective empowers leaders to develop solutions that address the entire ecosystem, not just isolated problems.

- **Enhanced stakeholder confidence:** When faced with challenging situations, stakeholders often crave transparency. A well-structured diagnosis demonstrates to stakeholders that leadership is committed to evidence-based decision-making. When stakeholders see that decisions are based on a thorough understanding of the organization's challenges, their trust in leadership increases. By presenting a clear picture of the organization's strengths and weaknesses, backed by data and analysis, diagnosis fosters trust and confidence. Stakeholders are more likely to support necessary changes and initiatives when they understand the reasoning behind them.

- **Foundation for effective solutions:** Diagnosis doesn't stop at identifying problems; it paves the way for effective solutions. By clearly defining what problems need to be solved and the underlying causes, diagnosis sets the stage for targeted interventions. This ensures that solutions are not one-size-fits-all approaches but rather tailored to address the specific needs of the organization. Furthermore, a thorough diagnosis helps leaders anticipate potential roadblocks and develop mitigation strategies. This promotes sustainable solutions with a higher chance of success in the long run.

Mastering the Discipline of Diagnosis in Public Sector Leadership

Mastering diagnosis begins with understanding that it involves engagement with both internal and external stakeholders. Leaders must harness the collective knowledge, perspectives, and experiences of these stakeholders to paint a complete picture of the organization's challenges. This includes collective deliberation, working with teams to validate findings, prioritize issues, and brainstorm potential interventions. By engaging both categories of stakeholders, leaders ensure that diverse viewpoints are considered, leading to more comprehensive and actionable insights.

Leaders must also recognize that the process of diagnosis is not a one-time effort but a critical ongoing practice that requires them to remain engaged, observant, and proactive. As organizations evolve, so do their challenges, making continuous diagnosis essential for sustained organizational health and effectiveness. This ongoing effort ensures that leaders are always equipped with up-to-date information to address emerging issues promptly.

With this understanding in place, the rest of this section delves deeper into the fundamental preparations, tools, techniques, and principles that leaders must become skilled at to effectively execute the diagnostic process. The first step is to define the scope of their diagnosis.

Defining the Scope of Diagnosis

Before embarking on the diagnostic journey, it is crucial to establish a well-defined scope. Defining the scope of diagnosis ensures that efforts are targeted and resources are used efficiently. Organizational challenges are multifaceted, and a clear scope helps prioritize the most critical areas for investigation. Whether it's declining citizen satisfaction with public programs or low employee morale, a well-defined scope allows leaders to focus resources where they can have the greatest impact.

Resource management is another key benefit. Conducting a thorough diagnosis can be resource-intensive, involving personnel, time, and budget.

Limiting the scope to essential areas prevents resource overextension and ensures that efforts are concentrated where they are most needed. Moreover, a well-defined scope aligns the diagnosis with the organization's strategic goals. By clarifying which aspects of the organization will be investigated, leaders can ensure that the findings contribute directly to refining and achieving strategic objectives.

A clearly defined scope makes managing the diagnosis process more feasible. It establishes realistic boundaries, enabling leaders to create a manageable timeline and allocate resources effectively. This ensures that the diagnosis phase progresses smoothly and concludes within the expected timeframe.

Defining the scope involves determining the breadth and depth of the diagnosis. The breadth refers to the range of areas under investigation— whether it's a specific department or a comprehensive view of the entire organization. The depth pertains to the level of detail and analysis required for each area, whether it's a high-level overview or an in-depth examination. By considering these factors and tailoring the scope to specific organizational needs, leaders set the stage for a focused, productive, and impactful diagnosis process.

After defining the scope, leaders need to understand the essential components that will ensure that their diagnosis is effective. This brings us to the next crucial aspect: understanding the breakdown of the core elements of the diagnosis process.

A Breakdown of the Core Elements of Diagnosis

For leaders to execute an effective diagnosis, they must deeply understand the following core elements and associated considerations:

1. Data Collection

Purpose: Data collection serves as the cornerstone for the entire diagnosis process, ensuring the acquisition of relevant and reliable data that accurately reflects the organization's current state.

Methods: To capture a comprehensive picture, a variety of data collection methods are utilized:

- **Surveys:** Structured questionnaires efficiently gather quantitative data from a large pool of participants.

- **Interviews:** In-depth interviews provide rich qualitative data, offering valuable insights into individual perspectives and experiences.

- **Observations:** Direct observation of processes and behaviors can uncover unspoken issues and hidden dynamics within the organization.

- **Document reviews:** Analyzing existing documents such as reports, policies, and procedures provides historical context and helps identify potential inconsistencies.

Challenges: Several challenges can arise in the data collection process:

- **Data reliability and comprehensiveness:** Ensuring data accuracy, completeness, and representability of the entire organization can be challenging.

- **Overcoming biases:** Both data collectors and participants can introduce unintentional biases. Mitigating these biases requires the careful design of data collection methods and a keen awareness of potential pitfalls.

2. Analytical Tools and Techniques

Purpose: After collecting data, apply analytical tools and techniques to extract meaningful insights.

Methods: This analytical toolkit encompasses various tools tailored to specific data and contexts:

- **Statistical methods:** Techniques such as correlation analysis and regression are employed to identify relationships between variables and evaluate their significance.

- **Content analysis:** This method systematically analyzes qualitative data from interviews, documents, and open-ended survey responses to uncover recurring themes and patterns.

- **Cause-and-effect diagrams:** These visual aids help visualize potential causes of an issue, aiding in brainstorming and root cause identification.

Challenges: Several challenges must be navigated:

- **Selecting the right tools:** Choosing the most suitable analytical tools requires a deep understanding of the data and the specific research questions.

- **Interpreting data:** Drawing accurate conclusions necessitates a critical assessment and awareness of inherent limitations in the chosen analytical techniques.

3. Stakeholder Involvement

Purpose: Stakeholders encompass individuals or groups who are either impacted by or have an impact on the issues being diagnosed. Their engagement is critical to the process.

Methods: Various approaches facilitate stakeholder involvement in the diagnosis:

- **Workshops:** Interactive sessions enable facilitated discussions and brainstorming, fostering collaboration and shared understanding of challenges.

- **Focus groups:** Bringing together smaller groups allows for deeper exploration of specific issues and experiences among stakeholders.

- **One-on-one interviews:** In-depth conversations with key stakeholders yield valuable insights from leadership, frontline staff, and external partners.

Challenges: Several challenges must be managed:

- **Managing differing opinions:** Addressing disagreements and varied perspectives requires facilitating constructive dialogue and ensuring inclusivity.

- **Ensuring meaningful participation:** Encouraging active engagement from all stakeholders demands effective communication and well-structured questioning.

- **Synthesizing inputs:** Integrating diverse stakeholder perspectives into a coherent understanding of organizational challenges necessitates meticulous analysis and synthesis of gathered information.

4. Issue Identification and Prioritization

Purpose: The objective is to systematically identify all issues unearthed during the diagnosis process. Once identified, these issues are ranked based on two key criteria:

- **Impact on organizational goals:** This involves assessing how each issue hinders the organization's ability to achieve its strategic objectives. Issues significantly impeding progress on critical goals are prioritized for immediate attention.

- **Urgency:** This criterion considers the timeframe within which each issue needs to be addressed. Urgent issues posing an immediate threat to the organization's stability or reputation require a swift response, while less time-sensitive issues can be addressed over a longer timeframe.

Methods: To achieve effective issue identification and prioritization, various techniques can be employed:

- **Prioritization matrices:** Visual tools, such as risk assessment matrices, allow issues to be plotted based on their impact and urgency.

- **Decision-making software:** Software applications can be utilized to objectively assess and rank issues based on predefined criteria, which is particularly helpful when dealing with complex data sets or numerous potential issues.

Challenges: Navigating this stage presents its own set of hurdles:

- **Balancing short-term fixes vs. long-term solutions:** The urge to address immediate problems can sometimes overshadow the need for sustainable, long-term solutions. The challenge lies in balancing the attention to pressing issues while also implementing solutions that address root causes and prevent future recurrence.

- **Aligning team perceptions:** Different team members may have varying perceptions of the severity and urgency of identified issues. Fostering open communication and utilizing objective data analysis is key to achieving consensus on prioritization.

5. Reporting and Recommendation Development

Purpose: After the most pressing issues have been identified and prioritized, the insights gleaned from the diagnosis process are communicated to a wider but relevant audience within the organization. This includes not only presenting the identified issues but also outlining a set of actionable recommendations for addressing them.

Methods: To achieve this objective, comprehensive reports are developed that include the following elements:

- **Executive summary:** A concise overview of the key findings and recommendations, targeted towards busy decision-makers.

- **Detailed findings:** An in-depth exploration of the data analysis presented clearly and understandably. Visual aids like charts and graphs can enhance comprehension.

- **Actionable recommendations:** The heart of the report, outlining specific actions to address the identified issues. Recommendations should be clear, measurable, achievable, relevant, and time-bound (SMART).

- **Implementation plan:** A roadmap for putting the recommendations into action, detailing timelines, resource allocation, and task ownership.

Challenges: Crafting impactful reports requires careful consideration of the audience:

- **Ensuring understandability:** The report should be written clearly and concisely, avoiding technical jargon that may alienate the reader. Tailoring the language and level of detail to the specific audience is crucial.

- **Actionability:** The recommendations should be practical and feasible to implement within the organization's existing resources and capabilities. Reports that propose unrealistic solutions are less likely to gain traction.

Having introduced the critical components for an effective diagnosis, we will now delve into the specific steps for executing the diagnosis process itself.

Executing Diagnosis: A Stage-by-Stage Guide

An effective diagnosis process unfolds in five distinct stages. By following this process, leaders can systematically uncover the root issues impacting their organizational performance and propose actionable solutions.

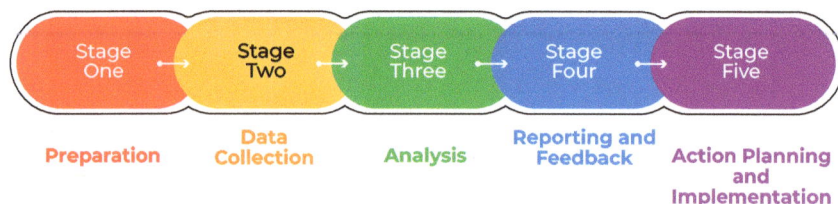

Stage One	Stage Two	Stage Three	Stage Four	Stage Five
Preparation	Data Collection	Analysis	Reporting and Feedback	Action Planning and Implementation

Figure 9. The Five Stages of Diagnosis

Stage 1: Preparing for Diagnosis

Before diving into the diagnosis process, it is crucial to lay a solid foundation through careful preparation. This stage ensures that the goals are well-defined, stakeholders are identified, and resources are allocated appropriately.

- **Objective setting:** Define specific goals for the diagnosis intervention. Goals should be aligned with the broader organizational objectives and clearly articulate the expected outcomes of the diagnosis.

- **Stakeholder identification:** Create a comprehensive list of stakeholders involved in or affected by the organizational issues under review, including employees, management, board members, and external partners.

- **Resource allocation:** Determine the resources necessary for the diagnosis, including personnel, technology, and budget. Assign roles and responsibilities to team members to ensure accountability.

Stage 2: Data Collection

Once the groundwork is laid, the next step is to gather relevant data. This stage focuses on planning, developing tools, and executing the data collection to ensure comprehensive and accurate information is obtained.

- **Data collection planning:** Choose appropriate data collection methods based on the objectives set in the Preparation Phase. Common methods include surveys, interviews, document analysis, and observational studies.

- **Tool development:** Develop or refine tools such as surveys, interview guides, and focus group questions that are tailored to the specific needs of the diagnosis.

- **Data collection execution:** Implement the data collection plan, ensuring that all data gathered is accurate, relevant, and comprehensive.

Stage 3: Analysis

With the data in hand, the focus shifts to analyzing and synthesizing the information. This stage is critical for transforming raw data into meaningful insights that can inform decision-making.

- **Data analysis:** Analyze the collected data using both qualitative and quantitative methods. Employ statistical tools for quantitative data and content analysis for qualitative data.

- **Synthesis of findings:** Synthesize data from various sources to form a coherent understanding of the diagnosed issues. Highlight key themes and patterns that emerge from the data.

Stage 4: Reporting and Feedback

Effective communication of the findings is essential for stakeholder buy-in and subsequent action. This stage involves compiling a comprehensive report and gathering feedback to ensure the findings are accurate and relevant.

- **Drafting the diagnosis report:** Compile the findings into a comprehensive diagnosis report that includes an executive summary, detailed findings, and actionable recommendations.

- **Stakeholder feedback:** Present the findings to key stakeholders to gather feedback and ensure the report's accuracy and relevance.

Stage 5: Action Planning and Implementation

The final stage focuses on translating insights into actionable plans. This involves developing detailed action plans and ensuring their effective implementation and monitoring.

- **Development of action plans:** Based on the diagnosis findings, develop detailed action plans that address the identified issues. Plans should include specific steps, timelines, and responsible parties.

- **Implementation:** Implement the action plans, ensuring that all activities are closely monitored and adjusted as necessary based on ongoing feedback.

Executing an effective diagnosis is not merely a procedural task but a strategic endeavor essential for organizational success. By diligently following the five stages outlined in the above section—from meticulous preparation and comprehensive data collection to rigorous analysis, insightful reporting, and decisive action planning—leaders can uncover deep-seated issues and pave the way for transformative change. Each stage reinforces the importance of clarity, stakeholder engagement, and systematic execution. Ultimately, embracing this structured approach empowers leaders to not only diagnose challenges accurately but also to implement sustainable solutions that drive organizational growth and resilience in an ever-evolving landscape of opportunities and challenges.

Integrating Diagnosis with Organizational Strategy

A critical aspect of the diagnosis process is its integration with the organization's broader strategic objectives. This ensures that the insights gained from diagnosis actively contribute to achieving the organization's overarching goals. This critical integration bridges the gap between identifying issues and implementing solutions, ultimately leading to more cohesive and impactful organizational improvements.

There are two key aspects to consider for successful integration:

Strategic alignment: The findings and recommendations from the diagnosis should be carefully aligned with the organization's long-term vision and strategic priorities. This alignment ensures that the actions taken as a result of the diagnosis are not only impactful in the short term but also contribute to the sustainable growth and advancement of the organization.

Feedback loops: Establishing effective feedback loops is essential for integrating diagnosis with organizational strategy. These mechanisms allow ongoing insights and lessons learned from the diagnosis process to inform and refine strategic planning and implementation. By continually feeding back findings into the strategy, organizations can adapt more swiftly to changing circumstances, optimize resource allocation, and ensure that strategic decisions remain well-informed and responsive to organizational needs.

By integrating diagnosis with organizational strategy through strategic alignment and feedback loops, organizations can maximize the impact of their diagnostic efforts, foster a culture of continuous improvement, and ensure that every action taken contributes effectively to overarching strategic goals.

Navigating Challenges in Diagnosis: Overcoming Common Obstacles

Diagnosing organizational issues in the public sector is a complex and intricate process that often encounters various challenges. Effective navigation and resolution of these challenges are crucial for ensuring that the diagnosis leads to meaningful and actionable insights. This section explores the common obstacles encountered during the diagnosis process and provides strategies for overcoming them to maintain the integrity and effectiveness of the endeavor.

1. Data Integrity and Quality Issues

Inaccurate or incomplete data undermine the reliability and validity of the diagnosis process. This can arise due to various factors such as data entry errors, outdated information, or bias in data collection methods. Misguided strategies emerge when decisions are based on faulty data, resulting in ineffective solutions that fail to address the real issues. Inaccurate data can obscure underlying problems or misidentify root causes, potentially exacerbating existing challenges. Moreover, reliance on flawed conclusions can waste resources and time, diverting efforts away from meaningful improvements.

Solution: Ensuring Data Accuracy and Completeness

- Implement robust data validation processes to ensure the accuracy and completeness of collected data.
- Utilize multiple data sources and triangulation techniques to cross-reference information and verify its reliability.

- Invest in training programs for data collectors to enhance their skills in data collection and entry.

- Regularly update data collection methods and tools to adapt to changing organizational needs and technological advancements.

2. Stakeholder Resistance

Resistance from stakeholders, including employees and management, poses a significant barrier to the diagnosis process. This resistance often stems from apprehension about potential negative outcomes, such as job insecurity, changes in roles or responsibilities, disruption to established routines, or skepticism about the effectiveness or relevance of the diagnostic efforts. Limited cooperation from stakeholders hampers data collection and compromises the validity of the diagnostic findings. Without active engagement from key individuals or groups, critical insights may remain undiscovered, leading to incomplete analyses or biased interpretations. Additionally, stakeholder resistance undermines the credibility of the diagnosis process, eroding trust in the outcomes and diminishing support for subsequent actions or interventions.

Solution: Engaging and Communicating with Stakeholders

- Proactively communicate the purpose, benefits, and expected outcomes of the diagnosis process to stakeholders to alleviate fears and uncertainties.

- Engage stakeholders early and involve them in the design and planning of the diagnostic efforts to foster ownership and buy-in.

- Address concerns and objections through open and honest dialogue, emphasizing the value of their input and participation.

- Provide opportunities for training and skill development to empower stakeholders to contribute meaningfully to the diagnosis process.

- Recognize and reward stakeholder contributions to reinforce positive behaviors and attitudes.

3. Resource Constraints

Limited budget, time, or personnel can severely constrain the resources available for conducting a comprehensive diagnosis. This constraint may result in difficulties accessing necessary data, conducting thorough analyses, or implementing corrective actions. The restricted scope and depth of the diagnosis may lead to overlooking critical issues or inadequately exploring underlying problems. Without sufficient resources, the diagnosis process may yield incomplete or inaccurate findings, hindering the development of effective solutions.

Solution: Optimizing Resource Allocation

- Prioritize resources based on the significance and urgency of identified issues, focusing efforts on areas with the greatest impact on organizational performance.

- Seek alternative sources of funding or leverage partnerships with external stakeholders to supplement limited resources and expand the scope of the diagnosis.

- Optimize resource allocation by streamlining processes, utilizing technology to automate repetitive tasks, and reallocating personnel to tasks aligned with their expertise.

- Conduct a thorough cost-benefit analysis to justify resource allocation decisions and ensure optimal utilization of available resources.

- Continuously monitor resource utilization and adjust plans as needed to address emerging needs or unexpected challenges.

4. Communication Breakdowns

Poor communication among stakeholders can lead to misunderstandings, conflicting interpretations of goals and processes, and a lack of clarity regarding roles and responsibilities within the diagnosis process. Communication breakdowns can result in misalignment, mistrust, and resistance among stakeholders, impeding collaboration and hindering progress in the diagnosis process. Without effective communication, stakeholders may feel disengaged or uninformed, leading to suboptimal outcomes.

Solution: Establishing Effective Communication Channels

- Establish clear channels of communication and protocols for sharing information, updates, and feedback among all stakeholders involved in the diagnosis process.

- Use platforms such as intranets, regular newsletters, and dedicated Q&A sessions to keep stakeholders informed and engaged.

- Foster an open and inclusive communication environment where stakeholders feel comfortable expressing their concerns, asking questions, and providing input.

- Provide regular updates and progress reports to stakeholders to keep them informed about the status of the diagnosis process, milestones achieved, and next steps.

- Encourage active listening and seek to understand the perspectives and viewpoints of all stakeholders, addressing any misunderstandings or misconceptions promptly to ensure effective communication throughout the diagnosis process.

By addressing these challenges with targeted solutions, organizations can enhance the effectiveness of their diagnostic efforts and achieve meaningful improvements.

Ethical Considerations in the Diagnostic Process

In public sector organizations, where decisions can significantly impact communities and the use of public resources, ethical considerations are paramount in the diagnosis process. This section examines the ethical dimensions of conducting diagnostics, focusing on maintaining integrity, confidentiality, and fairness throughout the process.

The Importance of Ethics in Diagnosis

Ethical practices in the diagnosis process ensure that the methods and outcomes not only comply with legal standards but also uphold public trust and organizational values. This is crucial for maintaining credibility and legitimacy in the eyes of stakeholders and the community at large.

Here, we delve into four key ethical considerations and propose strategies to ensure a trustworthy and unbiased diagnosis:

1. Confidentiality and Privacy

- **Challenge:** The heart of diagnosis lies in the data it gathers. However, this data often includes personal and potentially sensitive information. Protecting the confidentiality of this information is paramount.

- **Strategy:** Implement robust data handling and privacy policies. Ensure all data is stored securely using encryption and access is restricted to authorized personnel only. Consider anonymizing data whenever possible to further safeguard individual identities. Remember, building trust with stakeholders hinges on demonstrating your commitment to data privacy.

2. Informed Consent

- **Challenge:** Obtaining informed consent from all participants during the diagnosis process is essential for ethical data collection.

- **Strategy:** Provide clear and comprehensive information about the diagnosis. This should explain the purpose of the data collection, the methods used, and how the data will be utilized. Most importantly, participants must freely and willingly give their consent before any data collection commences. Transparency is key—let participants know that their involvement is voluntary and they have the right to withdraw at any stage.

3. Transparency and Accountability

- **Challenge:** Maintaining transparency throughout the diagnosis process fosters trust and stakeholder engagement. However, there may be times when discretion is necessary, especially when handling sensitive findings.

- **Strategy:** Develop a communication plan that keeps stakeholders informed about the progress of the diagnosis and the final recommendations. While complete transparency is ideal, be mindful of the need to protect confidentiality where appropriate. Establish clear accountability mechanisms to address any concerns that stakeholders may raise during the process.

4. Avoiding Bias

- **Challenge:** Bias can creep into the diagnosis process at various stages, from data collection to analysis and reporting. Biased results can lead to unfair recommendations and ultimately hinder the effectiveness of the diagnosis.

- **Strategy:** Utilize objective data collection methods such as standardized surveys and employ diverse teams in the analysis process. This cross-verification by individuals with different perspectives helps to mitigate the influence of any single bias. Additionally, employ statistical techniques to identify potential outliers or inconsistencies in the data.

By prioritizing these ethical considerations and implementing the suggested strategies, you can ensure that your diagnosis is conducted with integrity, fostering trust and confidence in the process and its outcomes. Remember, a trustworthy diagnosis is the foundation for effective change and a more efficient and citizen-centric public sector organization.

After thoroughly examining the principles and mechanics of an effective diagnosis process, we will now illustrate how diagnosis works through practical examples using two case studies: one showcasing a successful diagnosis and the other highlighting failures in diagnosis execution.

....

Case Study 1
Diagnosis Done Right

Background

The Omega State Utility Authority (OSUA), responsible for water and electricity services, faced escalating operational costs and service delivery challenges. With a new CEO, Mr. Emonike Oni, taking charge, a comprehensive efficiency diagnostic was initiated to uncover the root causes of inefficiencies and devise strategic solutions to enhance service delivery and operational effectiveness.

Key Players:

- **Mr. Emonike Oni (CEO):** Recently appointed, determined to revitalize OSUA by tackling core operational challenges.

- **Mr. Abdul Ibrahim (director of operations):** Oversees daily operations and coordinates data collection efforts across utility services.

- **Ms. Bola Ojo (chief financial officer):** Provides critical financial oversight for cost analysis and resource allocation.

- **Department managers and frontline staff:** Essential for providing operational insights and feedback on service delivery.

- **External consultants:** Engaged to provide specialized expertise in public sector operations and efficiency analysis.

The Diagnosis Process

Stage 1: Preparing for Efficiency Diagnostic

Objective setting: Mr. Oni, along with Mr. Ibrahim and Ms. Ojo, set clear objectives to uncover the root causes of escalating customer complaints and operational inefficiency. Meetings with department heads ensured alignment on goals and outcomes.

Stakeholder identification: Comprehensive mapping included engaging department managers, frontline staff, regulatory bodies, and community representatives to ensure inclusive decision-making.

Resource allocation: Mr. Oni, in collaboration with Ms. Ojo, defined resources for the initiative, including personnel for data collection, analytical tools, and budget allocations, with clear roles assigned for accountability.

Stage 2: Data Collection

Data collection planning: Mr. Ibrahim employed methods such as surveys, interviews, financial reviews, and performance analysis to gather comprehensive insights into service delivery and operational effectiveness.

Tool development: Under Ms. Ojo's oversight, tools like service performance assessment questionnaires and customer satisfaction surveys tailored to public utility operations were developed.

Data collection execution: Frontline staff actively participated in executing plans, ensuring accurate data collection across service points.

Stage 3: Analysis

Data analysis: Mr. Ibrahim and external consultants utilized quantitative methods for financial and operational metrics and qualitative analysis to assess service effectiveness and stakeholder perceptions.

Synthesis of findings: They synthesized data from reports and customer feedback, incorporating input from department managers and frontline staff to identify root causes impacting operational efficiency and service delivery.

Stage 4: Reporting and Feedback

Reporting: Mr. Oni, Ms. Ojo, and the team compiled findings into a comprehensive diagnostic report outlining inefficiencies and strategic initiatives.

Feedback: Presentation to stakeholders, including the State Assembly, ensured transparency and buy-in.

Stage 5: Action Planning and Implementation

Development of action plans: Detailed plans were developed with input from Mr. Ibrahim and department managers to streamline operations, optimize resources, and enhance service standards.

Implementation: Stakeholders actively participated in executing plans, with regular reviews and adjustments based on feedback from department heads and community representatives.

Outcomes

The diagnostic process, guided by Mr. Oni's leadership and collaborative efforts with Ms. Ojo, Mr. Ibrahim, and the entire team, uncovered network breaches in the billing system and work overload for call center staff as the foremost root causes of customer complaints and operational inefficiencies.

Key Success Factors

Strong leadership commitment: Mr. Oni's vision and proactive leadership, supported by Ms. Ojo, Mr. Ibrahim, and the team, were pivotal in driving the diagnostic process forward.

Effective stakeholder engagement: Engagement of department managers, frontline staff, and external consultants ensured comprehensive insights and informed decision-making.

Transparent communication: Regular updates facilitated by Mr. Oni and Ms. Ojo facilitated change management and maintained stakeholder trust.

Focus on training and development: Mr. Oni, Ms. Ojo, and department managers ensured staff were equipped to implement new processes effectively.

Conclusion and Lessons Learned

This case study underscores the importance of structured diagnostics in addressing organizational challenges. It highlights leadership vision, stakeholder engagement, and strategic data utilization in driving organizational improvement. By embracing these lessons, organizations can navigate complexities, address systemic inefficiencies, and achieve sustainable growth and customer satisfaction in their service delivery.

....

Case Study 2
Diagnosis Gone Wrong

Background

Kento National Trade Desk (KNTD), a public entity responsible for managing the nation's trade policies and operations, faced challenges including budget overruns, staffing shortages, and declining stakeholder satisfaction. Mr. Itoro Mark, the newly appointed Director, initiated a diagnosis intervention to address these issues. The objective was to diagnose operational inefficiencies, financial mismanagement, and improve trade services through comprehensive organizational analysis.

Key Players

- **Mr. Itoro Mark (newly appointed Director):** Eager to implement changes despite limited trade management experience.

- **Mr. Uwana Idara (Director of Finance):** Resistant to the intervention due to concerns about potential exposure of financial mismanagement.

- **Ms. Cynthia Raymond (Director of Operations):** Overwhelmed by staffing challenges and skeptical about the process's impact.

- **Staff members and stakeholders:** Directly affected by organizational issues but minimally consulted during the process.

The Diagnosis Process

Stage 1: Preparing for Diagnosis

Objective Setting: Mr. Mark announced the diagnosis process without a clear plan, causing confusion across departments. Objectives were vaguely defined, and roles and expectations were not communicated effectively.

Stakeholder Identification: Comprehensive mapping was lacking, resulting in minimal engagement of key stakeholders like frontline staff and external trade partners.

Resource Allocation: There was inadequate allocation of resources, with insufficient personnel and tools for effective data collection and analysis.

Stage 2: Data Collection

Data Collection Planning: Under pressure, Mr. Uwana Idara provided incomplete financial reports, obscuring the true extent of budget issues. Ms. Cynthia Raymond, grappling with staff shortages, struggled to allocate time for her team to participate, resulting in significant gaps in operational insights.

Tool Development: Tools for data collection and analysis were not developed, leading to incomplete and inaccurate data sets.

Data Collection Execution: Frontline staff and stakeholders were not actively involved in executing data collection plans, undermining the process's credibility.

Critical Moments and Turning Points

Resistance and Challenges: Resistance from department heads, particularly Mr. Uwana Idara, and lack of transparency during data collection severely compromised the integrity of the process. Staff and stakeholders felt ignored, leading to increased dissatisfaction and distrust.

Stage 3: Analysis

Data Analysis: Rushed analysis based on incomplete and inaccurate data failed to uncover the root causes of issues. Superficial assessments overlooked significant problems in trade service delivery.

Synthesis of Findings: The synthesis lacked input from critical stakeholders, resulting in recommendations that did not address the organization's core issues.

Stage 4: Reporting and Feedback

Reporting: The resulting report was incomplete and misleading, suggesting changes that were irrelevant or impractical. When presented to the board of directors, it faced criticism for lacking depth and understanding.

Feedback: There was minimal feedback from stakeholders, and no transparent communication on the report's findings and implications.

Stage 5: Action Planning and Implementation

Action Planning: Instead of improving organizational performance, the diagnosis process increased frustration and distrust among staff. There were no clear action plans developed or implemented to address the identified issues.

Implementation: Stakeholders were not actively involved in executing plans, leading to no visible improvements in trade service delivery or organizational performance.

Outcomes

The flawed diagnostic intervention aggravated existing issues without revealing root causes or providing guidance for effective design interventions. This led to decreased trust and morale within the Kento National Trade Desk and highlighted significant missteps in the diagnostic process.

Key Causes of Failures

Lack of Clear Objectives and Planning: Objectives were not clearly defined, and the planning phase was poorly executed.

Poor Stakeholder Engagement: Key stakeholders, particularly frontline staff and external partners, were not adequately involved in the process.

Resistance and Lack of Transparency: Resistance from department heads and lack of transparency during data collection severely compromised the integrity of the process.

Inadequate Analysis: Rushed and superficial analysis based on incomplete data led to irrelevant recommendations.

Conclusion and Lessons Learned

This case underscores the critical importance of meticulous planning, clear communication, thorough stakeholder engagement and effective data collection and analysis in the diagnosis process. Leaders must ensure transparency, involve all relevant parties meaningfully, and base their analyses on complete and accurate data to avoid missteps and achieve meaningful improvements.

Call to Action

Embrace Effective Diagnosis for Breakthrough Results

As we conclude our exploration of the diagnosis process within public sector organizations, one thing becomes abundantly clear: Embracing a thorough and continuous diagnostic approach is paramount for driving effective and transformational change.

Throughout this journey, we've emphasized the indispensable role of leadership in ensuring the success of the diagnosis process. Leaders must not only champion the cause but also foster a culture of transparency, open communication, and continuous improvement. By doing so, they pave the way for organizational growth and resilience in the face of challenges.

Looking ahead, the imperative for effective diagnosis and strategic management in public sector organizations will only intensify in an increasingly complex and demanding landscape. Leaders who embrace this process wholeheartedly will be better equipped to anticipate and address challenges, ensuring their organizations remain responsive and relevant to the needs of the communities they serve.

Undoubtedly, obstacles will arise along the path of diagnosis—from resource constraints to stakeholder resistance and data complexities. Apply the insights from this chapter to navigate these challenges with agility and adaptability.

Embrace the insights from diagnosis to drive meaningful progress and strengthen your organization's impact.

The Discipline of Diagnosis at a Glance

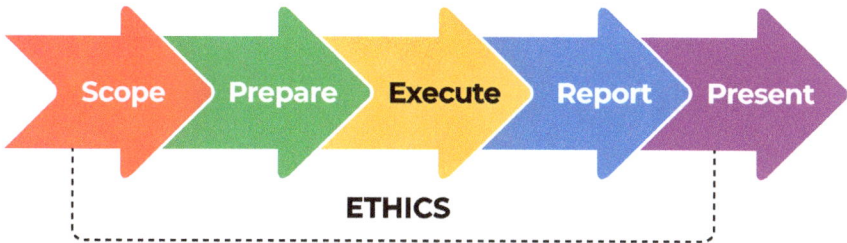

Figure 10. Framework for Mastering DIAGNOSIS: SPERP's Ethical Framework

⚡ WHY IS DIAGNOSIS IMPORTANT FOR PUBLIC LEADERS?

- **Precision in problem-solving:** Diagnosis goes beyond surface-level issues to identify the root causes hindering performance. This allows leaders to address core problems effectively, preventing wasted resources on temporary fixes.

- **Data-driven decisions:** By leveraging data collection and analysis, diagnosis paints a clear picture of the organization's strengths, weaknesses, and current state. This empowers leaders to make informed decisions based on evidence, fostering stakeholder trust.

- **Strategic alignment and impact:** Diagnosis ensures interventions directly address the organization's long-term strategic goals. This bridges the gap between identifying issues and implementing solutions, leading to impactful improvements aligned with the organization's vision.

- **Continuous learning and improvement:** Diagnosis is an ongoing cycle, not a one-time event. It allows leaders to stay informed about evolving challenges and adapt their strategies, promoting a culture of continuous improvement within the organization.

WHAT ARE THE BIG IDEAS?

- Active involvement from stakeholders throughout the diagnosis is crucial. Workshops, interviews, and surveys are effective tools to gather diverse perspectives, validate findings, and foster ownership of the solutions developed.

- High-quality data is the foundation for informed decision-making. Robust data validation processes, utilizing multiple sources, and training data collectors ensure data accuracy and integrity.

- Maintaining confidentiality, privacy, informed consent, transparency, and avoiding bias is paramount during diagnosis. Upholding these ethical principles builds public trust and strengthens the legitimacy of the diagnosis and its outcomes.

HOW DO I MAKE IT HAPPEN?

Follow a five-stage process to effectively diagnose your organization:

Stage 1: Preparing for Diagnosis

Stage 2: Data Collection

Stage 3: Analysis

Stage 4: Reporting and Feedback

Stage 5: Action Planning and Implementation

PART 3
EXECUTE

Chapter 5
Discipline 4 - Design

Albert Einstein once said, "We cannot solve our problems with the same level of thinking that created them." This profound insight captures the essence of the challenges public leaders face after diagnosing organizational issues. Identifying deep-seated problems is just the beginning. To truly address these issues, leaders must elevate their thinking and develop solutions that are not just effective but transformative. The transformation necessary for revitalizing organizations plagued by inefficiency or underperformance relies heavily on the discipline of **DESIGN**.

An organization's performance is intrinsically linked to its design, much like how a building's blueprint dictates its structural integrity and functionality. The equation is simple: No Design = No Results; Poor Design = Poor Results. Therefore, design is not just a component of leadership strategy; it is the foundation upon which all strategies are built and realized.

The Role of Design in Achieving Breakthrough Results

Effective design means seamlessly aligning the organization's core elements—mission, vision, and purpose—with its strategic goals and day-to-day operations. The design process involves meticulously structuring the organization to support and enhance its ability to execute its agenda effectively. This entails asking critical questions such as:

How should we organize ourselves to not only address our current challenges but also propel us toward long-term success?

What structures, processes, and systems need to be in place to transform our strategic vision into tangible outcomes?

This alignment between structure and strategy is crucial for organizational health. Just as a building with a flawed foundation risks collapse, an organization with misaligned structures will struggle to achieve its goals. This principle is aptly summarized by a saying popular in organizational design circles: "As naturally as day follows night, an organization's structure must follow its strategic agenda."

The Transition from Diagnosis to Design

Following a thorough diagnosis, leaders often experience a moment of stark clarity. They recognize the inadequacies in their organization's structure and realize how these flaws hinder their ability to function effectively. This recognition is usually followed by an urgent need to take action—to design or redesign the organization with a renewed focus on its core purpose.

The insights gained from the diagnosis phase are critical in identifying key issues and informing the design process. By understanding the root causes of inefficiencies and underperformance, leaders can create targeted solutions that address these specific problems. Engaging stakeholders from diverse backgrounds ensures a comprehensive understanding of the situation, helping to set clear objectives that align with both the organization's goals and the broader political context.

The Critical Need for Effective Design in Public Sector Organizations

Public sector organizations face unique challenges that require thoughtful and strategic design. These challenges include rigid hierarchies, bureaucratic inertia, and the need to balance multiple stakeholder interests. A well-designed organization can navigate these complexities by fostering a culture of innovation, agility, and accountability. Effective design in the public sector is essential for delivering high-quality services, meeting stakeholder expectations, and achieving sustainable results.

To appreciate the impact that design has on the health of organizations, imagine an organization aiming for rapid innovation but structured with rigid hierarchies and siloed departments. Information flow would be sluggish and collaboration would be stifled, hindering the agility needed for innovation. Misalignment between what an organization aims to achieve and how it is structured to achieve those aims can derail even the most well-intentioned strategies. Aligning an organization's structure with its mission is the essence of the discipline of design.

In a nutshell, design is crucial for any leader seeking to transform a diagnosis of problems into a delivery of results. It demands a visionary yet pragmatic approach to rethinking and restructuring organizations so that they are truly aligned with their missions, capable of meeting their mandates, and adept at navigating the complexities of their operational landscapes.

The rest of this chapter is devoted to supporting leaders with the knowledge and tools they need to execute the critical discipline of design.

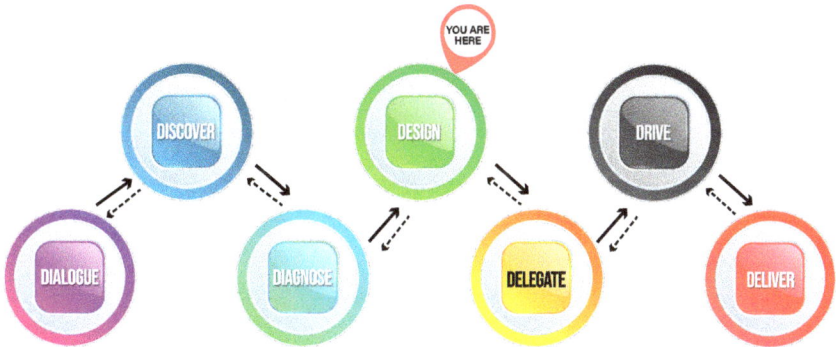

Figure 11. The Seven Disciplines of Breakthrough Results: Design

Introduction to Strategic Design in Public Sector Organizations

In the field of organizational design and development, the concept of design transcends aesthetics and simple organization charts. Instead, it is a strategic way of thinking about how an organization is built. It is akin to crafting a blueprint for a house where every essential element—from the foundation to the layout of rooms—is meticulously planned to ensure seamless functionality.

In the context of organizations, the discipline of design focuses on aligning the structure (how the organization is set up) with the core mission and vision (the organization's purpose and goals). This alignment ensures that all parts—people, processes, and resources—work together effectively to achieve an organization's goals.

At its heart, design is about creating a cohesive system where every component—people, processes, technology, and structure—works harmoniously toward the organization's strategic objectives. It involves crafting environments that not only support but actively enhance these objectives. In this context, design is not a one-time task but a continuous process of alignment that adapts to changing circumstances and new opportunities.

The Essence of Design in Public Leadership

Organizational design is critical because it directly affects an organization's efficiency, effectiveness, and ability to achieve its goals. The way an organization is structured shapes how work is divided, information flows, and decisions are made. This design is fundamental to operational success and long-term sustainability in a dynamic business environment.

The discipline of design is critical to the health of an organization for several reasons:

- **Alignment of vision and operation:** Strategic design ensures that every element of the organization's infrastructure is aligned with its purpose. This alignment is crucial because misalignments can lead to inefficiencies, employee dissatisfaction, and failure to meet stakeholder expectations. When the form and function of an organization are in sync, it significantly increases the probability of collective success.

- **Responsive and adaptive structure:** In today's dynamic world, public sector organizations face unprecedented challenges that require them to be nimble and adaptable. A well-designed organization can respond more swiftly to changes in the external environment, from shifts in government policy to rapid technological advancements. Design equips leaders with the framework to preemptively address these challenges rather than react when it may already be too late.

- **Engagement and empowerment:** A strategically designed organization dismantles bureaucratic barriers and fosters a culture of engagement and innovation. By designing systems that empower employees and encourage creativity, organizations can unlock the full potential of their human resources. Engaged employees are not only more productive but are also advocates for the organization's mission, driving it forward with passion and commitment.

Strategic design is never just about structuring for structuring's sake; it's about crafting a vision into a living, breathing reality. It is an essential practice for leaders who aim not only to manage but to transform their organizations in profound and lasting ways.

In the following sections, we will explore how leaders can effectively engage in the design process using the Four-Stage Organizational Design Model presented in this chapter. This model simplifies organizational complexities into manageable components, enabling the creation of organizations that are both visionary and high-performing.

Mastering the Discipline of Design in Public Sector Leadership

Design aims to answer the question, "What is the best way to organize our organization with a shared purpose to get things done and achieve our strategic intent?" Organizational design seeks to find the optimal form for an organization to maximize its performance. Therefore, leaders seeking to master the discipline of design must embrace the mindset that effective design is a collaborative process, requiring a deep understanding of the organization's unique needs, its service delivery mandates, and the expectations of the public it serves.

To empower organizations to achieve successful design, this section will equip leaders with the tools and knowledge for transformation through strategic design. We will begin by explaining the principles of effective organizational design, then transition to the critical preparation necessary for design, culminating in a deep dive into the design process itself.

The Principles of Effective Organizational Design

Effective organizational design is the bedrock of strategic management. It translates strategy into action by guiding how structures, processes, and people harmonize with an organization's mission and objectives. To ensure this critical translation occurs seamlessly, leaders must prioritize key principles in navigating the design process.

- **Alignment with strategic goals:** Aligning organizational design with strategic goals ensures that every facet of a public sector organization contributes directly to its mission and vision. For instance, a public agency aiming to lead in sustainable environmental practices should structure itself to prioritize initiatives, departments, and roles focused on sustainability efforts. This alignment sharpens focus, optimizes resource allocation, and propels long-term strategic success, ensuring the organization can effectively serve the public interest and achieve its mandated objectives.

- **Flexibility and adaptability:** In today's fast-paced world, public sector organizations must be nimble enough to pivot swiftly in response to technological advancements, regulatory shifts, or societal changes. Designing for flexibility involves adopting modular or matrix structures that enable agile responses to changing conditions without sacrificing efficiency or strategic coherence. This flexibility enhances resilience and positions the organization to proactively seize opportunities and address emerging public needs.

- **Efficiency and effectiveness:** Efficiency and effectiveness are foundational to optimizing performance in public sector organizations. Streamlining workflows, reducing redundancies, and leveraging technology to automate routine tasks are strategies that enhance operational excellence. By eliminating bureaucratic obstacles and optimizing resource utilization, public agencies can deliver high-quality services consistently and effectively, meeting the expectations of citizens and stakeholders.

- **Engagement and empowerment:** Creating a culture of engagement and empowerment in the public sector nurtures innovation, collaboration, and employee satisfaction. Encouraging open communication, involving employees in decision-making, and providing avenues for professional growth and development are essential. Empowered employees are motivated to contribute meaningfully, driving continuous improvement and organizational success in serving the public interest.

Leaders must carefully integrate these principles into organizational design to form a cohesive framework that aligns strategy with execution, adapts to change, optimizes performance, and fosters a dynamic and inclusive workplace culture. Mastery of these principles equips public sector organizations to navigate complexities effectively and achieve transformative results in today's dynamic environment.

With a solid understanding of these key principles in place, we will now dive into the essential preparation required before leaders can embark on the design of their organizations.

Preparing for the Design Process

Embarking on the organizational design process is a significant undertaking for public sector leaders. It requires thorough preparation to ensure the process is well-founded and strategically aligned. This section will guide you through the essential preparations needed to set the stage for a successful design process.

1. Comprehensive Diagnosis Review

Recap Key Findings from the Diagnosis Phase

Before initiating the design process, it is critical to revisit the findings from the diagnosis phase. This involves a detailed review of the key issues, strengths, weaknesses, opportunities, and threats identified during the diagnosis. Understanding these findings ensures that the design process addresses the root causes of organizational challenges and builds on existing strengths. Key questions to consider include:

- What are the critical issues that need addressing?
- What are the organization's core strengths?
- What opportunities can be leveraged for improvement?
- What threats must be mitigated?

2. Setting Clear Objectives

a. Define Goals for the Design Process

Setting clear, actionable goals for the design process is fundamental. These goals should be specific, measurable, achievable, relevant, and time-bound (SMART). They should reflect the desired outcomes of the design process and provide a clear direction for all involved. Consider the following when defining goals:

- What are the specific outcomes we aim to achieve through the design (redesign) of the organization?

- How will success be measured?

- What is the timeline for achieving these goals?

b. Align Objectives with Strategic Priorities

Aligning design objectives with the organization's strategic priorities ensures that the design process supports the broader mission and vision of the organization. This alignment helps in directing resources and efforts towards initiatives that contribute to long-term strategic success. Key considerations include:

- How do the design goals support the organization's mission and vision?

- Are the design objectives aligned with current strategic priorities and future aspirations?

- What adjustments are needed to ensure full alignment?

3. Stakeholder Engagement

Identify and Involve Key Stakeholders

Effective stakeholder engagement is crucial for the success of the design process. Identifying and involving key stakeholders from the outset helps in gaining diverse perspectives and securing buy-in. Consider the following steps:

- Identify key internal and external stakeholders who will be impacted by the design process.

- Engage these stakeholders early to understand their perspectives and concerns.

- Ensure ongoing communication and involvement throughout the design process.

4. Building the Design Team

a. Choose the Right Model for the Design Team

When assembling the design team, leaders can select between two effective models: the Conference Model and the Core Design Team Model. The choice should depend on the specific needs and dynamics of the organization.

Conference Model: In this model, senior leadership sponsors and leads the change process, with large groups of employees participating in real-time analysis, design, and implementation sessions. The major benefits of this model are:

- **Widespread involvement:** A significant number of employees are directly involved, fostering a strong sense of commitment and ownership.

- **Quick problem-solving:** Issues can be identified and decisions made swiftly, allowing for a short-cycle redesign that can be completed in weeks instead of months.

Core Design Team Model: Alternatively, the Core Design Team Model features a smaller, cross-functional team of employees chartered by senior management. This team undertakes the tasks of analysis, redesign, and implementation planning, presenting their proposals to senior leadership and the broader organization for feedback and approval. The benefits of this model include:

- **Continuity:** The design team provides consistency throughout the process and can conduct deeper analysis and planning.

- **Detailed planning:** This model allows for more thorough examination and design tasks, although it requires more ongoing communication with the rest of the organization and may take longer to complete.

Both models can effectively guide an organization through the design process, with timelines ranging from six weeks to six months depending on the organization's size, motivation, and available resources. Leaders must carefully choose the model that best suits their organization's specific needs and dynamics to ensure a successful design process.

b. Identify Necessary Skills and Expertise Needed on the Team

A successful design team comprises individuals with diverse skills and expertise relevant to the design process. This includes strategic thinkers, operational experts, HR experts and change management professionals. Key steps include:

- Identify the specific skills and expertise required for the design process.

- Select team members who bring these skills and have a deep understanding of the organization.

- Ensure a balance of strategic and operational perspectives within the team.

- Consider involving external experts or consultants for specialized knowledge.

5. Assigning Roles and Responsibilities within the Design Team

After deciding on the design team model, clearly defining roles and responsibilities within the design team ensures accountability and efficient collaboration. Consider the following:

- Assign specific roles based on individual expertise and strengths.

- Define clear responsibilities and deliverables for each team member.

- Establish mechanisms for collaboration and communication within the team.

- Implement infrastructures for regular check-ins and progress reviews to maintain alignment and address issues promptly.

6. Leadership and Governance

a. Establishing Leadership for the Design Process

Strong leadership is essential for guiding the design process and making critical decisions. Key considerations include:

- The chief executive officer/director-general is responsible for defining a clear vision and setting specific goals for the design process.

- The CEO/DG plays a key role in making informed decisions during the design process.

- The CEO/DG works with relevant parties to coordinate efforts and ensure effective implementation of the design.

b. Appointing a Design Process Leader

Appoint a design process leader with the authority and vision to drive the initiative. Ensure the leader has the support of senior management and key stakeholders. Provide the leader with the necessary resources and support to succeed. Facilitate leadership training and development to ensure leaders are equipped to handle the complexities of the design process.

7. Decision-Making Structures and Accountability

Effective governance structures facilitate decision-making and ensure accountability throughout the design process. Consider the following:

- Establish clear decision-making structures and processes.

- Define accountability mechanisms for tracking progress and outcomes.

- Ensure transparency and consistency in decision-making.

- Incorporate feedback loops to continuously improve the design process and address emerging issues.

Additional Considerations for Building the Design Team

- **Stakeholder engagement:** Continuously engage with stakeholders at all levels to gather input, manage expectations, and ensure buy-in.

- **Change management:** Integrate change management principles to support employees through transitions and mitigate resistance.

- **Technology and tools:** Utilize advanced tools and technologies to facilitate collaboration, data analysis, and project management.

- **Continuous learning:** Foster a culture of continuous learning and development within the team to keep up with the latest trends and best practices in organizational design.

8. Choosing the Organizational Design Framework

Choosing the right organizational design framework is crucial for success because it establishes the groundwork for how the organization will ultimately operate, evolve, and achieve its objectives. When making their choice, leaders must prioritize a robust framework that seamlessly integrates the organization's purpose, strategy, structure, and human resources without overly complicating the process. In this context, among the frameworks available, the Four-Stage Organizational Design Model stands out as particularly suitable for public sector entities. It guides leaders in addressing the following fundamental questions essential for organizational clarity and effectiveness:

- **Purpose:** What is the organization's mission, vision, and overarching objectives?

- **Strategy:** How will the organization accomplish its goals?

- **Structure:** How should departments and teams be organized within the organization?

- **People:** What skills and competencies are necessary to achieve success?

This model assists public sector leaders in aligning their organizational elements cohesively, ensuring efficient operations, strategic alignment, and effective resource utilization to meet public service objectives effectively. To elaborate further, the following highlights the core benefits of utilizing the Four-Stage Organizational Design Model.

Benefits of Using the Four-Stage Organizational Design Model in Public Sector Organizational Design

Implementing the Four-Stage Organizational Design Model in the public sector offers tailored advantages that address the unique challenges and goals of governmental organizations. This systematic approach provides a structured path towards optimizing organizational structure and performance.

Here are the key benefits of using this model:

1. **Mission and Values Alignment:** The Four-Stage Organizational Design Model begins with defining the organization's mission, vision, and values. This ensures that all design decisions align with public service objectives and legislative mandates. Establishing a clear purpose allows leaders to develop strategies for effective resource allocation, enhancing the organization's capability to meet citizen needs efficiently.

2. **Streamlined Structures:** A key outcome of this model is the creation of streamlined and transparent organizational structures. Improved decision-making processes and accountability in delivering services to citizens are achieved, reducing bureaucratic inefficiencies and enhancing operational effectiveness.

3. **Robust Organizational Culture:** The model promotes a robust organizational culture rooted in public sector values and ethical standards. By embedding integrity, transparency, and public trust into daily practices, it engages stakeholders—from citizens to community groups and elected officials—in decision-making processes. This inclusivity fosters broader support for governmental initiatives and strengthens overall organizational resilience.

4. **Clear Role Definitions:** Clear role definitions within the organization promote accountability and effectiveness. Every member understands their responsibilities in achieving organizational goals. Enhanced

transparency in operations builds trust among citizens and stakeholders, reinforcing confidence in governmental processes and outcomes.

5. **Strategic Public Policy Alignment:** The model is strategically aligned with long-term public policy objectives, supporting sustainable development and societal well-being. Its focus on continuous evaluation and adaptation fosters ongoing improvements in service delivery and governance practices, promoting innovation and adaptive solutions to community needs.

6. **Enhanced Organizational Resilience:** The model enhances organizational resilience by identifying and mitigating risks associated with public sector operations, ensuring compliance with legal and regulatory requirements. It promotes a citizen-centric focus, placing public value and satisfaction at the forefront of service delivery efforts, supported by evidence-based decision-making processes.

The Four-Stage Organizational Design Model enhances efficiency, improves service delivery, and strengthens governance practices in the public sector. By emphasizing strategic alignment, operational efficiency, stakeholder engagement, and continuous improvement, it fosters greater transparency, responsiveness, and public trust. Ultimately, these efforts contribute to effective service delivery and the well-being of communities served by governmental entities.

Now that we have explored the Four-Stage Organizational Design Model and its value proposition for public sector organizations, let's delve into the stage-by-stage blueprint with which leaders can design their organizations for breakthrough results.

Executing Design: A Stage-by-Stage Guide

As established in the preceding section, the Four-Stage Organizational Design Model helps public sector leaders create a cohesive and high-performing organization aligned with its purpose, strategy, structure, and roles. This model provides a systematic approach to organizational design, enabling leaders to optimize their organization's performance and deliver value to stakeholders. The following is a detailed stage-by-stage blueprint to guide leaders in designing their organizations using this model.

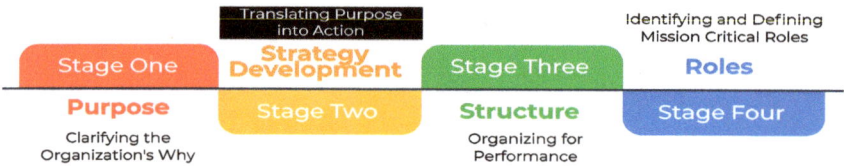

Figure 12. Four Stages of Organizational Design

Stage 1: Purpose Definition

This stage involves clearly defining the organization's purpose, mission, and vision, laying the foundation for all subsequent design decisions. At this stage, the design team championed by the CEO/DG must articulate why the organization exists, what it seeks to accomplish, and what values guide its actions. A well-defined purpose provides clarity and direction, guiding strategic decisions and shaping the organization's culture.

When defining the purpose of their organization, leaders and their teams must answer two fundamental questions:

- Why does this organization exist?
- What mission does it serve for the country and its citizens?

Key steps to take:

- **Clarify and communicate purpose:** Depending on the model of design team employed, leaders will typically hold workshops and discussions with members of the team and selected stakeholders to collaboratively define a clear and compelling purpose. After articulating the purpose, it must be disseminated through internal communication channels (e.g., emails, town halls) to ensure that all employees understand and align with it.

- **Implement reorientation programs:** Ensuring everyone within the organization is on the same page with the defined purpose is critical for the success of the design process. Leaders should implement ongoing reorientation programs for stakeholders and employees at all levels. These programs should ensure consistent understanding and commitment to the organization's purpose. Continuously running reorientation programs can foster a culture of commitment and shared goals throughout the organization.

Stage 2: Strategy Development

With the purpose established, the design team must then develop a comprehensive strategy to achieve the organization's goals. This involves identifying specific objectives, determining the resources needed, and outlining the actions required to achieve success. The strategy must be aligned with the organization's purpose and address both short-term priorities and long-term aspirations. For the strategy to be effective, it must never be developed in isolation. It requires a collaborative approach. The CEO/DG and the design team need to engage all critical stakeholders through:

- **Town hall meetings:** Gather citizen input on priorities and challenges.

- **Focus groups:** Facilitate discussions with experts from relevant sectors to identify opportunities and threats.

After developing a high-level strategy through a thorough process and incorporating inputs from critical stakeholders, the next crucial step is to "unpack" this strategy into actionable items. This involves breaking down broad goals into manageable tasks with clear deliverables, ensuring that the strategy transitions from vision to practical implementation that meets the needs of citizens and communities.

Stage 3: Structural Alignment

A well-designed structure is the backbone of any successful organization. When designing the organization's structure, public leaders must avoid the trap of building structures around people. This approach is a major cause of underperformance in many public organizations.

Key steps to take:

Leaders aiming for breakthrough results must shift from a people-centric structure to a deliverable-centric structure, ensuring each department and role has a clear mandate aligned with the organization's purpose and agenda. Here is how they can achieve this:

- **Design a deliverable-based structure:** Focus on the key outcomes the organization needs to achieve to fulfill its agenda. Structure departments and teams around these deliverables, ensuring each unit has clear ownership and accountability for specific results.

- **Define roles clearly:** For each role within the structure, clearly outline key responsibilities, accountabilities, performance indicators (KPIs), and decision-making authority. This clarity ensures everyone understands their contribution to the organization's success.

- **Avoid role pollution:** Resist the temptation to overload roles with competing objectives. For example, separating performance management from political lobbying allows key officials in the organization to focus on achieving results rather than managing external pressures.

Stage 4: Role Clarity

Once the structure is in place, the final step in the model is to identify mission-critical roles necessary for executing the strategy. Each role must be clearly defined, with explicit deliverables and success metrics. This clarity ensures that the right people are selected based on their ability to meet these defined expectations.

Key steps to take:

- **Define success for each role:** Clearly articulate what success looks like for each role, including key performance indicators and metrics. Clearly defined job descriptions outlining responsibilities, accountabilities, and performance expectations are essential.

- **Select competent people:** Choose individuals with the necessary expertise, experience, and behavioral profiles to fulfill the defined roles and deliver on the organization's agenda.

- **Ensure role clarity:** Ensure there is no ambiguity in role definitions to drive performance effectively.

By following these four stages, public sector leaders can effectively utilize the Four-Stage Organizational Design Model to create a high-performing organization that delivers exceptional public service. We will now explore the common challenges associated with the design process and provide strategies for navigating them.

Navigating Challenges in Design: Overcoming Common Obstacles

The process of organizational design in the public sector is fraught with challenges. From balancing diverse stakeholder interests to ensuring clear role definitions, leaders must navigate a complex landscape to build effective and high-performing organizations. Below are common obstacles and practical solutions for overcoming them.

1. **Balancing stakeholder interests:** Public organizations serve diverse stakeholders such as citizens and politicians, who often have conflicting priorities. To address this challenge, leaders should foster inclusive participation by conducting town hall meetings, focus groups, and stakeholder workshops. These activities ensure that the defined purpose reflects the needs and concerns of all relevant parties.

2. **Maintaining employee alignment**: Ensuring all employees understand and connect with the organization's purpose can be particularly difficult in large or geographically dispersed agencies. Implementing ongoing reorientation programs is essential. Leaders should utilize internal communication channels, such as emails and intranet, and hold regular leadership town halls to consistently reinforce the organization's purpose.

3. **Prioritization overload:** Balancing competing priorities from diverse stakeholders is a common challenge. Employing a data-driven approach can help leaders make informed decisions. By analyzing citizen feedback, budgetary constraints, and government priorities, leaders can prioritize strategies that address the most critical needs.

4. **Translating strategy into actionable steps:** Broad strategic goals need to be translated into practical, measurable initiatives. This can be achieved by breaking down the strategy into manageable steps and developing clear action plans with specific deliverables and timelines for each objective. This ensures smooth implementation and avoids ambiguity.

5. **Siloed structures**: Traditional department structures can create silos and hinder collaboration across teams. Adopting a deliverable-centric approach can mitigate this issue. Designing teams around specific outcomes fosters focused collaboration and accountability for achieving desired results.

6. **Role overload and ambiguity:** Assigning too many responsibilities to a single role can hinder performance. To combat this, roles and responsibilities must be clearly defined. Job descriptions should explicitly outline key tasks, performance indicators (KPIs), and decision-making authority for each role. This clarity reduces confusion and allows individuals to focus on delivering specific objectives.

7. **Talent management:** Attracting and retaining top talent in the public sector can be challenging due to salary limitations and a perceived

lack of career mobility. To attract and retain skilled individuals, it is important to highlight the impact potential of the roles. Emphasizing the opportunity to make a positive difference in the community and promoting clear career development paths within the organization can make public sector roles more appealing.

8. **Performance management:** Public sector performance management systems can be complex and bureaucratic. Developing clear and objective performance metrics for each role is crucial. This allows for performance evaluation based on tangible achievements aligned with strategic goals, ensuring that performance management is effective and fair.

By addressing these challenges with the proposed solutions, public sector leaders can effectively navigate the complexities of organizational design, ensuring that their organizations are well-positioned to deliver exceptional public service.

Having thoroughly examined the principles and mechanics of an effective design process, we will now illustrate how design works in practice with two case studies: One showcasing a successful design process and the other highlighting failures in design execution.

Case Study 1
Design Done Right

Background

The Ekan-City Transit Authority (ECTA), responsible for public transportation in the bustling metropolis of Ekan-City, faced significant challenges in meeting the demands of its growing population. With mounting customer complaints and operational inefficiencies, a new CEO, Dr. Adamu Dogo, was appointed to lead the organization. Dr. Dogo initiated a comprehensive organizational redesign using the Four-Stage Organizational Design Model to transform ECTA into a high-performing entity that delivers exceptional public service. In conjunction with other leaders, the decision was made to use the Core Design Team Model for the design process.

Key Players and Design Team

- **Dr. Adamu Dogo (CEO):** Visionary leader championing the transformation.
- **Dr. Funmi Okafor (design team leader**): Senior executive with expertise in organizational design.
- **Mr. Ufoma Okon (strategic advisor):** Renowned expert in strategic planning.
- **Mrs. Amina Abdullahi (HR director):** Overseeing structural changes and talent management.
- Mr. Kehinde Adeyemi (recruitment specialist): Responsible for talent acquisition.
- **Mr. Chukwudi Uche (head of operations):** Key manager involved in operational adjustments.
- **Mr. Timpa (politician):** Influential stakeholder with competing priorities.
- **Citizens and community groups:** Primary stakeholders providing feedback and support.

The Design Process

Stage 1: Purpose Definition

Objective setting: Dr. Adamu Dogo, with the support of Dr. Funmi, led sessions involving all members of the design team and stakeholders to define ECTA's purpose: "To provide safe, reliable, and sustainable transportation services that enhance the quality of life for Ekan-City residents."

Communicating purpose: The purpose was communicated through emails, town halls, and the intranet to ensure alignment across the organization.

Ongoing reorientation programs were also conducted to embed the purpose throughout the entire organization. Efforts were made to ensure that everyone, from top management to frontline staff, was on the same page.

Stage 2: Strategy Development

Led by Mr. Ufoma Okon, the team went through the following stages:

Objective identification: The team conducted workshops to define strategic objectives aligned with ECTA's purpose, focusing on service reliability, customer satisfaction, and operational efficiency.

Stakeholder engagement: Town hall meetings and focus groups were conducted with employees, community members, and local government representatives to gather input, identify opportunities, and highlight threats. Mr. Timpa nearly derailed the process by pushing for a focus on expanding services to his constituency. However, Dr. Dogo effectively facilitated a town hall meeting where he shared the data and broader mission, successfully aligning stakeholders with the strategic vision.

SWOT analysis: Mr. Okon performed a thorough SWOT analysis to ensure the strategy was robust and well-informed by internal and external factors.

Resource allocation: The team allocated financial resources, personnel, and technological tools based on the identified objectives.

Action planning: The team developed detailed action plans outlining initiatives, timelines, and responsible parties, covering service improvement, customer engagement, and operational enhancements.

Stage 3: Structural Alignment

Structure design: Once the strategy was finalized, Mrs. Amina Abdullahi championed the design of a deliverable-centric structure. The team organized departments around key outcomes to ensure clear ownership and accountability. They clearly defined responsibilities, accountabilities, KPIs, and decision-making authority for each role, making extra effort to avoid role pollution.

Addressing resistance: Mr. Chukwudi Uche voiced concerns about the new structure's potential impact on employees' jobs and overall performance. In response, Mrs. Amina Abdullahi facilitated team-building sessions and provided further clarification on role definitions, ensuring employees understood their new responsibilities and how they contributed to the organization's success.

Design oversight: Dr. Funmi Okafor ensured that the structural changes aligned with best practices in organizational design and facilitated cross-departmental collaboration.

Stage 4: Role Clarity

Articulating success metrics: Led by Mrs. Amina Abdullahi, the design team specified success metrics and KPIs for each role, ensuring alignment with organizational goals.

Competent people selection: The team identified competent staff members and strategically assigned them to critical roles that leveraged their strengths and expertise, thus maximizing their effectiveness within the redesigned organizational structure.

Overcoming recruitment challenges: Despite salary limitations, Mr. Kehinde Adeyemi successfully attracted top talent by offering non-monetary incentives, such as comprehensive professional development opportunities. This approach not only addressed recruitment challenges but also fostered a culture of continuous learning and growth among the workforce.

Outcomes

The design process rejuvenated organizational enthusiasm, evidenced by a 15% increase in employee engagement scores, indicating a more motivated and aligned workforce. Dr. Dogo's leadership and collaborative approach transformed the organizational culture, fostering openness, proactivity, and performance orientation.

Key Success Factors

- **Strong leadership commitment:** Dr. Dogo's clear vision and decisive leadership were pivotal in driving the transformation.

- **Effective stakeholder engagement:** Engagement with diverse stakeholders ensured comprehensive coverage and informed strategies.

- **Transparent communication:** Regular updates and transparent communication facilitated change management and maintained stakeholder trust.

Conclusion and Lessons Learned

This case study underscores the importance of a well-structured design process in transforming public sector organizations. It highlights the value of leadership vision, stakeholder engagement, and strategic data utilization in driving organizational change and improvement. By following a structured approach, ECTA successfully created a high-performing organization that delivers exceptional public service.

Case Study 2
Design Gone Wrong

Background

City Environmental Protection Agency (CEPA), responsible for overseeing environmental regulations and conservation efforts in a rapidly urbanizing area, faced significant challenges with policy implementation and operational efficiency. Dr. Sandra Ekaette was appointed as the new Director with a mandate to overhaul CEPA and improve service delivery. However, despite initial enthusiasm and a dedicated core design team, critical missteps in the design process led to unintended consequences.

Key Players and Design Team

- **Dr. Sandra Ekaette (Director):** Newly appointed leader with a vision for environmental reform.

- **Mr. Toyo-Abasi Nsini (design team leader):** Experienced in environmental management and process improvement.

- **Mrs. Uchechi Aliyu (HR director):** Overseeing structural changes and talent management.

- **Mrs. Ukeme Akan (community relations manager):** Focus on enhancing community engagement and satisfaction.

- **Mr. Ibrahim Abdullahi (facilities manager):** In charge of facility operations and infrastructure.

- **Frontline staff and community representatives:** Internal and external stakeholders who should have provided feedback and strategy support.

The Design Process

Stage 1: Purpose Definition

- **Objective setting:** Dr. Sandra and Mr. Toyo-Abasi led sessions to define CEPA's purpose: "To protect and enhance the environment through effective regulations and community partnerships." While initial objective-setting workshops were held, ongoing engagement with frontline staff and community representatives was minimal.

- **Communicating purpose:** The purpose was communicated through staff meetings and newsletters to align all internal stakeholders. However, minimal effort was made to embed the purpose within the organization and reorient employees to the updated purpose.

Stage 2: Strategy Development

Led by Dr. Sandra and Mr. Toyo-Abasi, the team made several critical mistakes during strategy development:

- **Objective identification:** Dr. Sandra focused heavily on financial sustainability, overlooking concerns raised by community advocates regarding service accessibility and environmental quality. The team formulated a strategy centered on cost-cutting measures and efficiency improvements, neglecting community engagement and regulations for environmental protection.

- **Stakeholder engagement:** The design team interacted minimally with frontline environmental officers and community members, resulting in disconnect and dissatisfaction among staff and the public. This lack of engagement with actual needs led to a strategy that prioritized operational efficiency over community-centric care, ultimately diminishing service quality.

- **Resource allocation:** Resources were predominantly allocated to IT upgrades and facility renovations, with little emphasis on environmental training and community outreach.

Stage 3: Structural Alignment

- **Structure design:** Led by Mrs. Uchechi Aliyu, the team developed a people-centric structure to execute the flawed strategy. However, these changes were made without sufficient consultation with department heads and staff, causing leaders like Mrs. Ukeme and Mr. Ibrahim to feel sidelined and excluded from decision-making processes. This oversight further deepened morale issues and decreased productivity within the team.

Stage 4: Role Clarity

- **Articulating success metrics:** Under Mrs. Uchechi Aliyu's leadership, the team focused primarily on financial targets and operational metrics when deciding on success metrics and KPIs.

- **Recruitment gap:** Recruitment efforts prioritized IT and administrative roles, neglecting specialized environmental positions and specializations.

Outcomes

The flawed design process at CEPA resulted in unintended consequences and organizational challenges. There was a disconnect between the organization's purpose and the strategy, structure and roles created. Subsequent evaluation revealed that operational efficiency goals were partially achieved but at the cost of diminished environmental protection quality and stakeholder trust. Employee morale declined, and community satisfaction scores stagnated, highlighting systemic issues in the design framework. High turnover among environmental professionals occurred due to dissatisfaction with workload and inadequate technical support.

Key Failures

- **Leadership oversight:** Dr. Sandra's focus on financial stability overshadowed environmental protection priorities and stakeholder engagement.

- **Poor stakeholder engagement:** Minimal involvement of frontline staff and community representatives led to overlooked concerns and resistance to change.

- **Misaligned strategy:** Emphasis on cost-cutting measures compromised service quality and community outcomes.

Conclusion and Lessons Learned

This case study underscores the critical importance of clear purpose definition, aligned strategy development, deliverable-centric structure and adequate focus on mission-critical roles for an integrated organizational design that drives environmental reform. Effective design in this context required a holistic approach that prioritized environmental protection alongside operational efficiency to achieve sustainable improvements in service delivery.

By learning from these mistakes, organizations can recalibrate their approach to design, ensuring that all stakeholders are heard, strategic priorities are balanced, and implementation aligns with organizational goals and community needs.

Call to Action
Embrace Strategic Design for Breakthrough Results

Breakthrough results begin with effective organizational design. The design of an organization plays a critical role in its success. Organizations that achieve remarkable results often have a well-defined purpose, a clear strategy, and a structure that aligns with their goals. They are also ruthless about role clarity and the right talent.

As we have seen, the discipline of design extends beyond superficial aesthetics or organizational charts; it entails a strategic approach to aligning organizations with their core purpose, mission, and strategic objectives. Through meticulous alignment of structure, strategy, and roles, leaders can establish cohesive systems that efficiently execute organizational agendas.

Utilize the Four-Stage Organizational Design Model to optimize your organization's performance. From articulating purpose and crafting strategy to designing structure and defining roles, each stage is crucial for fostering high-performing organizations that generate value for stakeholders.

The critical role of purpose in providing direction, strategy in translating purpose into action, structure in facilitating performance, and roles in delineating mission-critical responsibilities cannot be overstated. By adhering to this systematic approach and employing effective deliberation methods, public sector leaders can confidently navigate the complexities of organizational design.

The strategic design process is pivotal for public sector leaders striving to transform their organizations and achieve breakthrough results and outcomes for citizens.

Embrace strategic thinking, foster collaboration, and implement the Four-Stage Organizational Design Model to cultivate an adaptable, responsive, and mission-centric organization that is structured, capacitated and positioned for success in an ever-evolving landscape.

The Discipline of Design at a Glance

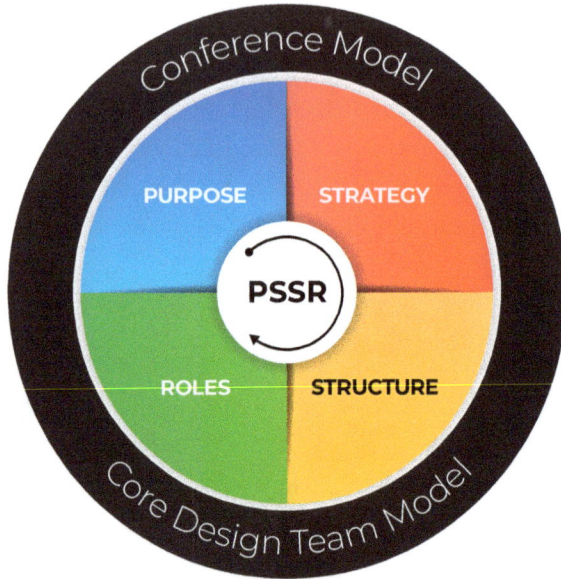

Figure 13. Framework for Mastering DESIGN: Purpose-Strategy-Structure-Roles (PSSR)

⚡ WHY IS DESIGN IMPORTANT FOR PUBLIC LEADERS?

- **Boosts performance:** Effective design aligns people, processes, and resources for efficient goal achievement and smooth adaptation to change.

- **Improves citizen service:** Clear structures and a focus on public needs lead to faster, more responsive service delivery.

- **Strengthens governance:** Design fosters transparency and accountability by aligning structures with purpose and mandates.

- **Empowers workforce:** Well-designed organizations create a culture of engagement and equip leaders with the skills to navigate complexities.

☀ WHAT ARE THE BIG IDEAS?

- **Public sector organizations need good design:** Just like a building needs a blueprint, organizations need a well-designed structure to function efficiently and achieve their goals. This design should be strategic and consider the organization's purpose, strategy, structure, and the roles of its people.

- **Design is about alignment:** A well-designed organization aligns all its parts—its mission, strategy, structure, and people—to work together seamlessly toward achieving its goals. This means everyone understands their role and how it contributes to the bigger picture.

- **The Four-Stage Design Model is a helpful framework:** After selecting the design team model of preference—Conference or Core Design Team—the model provides a step-by-step approach for leaders to design their organizations. It involves defining the organization's purpose, developing a strategy, designing the structure, and then clearly defining roles and responsibilities.

- **Benefits of good design in the public sector:** Public sector organizations that are well-designed can deliver services more efficiently, be more responsive to citizen needs, and operate with greater transparency and accountability. This ultimately leads to better outcomes for the public.

🔧 HOW DO I MAKE IT HAPPEN?

Follow a four-stage process to effectively design your organization:

Stage 1: Purpose Definition

Stage 2: Strategy Development

Stage 3: Structural Alignment

Stage 4: Role Clarity

Chapter 6
Discipline 5 - Delegate

A well-orchestrated design phase meticulously addresses two pivotal questions: **"What" initiatives are essential to propel the organization toward its goal**, and **"How" should these initiatives be executed to optimize outcomes?** However, as critical as these two elements are to the effectiveness of an organization, the true tipping point for success isn't just the strategic "What" or the tactical "How"—it's the "Who."

The "Who" refers to the focus on human capital—on the individuals whose skills and character bring the strategic plans of an organization to life. The right people (the "Who") with the skills and experience can ignite the potential of plans and processes, while the wrong team can dim their prospects from the start.

Effective leadership involves **identifying, nurturing,** and **empowering the right people.** It's about placing those who not only envision but can actualize those visions into tangible results. This isn't just about filling roles; it's about aligning human potential with the strategic goals of the organization.

Indeed, the significance of the "Who" cannot be overstated. When the right people are in the right places, the organization is poised not just to function but to flourish. These leaders and team members develop and execute initiatives that drive the organization forward, build formidable competitive advantages, and foster a culture of continuous development.

They are the architects of robust structures, creators of efficient systems, and upholders of high-performance standards.

Conversely, a misstep in the "Who" decision can ripple through the organization with devastating effects. The wrong "Who" leads to a myriad of organizational dysfunctions: Frustration permeates the ranks, strategic focus blurs, decision-making falters, and the balance between work and life is upset. Leaders find themselves perennially extinguishing fires rather than igniting sparks of innovation. The organization, stuck in a reactive stance, struggles with mediocrity and diminished productivity.

Thus, as we pivot to the fifth discipline essential for breakthrough results—**DELEGATE**—it becomes clear that this skill transcends mere task assignment. Effective delegation involves strategic alignment of people not just with tasks, but with the mission, vision, and core values of the organization. It demands a profound understanding of individual capabilities and a commitment to develop these capabilities in alignment with organizational needs.

In mastering the discipline of delegation, leaders must therefore ask not only "What needs to be done?" and "How should it be done?" but more crucially, "**Who is best equipped to undertake this?**" It is here, in the wise deployment of human resources, that leaders can transform potential into performance, aspirations into achievements, and challenges into victories. Delegation, then, is not just a managerial task—it is a pivotal leadership responsibility that directly shapes the organizational landscape and its future.

By focusing on the "Who," leaders ensure that the right people are empowered to drive the organization's strategic initiatives. This alignment of human resources with organizational goals creates a synergistic effect, where the collective efforts of a well-positioned team lead to exponential growth and success. It fosters an environment where innovation thrives and where employees are motivated and engaged, knowing that their contributions are valued and aligned with the organization's objectives.

In a nutshell, the "Who" in the organizational design and transformation process is the vital pillar that holds everything together. It is the catalyst that turns strategic plans into actionable realities and visions into tangible outcomes. Effective leadership, therefore, must prioritize the identification, development, and strategic placement of talent to harness the full potential of the organization. This people-centric approach not only enhances organizational performance but also ensures long-term sustainability and success.

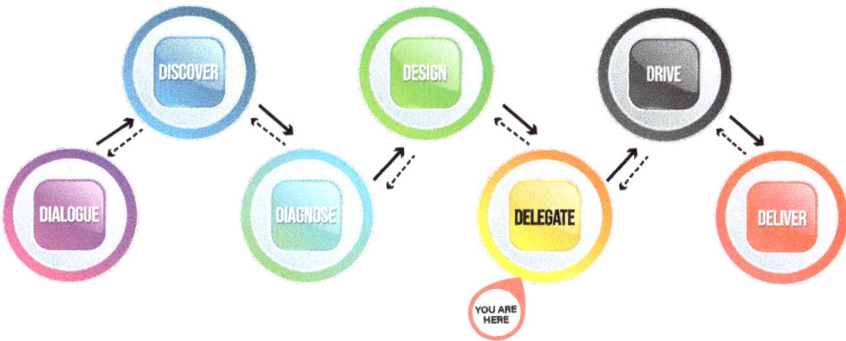

Figure 14. The Seven Disciplines of Breakthrough Results: Delegate

Introduction to Strategic Delegation

If "getting things done through people" is a solid definition of leadership, then effective delegation is the cornerstone of effective leadership.

Public leaders are under immense pressure to accomplish tasks efficiently and effectively. Since it is impossible to do everything themselves, they must master the art of amplifying their impact by tapping into the collective intelligence and expertise of their team. This, essentially, is what delegation means. To delegate effectively is to ensure that the right people are tackling the right tasks, maximizing efficiency, and leading to better outcomes.

It is important to emphasize that delegation is not merely about assigning tasks to others. If that were the case, it wouldn't warrant an entire discussion. Real delegation is the deliberate and strategic assignment of responsibility, authority, and accountability to employees or teams. When a leader delegates, they transfer their authority to empower others to take ownership of specific tasks and goals, fostering scalability, agility, and innovation within the organization. In light of this, it is easy to see why getting delegation wrong is courting disaster.

To delegate effectively, leaders must be adept at discerning what to delegate, to whom, and how. It requires a deep understanding of the strengths and capabilities of their team members, as well as clarity in communication and objectives.

When done well, the benefits of strategic delegation are far-reaching and transformational for organizations. This is perhaps why delegation is a highly rated skill in leadership development programs and has been tagged as a key differentiator between successful and unsuccessful leaders. It is a vital competence that can be learned and mastered with practice. The goal of this chapter is to help leaders master this skill so that they can effectively translate their carefully crafted strategic visions into tangible realities that deliver value for the public they serve.

The next section delves deeper into why public leaders must master the art of delegation and the tremendous benefits that will arise from doing so.

Why Public Sector Leaders Must Master Delegation to Drive Performance

While delegation is essential for leaders in all sectors, the public sector presents unique complexities and challenges. Leaders serving the public interest must leverage delegation to navigate challenges, optimize resources, and achieve their missions.

Effective delegation does more than lighten a leader's workload—it strategically positions the organization for scalable growth by:

1. **Enhancing Organizational Efficiency**: Public sector organizations tackle multifaceted issues requiring coordinated efforts. Effective delegation streamlines workflows, enabling leaders to distribute tasks according to team members' strengths, improving task completion and outcome quality.

2. **Enabling Strategic Focus**: By delegating routine tasks, leaders can focus on high-level strategic planning and decision-making. This allows them to address critical areas such as policy formulation, stakeholder engagement, and future planning, keeping the organization aligned with its broader objectives.

3. **Empowering and Developing Employees**: Delegation empowers employees by providing opportunities to develop new skills and take on leadership roles. This fosters a culture of trust and accountability, leading to motivated, engaged, and committed employees who drive performance and innovation.

4. **Enhancing Responsiveness and Agility**: Effective delegation enables quicker decision-making and agile responses to emerging issues. By entrusting team members with the authority to act, leaders reduce delays and enhance the organization's ability to respond promptly to public needs.

5. **Building Resilient Organizations**: Delegation builds resilience by creating an adaptable workforce. Employees accustomed to taking on responsibilities and making decisions are better equipped to handle unforeseen challenges, ensuring organizational stability and continuity.

6. **Promoting Innovation and Creativity**: Delegation fosters an environment where creativity and innovation thrive. By giving employees autonomy, leaders encourage diverse perspectives and out-of-the-box thinking, leading to innovative solutions and service improvements.

7. **Improving Public Trust and Accountability**: Effective delegation promotes transparency and accountability. Clearly defined

responsibilities and expectations build public confidence in the organization's ability to manage resources and deliver services effectively, reinforcing trust through responsiveness, efficiency, and continuous improvement.

By mastering the discipline of delegation, public sector leaders can drive their organizations toward greater success, ultimately better serving the communities and constituents they are dedicated to supporting. The rest of this chapter provides robust resources to help leaders master this essential capability.

Mastering the Discipline of Delegation in Public Sector Leadership

To truly master the discipline of delegation, the journey must begin with an understanding that delegation is not a haphazard act. It is a strategic tool for scaling performance. This means that delegation should be approached with careful planning and intentionality. Rather than simply offloading tasks to free up time, effective delegation involves deliberately assigning critical responsibilities to the right individuals based on their skills and strengths. This ensures that tasks are completed efficiently and effectively, contributing to overall organizational growth.

When leaders master the art of delegation, they master the business of time—time to think, plan, and achieve extraordinary results in record time. Done well, delegation is a powerful tool that drives organizational performance and fuels employee growth.

In this section, we systematically explore everything leaders need to know and understand to master the discipline of delegation. We will begin with an exploration of the six pillars of delegation.

The Six Pillars of Effective Delegation

It bears repeating effective delegation is more than just handing off tasks— it's about ensuring that these tasks are completed successfully and contribute positively to the organization's goals. This requires a foundational strategy built on six key pillars, which, when implemented correctly, can transform delegation from a managerial task into a powerful leadership tool in the public sector. The pillars are:

1. **Clear communication:** Essential to delegation is clear communication. It sets the stage for successful delegation. It ensures that both parties—the delegator and the delegate—understand the task, the expectations, and the reasons behind the delegation. This mutual understanding prevents misunderstandings and sets a clear path to follow.

2. **Assignment of responsibility and authority:** Delegation involves not just assigning a task but also granting the authority to make decisions related to it. This approach empowers employees, fostering a sense of ownership and demonstrating the leader's confidence in their abilities. It encourages proactive problem-solving and enhances employee engagement.

3. **Clarity of expectations:** Setting crystal clear expectations helps delegates understand not only what needs to be achieved but also how success will be measured. This alignment ensures that everyone is working towards the same objectives and standards.

4. **Competence and capability assessment:** Effective delegation requires a thorough understanding of an employee's skills and an assessment of their capability to handle the assigned task. Matching the right tasks with the right people ensures that the work is done efficiently and effectively.

5. **Trust and confidence:** Trust is crucial in delegation. Leaders must trust their employees to handle tasks independently, and employees must feel confident that they have their leader's support. A supportive environment encourages employees to take initiative and perform at their best.

6. **Provision of necessary support and resources:** Ensuring that employees have the necessary resources, information, and support

is indispensable for the successful completion of delegated tasks. Providing the right tools and guidance enables employees to perform their tasks effectively and reach their full potential.

A strong grasp of these six pillars lays the groundwork for public sector leaders to master delegation. The next section delves into the critical preparations leaders must take to ensure their delegation efforts translate into tangible improvements for the organization.

Planning and Preparing for Delegation

Leaders often underestimate thorough preparation and planning before extensive delegation, questioning its necessity. However, while planning and preparing for successful delegation might take a few hours or even a couple of days, recovering from the consequences of a failed delegation can take weeks or even months.

The significant efforts invested in the phases of discovery, diagnosis, and design will be futile if leaders do not dedicate sufficient time to effectively delegate the responsibilities necessary to implement new initiatives, projects, and tasks arising from these processes.

Without effective delegation, there is no effective execution, and without execution, nothing is accomplished.

This section provides critical preparatory steps that must be in place for before leaders embark on the delegation process.

1. Identifying Delegation Opportunities

The first step is to identify what should be delegated and what should not be. This step ensures that delegation is strategic and aligned with both organizational goals and individual capabilities.

- **Task analysis:** Leaders should begin by conducting a thorough review of their daily activities as well as those of their team members. This involves breaking down all tasks and responsibilities to understand their nature and demands. Key questions to ask include: "Which tasks are essential for me to handle personally, and which can be effectively delegated without compromising quality or organizational integrity?" This analysis helps to distinguish between tasks that require your direct involvement and those that can be managed by others within your team.

- **Focus on efficiency and value:** After identifying potential tasks for delegation, prioritize those that are repetitive, time-consuming, or better suited to the specific skill sets of your team members. Delegating such tasks can significantly enhance operational efficiency and ensure that you and your team are utilizing your time effectively.

- **Alignment with public sector goals**: In the public sector, it is essential to ensure that delegation aligns with broader organizational goals. This involves considering how delegation can enable you to focus on high-impact areas such as community engagement, policy development, or strategic planning. By delegating routine tasks, you free up valuable time to concentrate on initiatives that directly contribute to the public sector's mission and objectives.

By systematically identifying delegation opportunities through these lenses, leaders can ensure that they are making informed decisions that enhance both personal productivity and organizational effectiveness.

2. Assessing Delegation Readiness

Ensuring that both your organization and individual team members are ready for delegation is a crucial step. This involves assessing the current workload, infrastructure, resources, and skill levels of your team. Proper assessment ensures that delegation becomes a good opportunity for growth and efficiency.

- **Assessing organizational readiness:** Before delegating tasks, evaluate your team's current workload to ensure they can take on additional responsibilities. Overloading your team can lead to burnout, decreased morale, and a drop in overall performance. Effective workload management involves balancing existing tasks with new assignments to maintain productivity and job satisfaction.

- **Assessing individual readiness:** Match tasks to individuals who possess the requisite skills and experience to perform them effectively. Conduct skills assessments or hold one-on-one conversations to gauge the capabilities and readiness of your team members. This step ensures that the tasks are delegated to the right people, maximizing efficiency and minimizing errors.

- **Identify development opportunities:** View delegation not only as a means to distribute workload but also as a tool for employee development. Delegating tasks that provide exposure to new challenges can help individuals develop the necessary skills and grow professionally.

It is recommended that these steps be taken ahead of the delegation process. Taking the time to plan and prepare for delegation is as critical as any other strategic move. By making these preparations, leaders can create an environment where delegation fosters growth, efficiency, and accountability within their teams. This approach enhances individual performance and drives organizational success.

With this foundation in place, the next section will provide a detailed step-by-step guide to effective delegation.

Executing Delegation: A Stage-by-Stage Guide

Many leaders view delegation as a one-time event where they give instructions and wait for a report. However, effective delegation is the exact opposite. It is an ongoing process that relies on clear communication, continuous support, and a strong commitment to accountability, as captured in the six-stage process below.

By following the steps in this guide, leaders can transform delegation from a chore to a powerful tool for achieving organizational goals efficiently. Not only will this boost productivity, but it will also foster a culture of growth and empower team members."

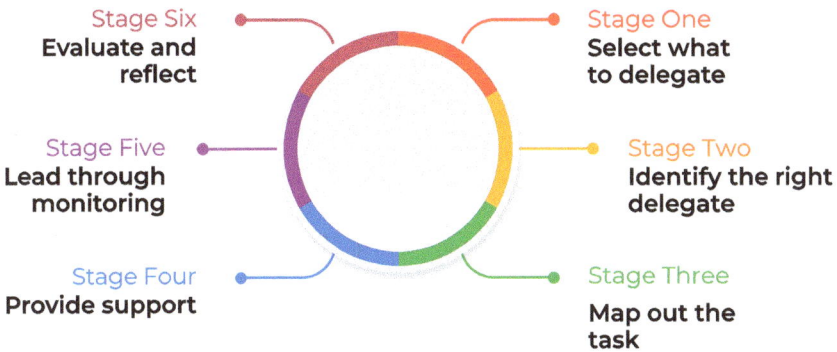

Figure 15. The Six Stages of Delegation

Stage 1: Select What to Delegate

If leaders meticulously follow the first step in the planning and preparation phase, deciding what to delegate becomes straightforward. This crucial step involves:

- **Identifying appropriate tasks for delegation:** Distinguish between tasks that require your direct involvement and those that can be effectively managed by others.

- **Selecting tasks with specific, measurable goals:** Clearly defined objectives ensure that delegated tasks have a purposeful direction and expected outcomes. This clarity not only facilitates progress tracking and success evaluation but also empowers team members to understand their responsibilities and the standards they need to meet.

Stage 2: Identify the Right Delegate

Choosing the right delegate is a make-or-break decision for a successful delegation. This, again, underscores the importance of the planning stage, where leaders must invest time in thoroughly assessing their employees' readiness. Identifying those with the appropriate combination of capabilities is paramount.

- **Evaluate interests and work loads of team members:** Leaders should evaluate not just the requisite skill set, but also the interests and current workloads of potential delegates. Match the task to someone who possesses the necessary skills and demonstrates enthusiasm and a willingness to learn. This approach ensures that the task is handled competently and with commitment.

- **Align delegated tasks with career goals:** For high-stakes tasks, it is even more crucial to align the delegated tasks with the career goals of your team members. When tasks contribute to their professional growth, it boosts team members' motivation and ownership. For example, assigning a leadership task to someone aspiring to be a manager provides them with valuable experience and fosters their development.

Given the importance of selecting the right delegate, a subsequent section in this chapter will delve deeper into this topic, offering practical guidance on making optimal choices.

Stage 3: Map out the Task Clearly

After selecting the delegate, the next critical step is to provide a comprehensive explanation of the task. This involves detailing the scope of the task, any limitations, and the extent of the delegate's authority. Clear communication at this stage is essential to prevent misunderstandings and to set the foundation for successful task completion. Be sure to communicate the following:

- **Clear parameters for success:** Leaders must take the time to clearly outline what successful completion of the task would look like. This involves using examples or benchmarks to provide a concrete understanding of the desired results. By doing so, you help set clear expectations and establish criteria for measuring performance.

- **Specific deadlines and milestones for the task:** This will ensure timely completion and facilitate progress tracking. Regular milestones also allow for necessary adjustments to be made along the way, ensuring the task stays on track and meets the established goals.

This structured approach not only helps the delegate stay focused but also enables the leader to monitor progress effectively and provide support as needed.

Stage 4: Provide Adequate Support and Resources

Once delegates begin working on their assigned tasks, leaders must ensure that they have access to all necessary resources and support:

- **Provide the right tangible resources:** Ensure that relevant personnel have access to the required tools, data, reports, and connections to complete the task. Access to these resources is essential for efficient task execution and for achieving high-quality outcomes.

- **Offer continuous mentorship and coaching:** This involves not only being available to answer questions but also proactively checking in with delegates to offer guidance and support. Facilitating access to subject matter experts can further enhance the delegate's ability to perform well, as they can draw on specialized knowledge and experience as needed.

- **Create a supportive environment:** Leaders should foster a safe space where delegates feel comfortable asking questions and seeking advice without fear of judgment. This open communication channel helps address challenges promptly, preventing minor issues from escalating into major obstacles. By maintaining this ongoing support, leaders can ensure delegates remain motivated and focused, ultimately contributing to the success of the delegation process.

Stage 5: Lead through Monitoring Progress

It is important to consistently monitor delegates' progress to maintain momentum and ensure the task stays on track toward completion. Do this through:

- **Regular check-ins and meetings:** These check-ins are essential for monitoring delegates' progress, addressing challenges, and providing guidance for the duration of the task.

- **Positive reinforcement and constructive feedback:** Recognizing and acknowledging achievements with positive reinforcement boosts morale and motivation. Conversely, offering constructive feedback helps delegates learn and grow by identifying areas for improvement.

- **Encouraging open communication:** Keeping the lines of communication open throughout the process is crucial for fostering a culture of learning and continuous improvement. By creating a safe space for delegates to share their thoughts, concerns, and ideas, leaders can cultivate an environment where feedback is valued and acted upon. This collaborative approach not only enhances individual performance but also strengthens team cohesion and effectiveness.

Stage 6: Evaluate and Reflect

After the task is completed, it's crucial to assess the results against the established goals and expectations. This evaluation process provides valuable insights into the effectiveness of the delegation and enables leaders to make informed adjustments for future tasks.

- **Review outcomes:** Take the time to thoroughly review the outcomes, discussing what went well and identifying any areas for improvement.

- **Reflect on the overall process:** Gather feedback from the delegate and encourage them to share their perspectives on what worked well and what could be improved. This collaborative reflection fosters a culture of continuous learning and improvement within the team.

By engaging in this review and evaluation process, leaders demonstrate a commitment to ongoing improvement and development. They can leverage lessons learned to refine their delegation strategies, optimize team performance, and drive future success.

The six steps described above are what it means and what it takes to delegate effectively. This comprehensive process unfolds from meticulous planning and preparation to thorough review and evaluation. When executed proficiently, public leaders can expect a notable enhancement in the success rate of their delegated initiatives and overall organizational performance.

However, some inherent pitfalls and challenges have the potential to derail the delegation process. Leaders must be cognizant of these challenges. In the subsequent section, we delve into the various factors that can lead to delegation failure and explore proactive solutions to mitigate these risks. By understanding these challenges and implementing effective strategies to address them, leaders can safeguard against potential setbacks and maximize the effectiveness of their delegation efforts.

Navigating Challenges in Delegation: Overcoming Common Obstacles

Delegation, while straightforward in theory, often presents challenges that can impede its effective implementation. Addressing these challenges proactively fosters operational smoothness and cultivates a culture of empowerment and growth within the organization.

Here are the challenges that often arise during the process of delegation and strategies to mitigate them:

1. Resistance from employees: Delegation often meets resistance from employees who may feel overwhelmed or uncertain about taking on new responsibilities. To overcome this challenge:

- Engage employees in the delegation process by soliciting their input and involving them in decision-making. Recognize and appreciate their contributions to boost morale and motivation.

- Address any fears or uncertainties by clearly communicating the benefits of delegation for both individual growth and organizational success. Emphasize how delegated tasks align with employees' career development goals and contribute to their professional advancement.

2. Inadequate follow-up: Inadequate follow-up can lead to communication breakdown, with tasks being overlooked or completed incorrectly. To ensure effective follow-up without resorting to micromanagement:

- Implement structured follow-up mechanisms to monitor progress and provide support as needed. This could include setting up regular check-in meetings, using project management tools to track milestones, or utilizing digital dashboards for real-time updates. These mechanisms provide a framework for accountability while allowing employees autonomy in task execution.

3. Mismatched skills and tasks: Assigning tasks that do not align with employees' skills or interests can lead to inefficiency and frustration. To address this challenge:

- Continuously assess and update your understanding of employees' skills and capacities. Conduct regular skills assessments or performance reviews to identify areas of strength and areas needing improvement. Provide targeted training and development opportunities to bridge skill gaps and ensure employees are equipped to handle delegated tasks effectively.

4. Distraction of activity over results: One significant challenge frequently experienced in public organizations is delegates' tendency to prioritize activities over impact. They focus on completing tasks without considering the impact on citizen satisfaction or community development. To keep this in check:

- Align delegated tasks with the broader goals and priorities of the government, such as improving service delivery, promoting equity, or addressing societal challenges. Emphasize the importance of outcomes and measurable results in evaluating task performance. Implement performance management systems that reward results-oriented behavior and innovation.

5. Conflicts of interest: Public servants may encounter conflicts of interest when delegated tasks involve regulatory enforcement, procurement decisions, or public policy development. The following are ways to mitigate this problem:

- Establish robust conflict-of-interest policies and ethical guidelines to govern public servants' conduct. Provide training and guidance on ethical decision-making and impartiality. Implement mechanisms for disclosing and managing conflicts of interest transparently. Foster a culture of integrity, accountability, and public trust within the organization.

Mapping Competence: How to Choose the Right Person for the Task

Some of the best leaders the world has seen have been noted for being talent masters. They were exceptionally skilled at identifying and nurturing the unique strengths and abilities of their team members. These leaders understood that the success of their organization depended not just on their vision and strategy, but on their ability to place the right people in the right roles. By leveraging competence mapping, they could meticulously analyze the skills, potential, and development needs of their employees. This allowed them to build cohesive, high-performing teams tailored to the specific demands of their projects and objectives.

Competence mapping is a crucial skill for leaders to master in order to delegate tasks effectively. This section breaks down the concept of competence mapping, providing leaders with clear and practical insights for selecting the right delegates based on their team members' specific competencies.

Understanding Competence Mapping

Competence mapping is a systematic process used to identify, assess, and document the skills, knowledge, abilities, and behaviors required for individuals to perform their roles effectively within an organization. It involves evaluating the current competencies of employees and comparing them to the competencies needed to achieve organizational goals and objectives.

Key Components of Competence Mapping

To understand competence mapping more thoroughly, it's essential to break down its key components. These components form the foundation of the competence mapping process and ensure its effectiveness in achieving organizational goals:

1. Skill Inventory

A skill inventory is a systematic record of the skills, qualifications, and experience of all the employees within an organization. It's essentially a database that compiles information about what each individual can do and what areas of expertise they possess. To build a skill inventory, follow these steps:

- Maintain a current and detailed list of each employee's skills. This should capture technical skills, soft skills, and specialized knowledge. Consider using self-assessment surveys, skills tests, or one-on-one discussions to gather this information.

Document relevant work experience, educational qualifications, and any professional certifications your employees possess. This can highlight specific areas of expertise that might be perfect for delegated tasks.

2. Performance History

- Review past performance evaluations and project reports to gain insights into each team member's reliability, work ethic, and ability to meet deadlines.

- Analyze the quality of work delivered on past projects. This can reveal strengths in areas like attention to detail, problem-solving skills, and analytical abilities.

- Identifying areas where team members have struggled in the past can help you tailor delegations to avoid potential pitfalls. However, it's also important to consider growth since those evaluations.

3. Developmental Potential

Competence mapping goes beyond just current skill sets. It encompasses a comprehensive assessment of team members' potential for future growth. This involves identifying individuals who not only possess the necessary skills for their current roles but also demonstrate a strong potential for development.

The three key components of competence mapping outlined above provide a robust framework for organizations to harness the full potential of their workforce. By maintaining a thorough skill inventory, leveraging insights from past performance history, and recognizing developmental potential, leaders can make informed decisions when delegating tasks and responsibilities.

How to Implement Competence Mapping During the Delegation Process

- Define the task requirements:
  - **Outline task details**: Clearly articulate what the task involves, including the specific skills needed, the level of authority required, and the expected outcomes.
  - **Identify challenges**: Recognize any unique challenges associated with the task that might require specialized skills or experiences. Understanding these nuances ensures a precise match between the task and the individual's competencies.
- Assess available talent:
  - **Skill inventory comparison**: Compare the task requirements with your existing skill inventory to identify potential candidates who possess the necessary competencies.
  - **Consider soft skills:** Evaluate personality traits and interpersonal skills, especially if the task involves teamwork or leadership. These traits can be crucial for task success and team dynamics.

- Choose the delegate:

  - **Align skills and interests**: Select the individual whose skills, interests, and developmental trajectory align most closely with the task requirements. This alignment ensures that the delegate is both capable and motivated.

  - **Consider team impact:** Evaluate the broader impact on the team and ensure that the individual's current workload is balanced. Overloading a capable employee can lead to burnout and reduced overall team efficiency.

- Communicate the decision:

  - **Transparency in selection**: Clearly communicate why the individual was chosen for the task, highlighting their strengths and the trust the organization has in their capabilities. This transparency fosters trust and motivation.

  - **Discuss developmental aspects**: Discuss any developmental aspects of the assignment, aligning the task with the individual's growth objectives and the organization's goals. This alignment ensures mutual benefit and engagement.

By following these structured steps, organizations can effectively map competencies, ensuring that tasks are assigned to the right individuals. This not only enhances task performance but also contributes to the personal and professional growth of employees, ultimately driving organizational success.

How to Monitor Progress Effectively During the Delegation Process

The success of delegation hinges heavily on proactive monitoring and constructive feedback. While delegation itself can be a powerful tool, a weak monitoring infrastructure is a frequent culprit in delegation failures. Effective monitoring and feedback provide several critical benefits:

- **Ensuring task alignment:** Regular monitoring ensures that delegated tasks remain aligned with the original goals and objectives. It allows for quick adjustments if the task is veering off course, thereby preventing minor issues from developing into significant problems.

- **Course correction opportunities:** Early identification of roadblocks allows for timely adjustments, keeping the project aligned with its goals.

- **Supporting delegate development:** Feedback is crucial for the professional growth of the delegate. Constructive feedback helps them understand what they are doing well and where they can improve, fostering a learning environment that encourages personal and professional development.

The rest of this section offers insights and strategies to assist leaders in effectively monitoring and managing feedback during the delegation process.

Key Strategies for Effective Monitoring During Delegation

Monitoring delegated tasks effectively involves three key strategies that seamlessly integrate into the delegation process. First, setting clear milestones is essential. By breaking down tasks into manageable segments with specific milestones, you create natural checkpoints for review and assessment. These milestones not only track progress but also help in evaluating whether the task is proceeding according to schedule.

Second, leveraging technology enhances monitoring capabilities. Implementing project management tools enables real-time tracking of tasks. These tools provide visual progress updates and promptly notify you of any delays or issues that may arise. This technological support ensures that you stay informed and can intervene when necessary, maintaining task alignment with overall objectives.

Maintaining open lines of communication is another critical strategy for effective monitoring. Encourage regular updates from the delegate on their progress. Establishing a communication routine—whether daily, weekly, or as fits the task's timeline—ensures you are kept informed without resorting to micromanagement. This approach fosters transparency, supports the delegate in overcoming obstacles, and reinforces accountability throughout the delegation process. By employing these strategies cohesively, leaders can effectively monitor delegated tasks, promoting efficiency, accountability, and successful task completion within the organization.

How to Craft Constructive Feedback

Crafting constructive feedback requires a strategic approach that supports team growth and development. Begin by focusing on the feedback's objective, ensuring it remains specific, objective, and relevant to the task at hand. This approach helps avoid defensiveness and encourages a positive response by emphasizing outcomes and behaviors over personal attributes.

Balancing positive reinforcement with constructive criticism is equally crucial. Recognizing the delegate's achievements alongside areas for improvement motivates them and reinforces effective behaviors. This dual approach ensures feedback remains constructive and supportive, fostering a conducive environment for growth.

Additionally, adopt a solution-oriented mindset when delivering feedback. Alongside identifying areas needing improvement, offer practical solutions or additional support. This proactive stance empowers delegates to view feedback as a tool for development, promoting continuous learning and enhancing team effectiveness.

By employing these strategies cohesively, leaders can effectively craft feedback that nurtures professional growth, enhances performance, and strengthens team dynamics.

Overcoming Challenges in Monitoring and Feedback

Overcoming challenges in monitoring and feedback involves navigating various dynamics to foster a productive and supportive environment. Addressing resistance from delegates, particularly when feedback involves areas needing improvement, requires empathy and clear communication. By involving the delegate in formulating solutions and emphasizing the developmental purpose of feedback, leaders can enhance buy-in and engagement in the improvement process.

Avoiding the pitfall of micromanagement is essential in effective monitoring. While staying informed about progress is crucial, it's equally important to trust delegates with autonomy in their daily activities. Leaders should focus on outcomes rather than overly controlling processes, allowing room for individual initiative and innovation.

Managing feedback fatigue is another critical aspect of effective monitoring and feedback practices. Too frequent or overly detailed feedback sessions can overwhelm delegates, potentially diminishing the effectiveness of the feedback. Leaders should ensure that feedback sessions are appropriately spaced out and should focus on highlighting key developments or changes since the last meeting. This approach not only prevents overload but also ensures that feedback remains meaningful and actionable.

By addressing these challenges thoughtfully and proactively, leaders can cultivate a culture where monitoring and feedback are constructive tools for continuous improvement and professional growth.

After thoroughly examining the principles and mechanics of effective delegation, we will now illustrate how delegation works through practical examples using two case studies: One showcasing successful delegation and the other highlighting failures in delegation execution.

....

Case Study 1
Delegation Done Right

Background

As the nation approached the peak harvest season, the National Agricultural Development Board (NADB) encountered significant challenges due to a fast-spreading pest infestation threatening large portions of crops. Director Amina Yusuf, aware of the pressing nature of the crisis, which spells nationwide havoc of food insecurity if not curtailed, and the board's operational limitations, recognized an opportunity to enhance response efficiency and resource management through strategic delegation. She initiated a comprehensive effort aimed at empowering her team and improving the overall national response to the agricultural crisis.

Key Players

- **Mrs. Amina Yusuf (Director, Agricultural Field Services):** Initiator of the delegation initiative aimed at ensuring the adequacy, efficiency and effectiveness of the response to the pest infestation.

- **Mr. Chike Obi (Chief Operations Officer):** Responsible for overseeing operational changes and the direct implementation of delegated tasks.

- **Mrs. Maryam Bello (Senior Agronomist):** Selected for delegated responsibilities related to pest control and resource allocation alongside other NADB staff.

- **Mr. Mekana Aluya (Senior Partnerships Manager):** Responsible for coordinating engagements and joint efforts with partner organizations.

- **External Partners (other agricultural agencies and national emergency response institutions):** Invited to provide a concerted response and backstopping support to NADB.

- **Local farmers and citizens (audience):** Beneficiaries of improved pest management and resource distribution strategies.

The Delegation Process

Stage 1: Select What to Delegate

Set Clear Objectives: To effectively manage the pest infestation and optimize resource use during the crisis.

Identify Delegation Opportunities: Mrs. Amina organized workshops to pinpoint delegation opportunities and evaluate the organization and her team's readiness to handle critical pest control tasks.

Identify Key Tasks: She identified key tasks suitable for delegation, focusing on pest control strategies and coordination of resources.

Stage 2: Identify the Right Delegate

Assess Capabilities: During the workshops, Mrs. Amina assessed staff capabilities and identified Mrs. Maryam due to her expertise in agronomy and experience with pest management. She identified Mr. Mekana Aluya, Director of Partnerships as the most qualified to manage collaboration with other institutions in planning an expanded response.

Empower the Delegate: Mr. Chike delegated pest management and resource allocation tasks to Mrs. Maryam, empowering her to make real-time decisions on pest control measures and resource distribution. Mrs. Amina set up the joint task force and at the emergency meeting, announced Mr. Mekana as the focal point for all inter-agency efforts for the management of the crisis at hand.

Stage 3: Map Out the Task Clearly

Communicate Goals and Expectations: Mrs. Amina clearly communicated the goals and expectations to Mr. Chike, who oversaw operational changes. He conducted training sessions for Mrs. Maryam, emphasizing effective pest management techniques and resource allocation strategies. Both Mrs. Amina and Mr. Chike clearly communicated the scope of support required from external partners and boundaries of work to Mr. Mekana.

Set Up a Monitoring System: A robust monitoring system was implemented to track outcomes from the new delegation strategy, including daily reports on pest control effectiveness, resource utilization and partner coordination efforts to ensure that risk mitigation progressed adequately and immediate adjustments were made, where necessary.

Stage 4: Provide Adequate Support and Resources

Access to Relevant Tools and Data: Mr. Chike ensured that Mrs. Maryam had access to necessary tools, pest management data, and resources needed to address the infestation efficiently. He also ensured that Mr. Mekana had relevant communication tools and received timely approvals for approved activities.

Continuous Mentorship: Ongoing mentorship sessions were provided to strengthen Mrs. Maryam's decision-making abilities and Mr. Mekana's stakeholder coordination skills in managing the crisis.

Access to Experts: Access to pest control experts and agronomy specialists further enhanced the delegation process and support for Mrs. Maryam.

Stage 5: Lead Through Monitoring Progress

Continuous Progress Monitoring: Mr. Chike conducted regular check-ins with Mrs. Maryam and Mr. Mekana to monitor progress, address challenges, and provide guidance. These sessions ensured that all pest management efforts stayed on track. Mrs. Amina reviewed weekly reports to ensure alignment with crisis management objectives.

Feedback: Positive achievements were acknowledged, and constructive feedback was given to foster continuous improvement in pest control strategies.

Constant Communication: Open communication channels were maintained to encourage collaboration and problem-solving among team members, partners and local farmers.

Stage 6: Evaluate and Reflect

Review Performance Metrics: Performance metrics were reviewed to assess the impact of all response actions on crop protection, recovery and resource management.

Evaluate Outcomes Against Established Goals: Mrs. Amina and Mr. Chike evaluated outcomes against the established objectives, reflecting on successes and areas for improvement to refine future crisis response strategies.

Document Lessons Learned: Lessons learned were documented and shared to optimize delegation strategies and crisis management processes across NADB.

Conclusion and Lessons Learned

The delegation initiative at NADB significantly improved the response to the pest infestation crisis. Mrs. Amina's strategic approach to delegation, supported by Mr. Chike's diligent oversight and the effective execution by Mrs. Maryam and Mr. Mekana, transformed the crisis into an opportunity for improved operational efficiency and agricultural management. By following a structured delegation process, NADB fostered a culture of collaboration and responsiveness, paving the way for sustained success in managing agricultural crises and improving overall productivity and resilience.

Case Study 2
Delegation Gone Wrong

Background

Under the direction of Mr. Owei Sele, the Credit Control Unit of the Federal Savings & Credit Scheme (FSCS) was tasked to set up a line of credit for a novel and specialized public-private partnership transaction through strategic delegation. This initiative was driven by the organization's commitment to improving and expanding service delivery amidst a growing customer base. However, due to insufficient planning and execution, the effort encountered significant hurdles, resulting in internal conflicts and operational setbacks that affected the organization's ability to meet its objectives effectively.

Key Players

- **Mr. Owei Sele (executive director, risk and compliance at the FSCS):** Enthusiastic about the potential benefits of delegation but lacked a clear implementation plan.

- **Ms. Funke Umukoro (senior credit control officer):** Tasked with additional responsibilities in an unfamiliar terrain without proper authority or resources.

- **Other credit control staff and PPP transaction parties (audience):** Directly affected by the outcomes of the delegation strategy.

The Delegation Process

Stage 1: Select What to Delegate

Unclear scope and tasks: Mr. Owei initiated the delegation process without a thorough assessment of the scope of work covered by the delegation, clarity of expected outcomes and defined strategy for execution.

Missed delegation opportunities: He took no special measures to identify tasks that should be delegated.

Stage 2: Identify the Right Delegate

Assess capabilities: Mr. Owei did not evaluate Ms. Funke's readiness for the delegated tasks or consider other potential candidates. Ms. Funke was chosen without assessing her skills, interests, or current workload. She lacked the necessary experience and authority for the role.

Lack of empowerment: There was no training provided to Ms. Funke or other staff of the credit control unit about the specialized transaction. Mr. Owei delegated critical responsibilities to her without ensuring she had the necessary knowledge or authority to make credit appraisal decisions.

Stage 3: Map Out the Task Clearly

Unclear goals and expectations: The tasks were not clearly defined, and Ms. Funke was given incomplete information. Mr. Owei failed to provide a comprehensive explanation of the task, its scope, and the expected outcomes. There were no specific deadlines or milestones set for Ms. Funke to follow.

No monitoring system established: Mr. Owei failed to map out a monitoring system or schedule, setting the delegation up for failure due to a lack of continuous monitoring and feedback.

Stage 4: Provide Adequate Support and Resources

Access to relevant tools and data: Ms. Funke received no additional resources or support to manage her new responsibilities and struggled to manage them.

Mentorship and support: There was no mentorship or coaching provided to help her navigate the new assignment. She did not have access to experts to assist her in her task.

Stage 5: Lead through Monitoring Progress

Failure to monitor progress: Ms. Funke did not have regular check-ins with Mr. Owei to discuss progress and challenges, preventing Mr. Owei from recognizing and addressing issues early on. This lack of oversight led to frequent conflicts and operational failures.

Lack of feedback mechanisms: There was also no system in place to provide constructive feedback or address problems as they arose.

Tensions and Challenges

Crisis moments: After weeks of credit analysis and creating the line of credit, a significant error was discovered in the offer letter by the transaction parties, leading to outrage and complaints about the prolonged process and lack of professionalism. Overwhelmed and unsupported, Ms. Funke confronted Mr. Owei in a heated argument, resulting in her receiving a query that further affected staff morale.

Stage 6: Evaluate and Reflect

Lack of assessment: After the initiative failed, there was no evaluation or reflection on what went wrong. This lack of assessment prevented learning from the mistakes made during the delegation process.

Review outcomes: Mr. Owei did not review the outcomes against the established goals or gather feedback from Ms. Funke and other team members.

Lessons learned not captured: There was no reflection on the overall process or discussion on improvements for future delegation efforts.

Final Outcomes of the Delegation Process

Decreased operational efficiency: The delegation led to significant inefficiencies, major errors, delays and conflicts.

Low morale and high turnover: The failed initiative led to a significant drop in morale and dissatisfaction among staff, resulting in high turnover.

Public confidence erosion: The visible failures and errors eroded customer confidence in FCSC's ability to create specialized credits within defined timeframes.

Conclusion and Lessons Learned

The delegation initiative at FCSC failed primarily due to the absence of clear objectives, thorough planning, and effective communication. Delegating tasks without providing the necessary support and authority resulted in operational paralysis, low staff morale and customer complaints.

This troubled initiative serves as a cautionary tale about the risks associated with poorly planned and executed delegation. Mr. Owei's failure to properly assess, plan, and support the delegated tasks led not only to operational failures but also to significant staff dissatisfaction and public discontent.

This case underscores the critical importance of meticulous preparation, clear communication, and adequate empowerment and support in the delegation process. For delegation to be successful, leaders must ensure that tasks are clearly defined, appropriate delegates are chosen, and continuous support and monitoring are provided throughout the process.

Call to Action
Master Delegation for Breakthrough Results

In my work with leaders across sectors, I've observed many potential breakthrough leaders limit their performance and success by not mastering the art of delegation. Delegation is about leveraging the strengths of others to get the job done. It is a fundamental skill for every leader's success and is worth practicing until it is refined.

The true power of delegation lies in its ability to transform the organizational landscape. By entrusting team members with meaningful responsibilities and the autonomy to execute them, leaders instill a sense of ownership that drives innovation and commitment. This empowerment leads to a dynamic where teams are not only executing tasks but are also motivated to find new ways to contribute positively to their organization's goals.

Moreover, successful delegation supports organizational resilience and adaptability, qualities that are increasingly crucial in today's fast-paced and ever-changing world. By distributing decision-making across various levels, public leaders and their organizations can respond more swiftly and effectively to challenges and opportunities. This decentralized approach allows for quicker adjustments and enhances the organization's ability to navigate complexities with agility.

However, effective delegation requires a thoughtful balance of giving autonomy while maintaining alignment with the organization's goals and culture. It demands clear communication of expectations, ongoing support, and a constructive feedback loop where learning and development are continuous. Leaders must be diligent in not only choosing the right tasks to delegate but also in selecting the right individuals for these tasks and supporting them toward successful outcomes.

Delegation is a critical leadership discipline that extends beyond operational management to touch on the very essence of leadership itself—trust, respect, and empowerment. Therefore, embracing and refining the practice of delegation is not just a pathway to organizational efficiency; it is a commitment to nurturing a thriving, resilient, and adaptable organizational culture. Master the art of delegation, unlock the potential of your teams and drive your organization toward greater heights of performance and innovation.

The Discipline of Delegation at a Glance

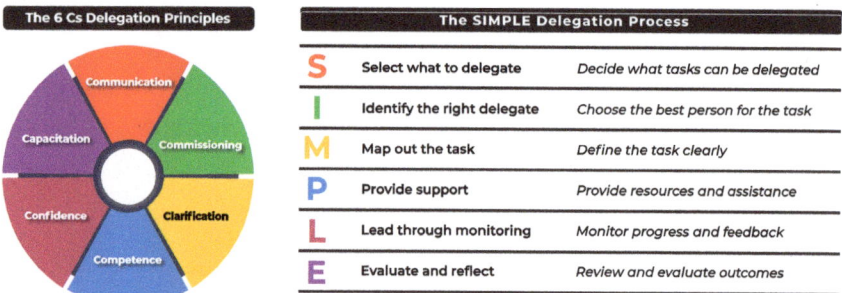

The 6 Cs Delegation Principles	The SIMPLE Delegation Process	
	S Select what to delegate	Decide what tasks can be delegated
	I Identify the right delegate	Choose the best person for the task
	M Map out the task	Define the task clearly
	P Provide support	Provide resources and assistance
	L Lead through monitoring	Monitor progress and feedback
	E Evaluate and reflect	Review and evaluate outcomes

Figure 16. Frameworks for Mastering Delegation: 6 + 6 MODEL

⚡ WHY IS DELEGATION IMPORTANT FOR PUBLIC LEADERS?

- **Enables strategic focus:** Public leaders balance immediate needs with long-term goals. By delegating routine tasks, they free up time to concentrate on high-level strategic planning, ensuring the organization remains aligned with its objectives.

- **Enhances responsiveness and agility:** Public leaders need to respond quickly to emerging issues. Delegation allows them to make faster decisions and give more agile responses by entrusting team members with the authority to act within their areas of responsibility.

- **Enhances organizational efficiency:** Public sector organizations deal with complex issues requiring expertise from various departments. Delegation allows leaders to distribute tasks based on team members' strengths, leading to faster completion and improved quality of outcomes.

- **Improves public trust and accountability:** Clear communication during delegation defines responsibilities and expectations. When employees understand their roles and are accountable for their actions, it builds public confidence in the organization's ability to manage resources and deliver services effectively.

☀ WHAT ARE THE BIG IDEAS?

- To be truly effective, leaders must focus on the "Who" not just "What" and "How". This involves identifying and empowering the right people with the skills and experience to execute strategic plans.

- Delegation is a strategic leadership tool, not just task assignment. It is about empowering the right people with the right tasks to achieve organizational goals. Leaders must transition from "doing everything" to "leading and enabling others" to achieve results.

- To delegate effectively, leaders must be guided by six principles: Capacitation, Communication, Commissioning, Clarification, Competence, and Confidence.

- The acronym SIMPLE is a memorable way for leaders to memorize and master the six stages of delegation.

⚲ HOW DO I MAKE IT HAPPEN?

Follow a six-stage process to delegate effectively within your organization:

Stage 1: Select What to Delegate

Stage 2: Identify the Right Delegate

Stage 3: Map Out the Task Clearly

Stage 4: Provide Adequate Support and Resources

Stage 5: Lead through Monitoring Progress

Stage 6: Evaluate and Reflect

Chapter 7
Discipline 6 - Drive

Why do public sector goals often fall short?

It cannot be because public leaders set out to fail. Most leaders start with clear, ambitious goals, meticulously crafting strategic plans to chart a path to organizational success. They set specific objectives for their teams and provide the necessary resources to achieve these goals. Despite these well-intentioned efforts, a troubling pattern often emerges: A routine failure to meet organizational objectives. Even when targets are met, there's a lack of understanding of how to replicate this success. This cycle of unmet expectations reveals a chronic issue not just in setting goals, but crucially, in delivering them.

The reason why so many public sector organizations falter in achieving their desired outcomes, often lies not in the inadequacies of their strategic plans or the capabilities of their people, but in a failure of implementation—a lack of a consistent, well-orchestrated rhythm to drive performance. This missing element is what the discipline of **DRIVE** seeks to address.

The Criticality of Drive to Breakthrough Public Leadership

Drive is the crucial discipline where strategies and intentions are transformed into measurable and meaningful results that align with an organization's mandate. This discipline enables leaders to establish a performance rhythm that ensures initiatives are not only launched but also sustained and brought to their intended conclusions. Without it, leaders cannot convert plans into actions and ambitions into realities. Drive goes beyond mere incremental improvements; it is about making significant leaps in performance and achieving dramatic strategic advantages that propel the organization forward.

Furthermore, drive is not just about achieving any results, but about reliably achieving the most ambitious organizational objectives. It entails putting plans into action swiftly and effectively, ensuring rapid and intentional outcomes consistently. This discipline provides a blueprint for leaders—a structured approach to not just dream big but to actualize these dreams systematically and consistently through a culture of execution.

Building a Culture of Execution

The secret of leaders who deliver breakthrough results is that they have mastered how to embed a robust, relentless execution culture within their organizations. A culture of execution is the hallmark of breakthrough results. This requires setting up systems that ensure actions are regular, intentions are clear, and follow-through is rigorous. Such an approach shows leaders how to operationalize their strategies into routine practices that yield consistent results. It transforms the sporadic success of individual projects into a reliable, repeatable formula for ongoing excellence.

To drive people, leaders must transcend traditional administrative oversight to foster a culture of high performance and ownership—a culture where results are not hoped for but expected, planned, and achieved. To instill such a culture, leaders must first ensure that every member of the organization understands its core mandates and priorities. This alignment of individual roles with organizational goals sets the foundation for accountable performance.

Next, it is essential to establish transparent systems for tracking progress. Implementing key performance indicators (KPIs) and visible scoreboards allows everyone in the organization to see, understand, and engage with these metrics regularly, creating shared responsibility for achieving these goals. Aligning incentives with organizational performance is also crucial. Broad-based incentive plans intricately tied to the organization's success can motivate employees and align their contributions directly with institutional success, reinforcing their stake in the outcomes. Furthermore, effective consequence management ensures that there are real implications for performance outcomes, further solidifying the organizational commitment to achieving results.

Establishing an "adult contract" is also vital for entrenching the discipline of execution. An "adult contract" refers to an implicit agreement or understanding within an organization that treats employees as responsible, autonomous adults rather than as individuals who need constant supervision and motivation. This concept is built on the principle that professional adults are expected to take ownership of their roles and responsibilities, perform their duties diligently, and contribute to the organization without needing to be coerced or constantly incentivized.

In today's culture where entitlement often undermines productivity, entrenching an adult contract is imperative. This mindset fosters an environment of professionalism and maturity where duties are performed because they are integral to personal and collective success, not because of extrinsic rewards or penalties.

As public leaders move to establish this contract, they may find the need to dismantle the entitlement mentality in their organization. This mentality, characterized by expectations of receiving benefits based on status rather than contribution, breeds dependency and stifles potential. Creating a culture of earning, where rewards are the direct results of one's contributions, shifts the organizational dynamic from one of dependency to one of empowerment. This shift enhances productivity and fosters a sense of pride and ownership among employees.

As we delve into the discipline of drive in this chapter, we explore crucial strategies to help leaders establish this culture of implementation within their organization. We discuss how to transition from the planning phase to action, from aspiration to measurable success, ensuring that every layer of the organization is aligned and committed to delivering on its promises. The ultimate goal is to equip leaders with the tools and methodologies to not just aim for exceptional performance but to guarantee it, time and again.

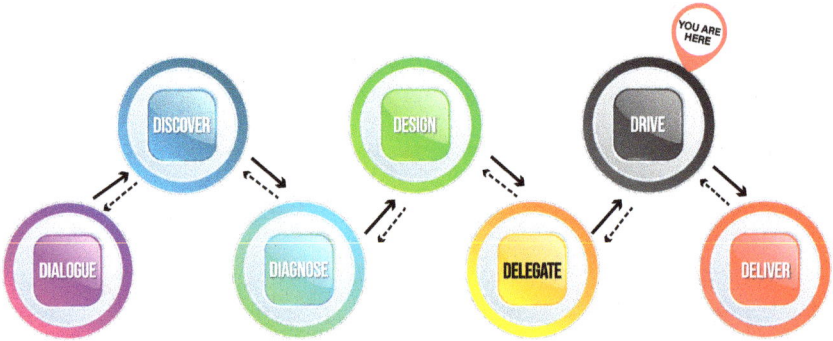

Figure 17. The Seven Disciplines of Breakthrough Results: Drive

Introduction to Strategic Drive: Catalyzing Performance in Public Sector Leadership

Words convey intentions, explanations rationalize plans, and activities demonstrate effort, but ultimately, in public sector leadership, only results reflect reality. Leadership is fundamentally an outcome-based endeavor. At the end of the day, leaders are appraised and remembered not for their eloquence or efforts, but for the tangible results they achieve.

In the public sector, where the stakes involve public trust and societal progress, results are not just an expectation but the very metric by which effectiveness is gauged. This unwavering focus on outcomes underpins the sixth discipline of breakthrough results: Drive.

Drive as a leadership competence transcends simple motivation. It is not merely about ambition or persistence; it embodies a systematic, strategic approach to ensuring that organizations not only set ambitious goals but also achieve them. In the public sector, where outcomes directly impact community welfare and societal progress, the significance of drive cannot be overstated. The following section explores the essence of drive and its transformative impact on public sector organizations.

The Essence of Drive

Drive is characterized by a relentless pursuit of results, orchestrated through meticulously planned activities that align with the overarching goals of an organization. It is not merely about pushing employees to work harder; it is about fostering an environment where strategic execution, accountability, and continuous improvement are part of the organizational ethos.

Understanding the essence of drive involves delving into several key components:

- **Meticulous planning and alignment:** At the heart of drive is meticulous planning. This involves breaking down broad organizational goals into specific, actionable tasks. Leaders must create detailed roadmaps that outline the steps required to achieve these goals, complete with timelines and resource allocation. This level of planning ensures that every action taken by the organization is purposeful and contributes directly to its strategic objectives. Additionally, it is crucial to align these activities across all levels of the organization, ensuring that every department and team is working towards the same goals in a coordinated manner.

- **Strategic execution:** Strategic execution is another cornerstone of drive. This means implementing meticulously planned activities in a way that maximizes efficiency and effectiveness. It's about making informed decisions, prioritizing high-impact tasks, and optimizing the use of resources. Leaders must ensure that the organization operates like a well-oiled machine, where every part works harmoniously towards the common objectives. This requires clear communication, robust processes, and the ability to adapt quickly to changing circumstances.

- **Fostering accountability:** A culture of accountability is essential for drive to be effective. This involves setting clear expectations for performance and establishing mechanisms for monitoring and evaluating progress. Employees at all levels should understand their roles and responsibilities and how their contributions fit into the larger organizational goals. Regular performance reviews, feedback sessions, and transparent reporting systems are critical components that help maintain accountability. When everyone is held accountable for their performance, it fosters a sense of responsibility and drives individuals to achieve their best.

- **Continuous improvement:** Drive also encompasses a commitment to continuous improvement. Organizations must foster an environment where learning and development are prioritized. This means encouraging employees to seek out new solutions, innovate, and continuously refine their skills and processes. Leaders should create opportunities for professional development, provide access to training resources, and promote a culture where constructive feedback is valued. Continuous improvement ensures that the organization remains agile, adapts to new challenges, and stays ahead in a rapidly changing environment.

The Transformative Impact of Drive on Public Sector Organizations

The transformative impact of drive on public sector organizations cannot be overstated. When fully embraced, drive can revolutionize the way these organizations operate, leading to significant improvements in performance and service delivery. By embedding the principles of drive into the organizational ethos, public sector leaders can build a culture of excellence. This culture is characterized by high standards, a commitment to continuous improvement, and a relentless focus on achieving results. Employees are motivated to perform at their best, knowing that their efforts are contributing to meaningful and measurable outcomes. This cultural shift not only enhances individual performance but also elevates the overall effectiveness of the organization.

Drive also ensures that public sector organizations can achieve their most ambitious strategic objectives. By providing a clear framework for planning, execution, and accountability, drive helps leaders translate their vision into reality. This disciplined approach enables organizations to tackle complex challenges, implement innovative solutions, and deliver on their promises to the community.

Finally, drive enhances public trust and confidence in public sector organizations. When these organizations consistently deliver results and demonstrate transparency and accountability, they build credibility and trust with the public. This trust is essential for maintaining support and cooperation from the community, which is vital for the successful implementation of public policies and programs.

Having established the critical importance of drive for the health of public sector organizations, we will now explore how leaders can master this discipline to position their organizations for high productivity and success.

Mastering the Discipline of Drive in Public Sector Leadership

While several key qualities contribute to a leader's success, the ability to consistently organize and drive the organization to peak performance stands out as a crucial differentiator. Leaders who deliver breakthrough results go beyond simply setting goals; they possess the capability to propel their teams toward achieving those goals with enthusiasm and focus. This involves providing clear direction, fostering a culture of accountability, and removing roadblocks that impede progress. By effectively driving performance, leaders can transform strategies from blueprints on paper to tangible results in the real world.

The discipline of drive comprises three components that, when well understood, integrated, and executed, automatically translate into consistent performance. To master the art of drive, leaders must thoroughly comprehend these three building blocks.

The Building Blocks of Drive

To cultivate a culture where employees consistently deliver results and fulfill commitments, three key elements must be established:

1. **Execution rhythm:** Establish a regular operational cycle that ensures all activities are directly linked to the organization's strategic objectives. This rhythm acts as a heartbeat, keeping everyone focused on achieving the overall goals.

2. **Reporting systems:** Implement robust systems that provide up-to-date data on progress. This enables informed decision-making and allows for timely adjustments as needed.

3. **Consequence management system:** Develop a framework that clearly links performance outcomes with rewards or corrective actions. This reinforces accountability and motivates consistent high performance across the organization.

Mastering the discipline of drive requires leaders to proactively entrench these elements within their organization. The following section explores each of these components in detail, providing actionable strategies for public sector leaders to effectively instill and manage these elements within their organizations.

Understanding and Mastering the Concept of an Execution Rhythm

By definition, an execution rhythm is a structured, consistent approach to managing and completing tasks within an organization. It involves establishing regular, predictable cycles of planning, execution, and review to ensure that initiatives progress smoothly and objectives are met on time. This rhythm helps create a disciplined workflow where everyone knows their responsibilities, deadlines, and the sequence of activities necessary to achieve the organization's goals.

An execution rhythm can be likened to the heartbeat of an organization, pumping energy and direction through its operations. It provides a predictable and steady framework that helps maintain focus and momentum, even in the face of challenges and changes. This rhythm ensures that every team member is on the same page, working towards the same objectives with clarity and purpose.

Key Characteristics of an Effective Execution Rhythm

An effective execution rhythm is built on several key characteristics that together create a cohesive and productive working environment:

- **Consistency:** Consistency is at the heart of this rhythm. Regular cycles of activity keep all team members aligned and focused, building reliability and trust within the team. Consistent execution ensures everyone knows what to expect and when, reducing uncertainty and enhancing coordination.

- **Predictability:** A well-understood schedule allows staff to anticipate tasks and prepare adequately. This fosters a sense of security and readiness, enabling employees to plan their work effectively and meet deadlines without undue stress. Predictability helps manage resources efficiently and avoids last-minute rushes, contributing to a smooth operational flow.

- **Responsiveness:** This is crucial for maintaining momentum while adapting to feedback and changing circumstances. This characteristic ensures that the organization remains agile and capable of pivoting when necessary, all while maintaining steady progress toward its goals. Responsiveness involves continuous monitoring and adjusting of plans to address emerging challenges and opportunities, ensuring that the execution rhythm is not rigid but dynamic and adaptable.

Benefits of an Execution Rhythm

Establishing an effective execution rhythm can be transformative for an organization, significantly enhancing how work is accomplished in a short period. Leaders who successfully implement an execution rhythm can expect several proven benefits that contribute to overall organizational success:

- **Enhanced productivity:** By following a regular cycle of planning, execution, and review, organizations can streamline processes and reduce downtime. This structured approach leads to higher productivity as tasks are completed more efficiently and effectively.

- **Improved accountability:** Clear responsibilities and deadlines ensure that everyone is accountable for their tasks, fostering a culture of ownership and responsibility. When team members know what is expected of them and by when, they are more likely to stay on track and deliver quality results.

- **Better communication:** Regular review meetings and updates keep all team members informed and engaged, improving communication and collaboration across the organization. This ongoing dialogue helps to align everyone's efforts and ensures that any issues are promptly addressed.

- **Increased efficiency:** Efficiency is achieved through predictable workflows and schedules. This predictability enables better resource allocation and time management, ensuring that all efforts are directed towards achieving organizational goals. By optimizing the use of resources and time, organizations can operate more smoothly and effectively.

In summary, an effective execution rhythm brings enhanced productivity, improved accountability, better communication, and increased efficiency, all of which contribute to the overall success and transformation of an organization.

Critical Steps to Establish an Execution Rhythm

Establishing a strong execution rhythm is not just about implementing a few tactics; it is about constructing a high-performance engine that drives consistent progress toward organizational goals. Below is a breakdown of the critical steps to establish this:

Step 1: Define Clear Objectives

- **Vision and alignment**: Begin by outlining the organization's short, medium, and long-term objectives. Ensure these objectives are aligned with the organization's core mission and strategic goals. This creates a clear picture of the desired destination and ensures everyone is working in unison.

Step 2: Break Objectives into Actionable Tasks

- **Task decomposition**: Each objective needs to be deconstructed into a series of well-defined tasks. These tasks should be specific, actionable, manageable, and understandable. This allows for a step-by-step approach, making the overall goal seem less daunting.

- **Assign roles and define timelines**: Assign clear responsibilities for each task. Who owns what? Define realistic timelines for completion, ensuring everyone is working towards the same deadlines. This fosters a sense of urgency and keeps the project moving forward.

Step 3: Implement Scheduling Tools

- **Project management tools**: Utilize scheduling tools and project management software to create visible and shared calendars that include all critical tasks and milestones. This allows everyone involved to see the big picture of tasks, deadlines, and dependencies.

- **Accessibility and transparency**: These tools should be accessible to all relevant team members and stakeholders. Easy updates and tracking are crucial to ensure everyone has access to the latest information. This fosters transparency and a sense of being "in the know."

Step 4: Regular Progress Reviews

- **Check-ins and meetings**: Establish regular check-in points to assess progress against the plan. Daily stand-up meetings for smaller teams, weekly team meetings, and monthly review sessions for larger initiatives are all crucial elements.

The framework below captures this effectively.

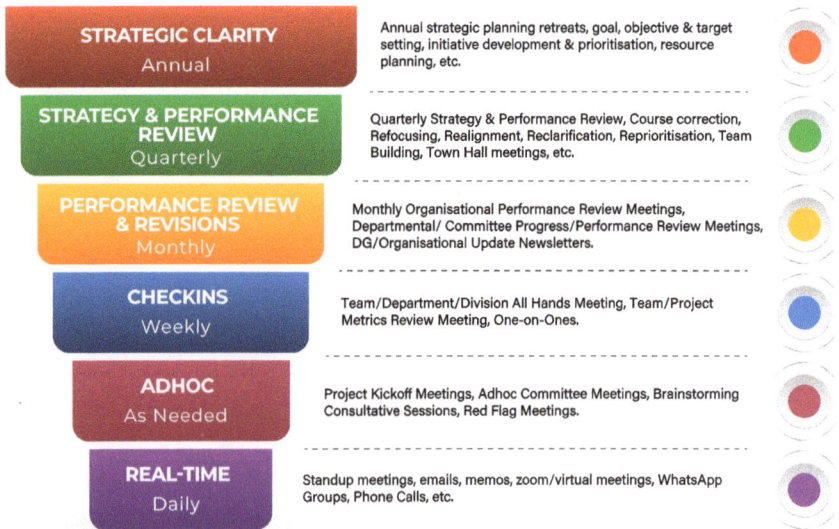

STRATEGIC CLARITY Annual	Annual strategic planning retreats, goal, objective & target setting, initiative development & prioritisation, resource planning, etc.
STRATEGY & PERFORMANCE REVIEW Quarterly	Quarterly Strategy & Performance Review, Course correction, Refocusing, Realignment, Reclarification, Reprioritisation, Team Building, Town Hall meetings, etc.
PERFORMANCE REVIEW & REVISIONS Monthly	Monthly Organisational Performance Review Meetings, Departmental/ Committee Progress/Performance Review Meetings, DG/Organisational Update Newsletters.
CHECKINS Weekly	Team/Department/Division All Hands Meeting, Team/Project Metrics Review Meeting, One-on-Ones.
ADHOC As Needed	Project Kickoff Meetings, Adhoc Committee Meetings, Brainstorming Consultative Sessions, Red Flag Meetings.
REAL-TIME Daily	Standup meetings, emails, memos, zoom/virtual meetings, WhatsApp Groups, Phone Calls, etc.

Figure 18. Execution Rhythm Framework

- **Continuous improvement:** Focus these meetings on evaluating what is working, what is not, and what adjustments need to be made to stay on track.

Step 5: Foster Team Alignment and Commitment

- **Reinforce goals:** Regularly reinforce the importance of each team's contributions to the broader organizational goals to maintain motivation and focus.

- **Encourage collaboration:** Promote open communication and collaboration across departments to ensure that the execution rhythm is cohesive and integrated, fostering a unified approach to achieving objectives.

Challenges in Establishing an Execution Rhythm

Establishing a strong execution rhythm is a powerful driver of success, but it is not without its hurdles. Anticipating and overcoming these key challenges is essential for creating an effective and sustainable rhythm.

One significant challenge is resistance to change. Staff may initially resist new processes and schedules as they adapt to changes. This resistance is a natural human response to change and can hinder the implementation of an execution rhythm. To overcome this resistance, open and transparent communication is crucial. Clearly explain the benefits of the new execution rhythm, emphasizing how it will improve efficiency, focus, and ultimately, success. Additionally, involving team members in the planning process can foster a sense of ownership over the rhythm, making them more likely to embrace and support it.

Another common challenge is over-complexity. Creating an execution rhythm that is too rigid or overly complex can stifle productivity and lead to frustration among staff. The goal of an execution rhythm is to guide action, not to strangle it with bureaucracy. Simplifying processes where possible and allowing for flexibility where necessary to accommodate unforeseen circumstances or evolving priorities is essential. The rhythm should be a living document, adaptable to the realities of daily operations.

By addressing these challenges through clear communication, involvement, simplification, and flexibility, organizations can establish a strong execution rhythm that drives success and enhances overall performance.

Monitoring and Adjusting the Rhythm

Recognizing the dynamic nature of an execution rhythm is crucial for optimizing organizational performance. Rather than treating it as a static procedure, leaders should embrace it as a continuously evolving tool that requires ongoing refinement.

First, it's essential to view the execution rhythm as a dynamic component of operations, open to continuous improvement. This mindset shift allows leaders to adjust and refine processes in response to changing operational needs and emerging challenges. Regularly seeking feedback from team members is integral to this process. By listening to their perspectives on how the rhythm can better align with operational realities and employee needs, leaders can glean valuable insights for ongoing enhancement.

Second, adapting to external changes is paramount. The external environment is constantly evolving, presenting new challenges or unexpected opportunities that can impact organizational goals. A robust execution rhythm should be adaptable enough to accommodate these external forces. Leaders must remain vigilant and responsive, ready to swiftly adjust plans to capitalize on opportunities or mitigate risks.

By treating the execution rhythm as a dynamic and adaptable framework, informed by regular feedback and responsive to external changes, organizations can maintain agility, optimize performance, and drive sustainable success.

We have just explored the concept of an execution rhythm, the first building block required to implement the discipline of drive, and detailed how leaders can establish this essential rhythm. Next, we will delve into the second pillar of drive: Reporting systems.

Understanding and Mastering Reporting Systems

For public leaders looking to drive peak performance in their organizations, mastering the discipline of reporting is an essential skill. It goes beyond simply tracking progress. Effective reporting fosters a culture of transparency and accountability, enabling informed decision-making that keeps the organization aligned with its mission.

More than just documenting outcomes, insightful reports shape strategic directions and policy adjustments. They become the compass guiding leaders to adapt and respond effectively to the evolving needs of the communities they serve. Understanding strategies to enhance reporting mechanisms empowers leaders to ensure their organizations remain agile and responsive in this dynamic landscape.

The Importance of Reporting in Public Sector Organizations

Effective reporting systems act as the central nervous system of an organization, transmitting vital information crucial for informed decision-making and operational efficiency. In the public sector, where every action directly affects community well-being, robust reporting mechanisms become indispensable. They ensure resources are used responsibly and public services are delivered effectively.

Transparency lies at the heart of effective reporting, offering stakeholders clear insights into organizational operations and outcomes. This transparency builds trust and credibility, showcasing the organization's commitment to accountable governance. Furthermore, reporting systems uphold accountability by tracking performance against objectives and regulatory compliance, ensuring that public servants fulfill their commitments ethically and legally.

Beyond historical tracking, effective reporting provides strategic insights that guide future actions. Through detailed data analysis, reports uncover trends, pinpoint areas for enhancement, and inform strategic resource allocations. This strategic approach ensures that organizational efforts are precisely targeted to achieve maximum impact for the communities they serve.

How to Develop an Advanced Reporting Mechanism

In addition to the benefits discussed above, leaders who prioritize establishing an effective reporting system within their organizations will significantly enhance their ability to make effective decisions based on real-time data and insightful analysis. To achieve this, they must move beyond traditional reporting methods and adopt advanced reporting mechanisms. Below is a roadmap to building an advanced reporting system:

1. Implement Real-time Data Collection Systems

Leverage modern technology solutions to collect and analyze data in real-time. This allows for a more dynamic approach to decision-making, where leaders can adapt and respond swiftly to emerging needs or unforeseen challenges.

Integration is key. Consider implementing systems like enterprise resource planning (ERP) and customer relationship management (CRM) software. These systems excel at integrating data streams from various departments, providing a comprehensive and unified view of organizational performance. This holistic perspective empowers leaders to identify cross-departmental trends and make strategic decisions that optimize overall effectiveness.

2. Design Tailored Reporting Dashboards

Move away from "one-size-fits-all" reporting. Design customized dashboards that cater to the specific needs of different departments and stakeholders. Tailored dashboards ensure everyone has the critical information they need at their fingertips, facilitating quick assessment and informed action.

Ensure each dashboard prominently displays key performance indicators (KPIs) relevant to its specific audience. KPIs act as the guiding lights, allowing users to quickly gauge performance against established goals and identify areas requiring attention.

3. Standardize Reporting Formats

Develop and enforce standardized reporting formats across the organization. This ensures consistency in data collection and presentation, allowing for comparability of information across departments and over time.

Regularly conduct training sessions to familiarize staff with these reporting formats and the importance of accurate and timely data entry. Empowering staff with the knowledge and skills necessary for effective reporting is crucial for the success of the entire system.

Ensuring Accuracy and Timeliness in Reporting

Effective reporting relies fundamentally on two pillars: Accuracy and timeliness. These elements are critical for leaders who depend on reliable data to make informed decisions. Below, we outline strategies to establish a solid foundation in reporting.

- **Establish a mechanism for data integrity checks:** To ensure data accuracy, start by implementing robust mechanisms for data integrity checks. Establish rigorous data validation processes that encompass every stage from data collection to analysis. Incorporate both automated checks and manual reviews to swiftly identify and rectify any errors that may arise. Additionally, provide regular training sessions for staff on best practices in data collection and entry. Emphasize the significance of accuracy and how it directly influences organizational decision-making. Utilize advanced analytical tools capable of identifying patterns and anomalies, facilitating early detection and correction of inaccuracies.

- **Establish a mechanism for prioritizing timeliness:** Prioritize timeliness by instituting mechanisms that expedite data collection and reporting. Implement automated systems that streamline the gathering and dissemination of real-time data. Automation not only minimizes delays but also ensures stakeholders have access to the most current information available. Establish clear and achievable deadlines for data submission and report generation. Consistent adherence to these deadlines will guarantee timely production and distribution of reports.

- **Streamline reporting processes:** Review and optimize workflows to eliminate bottlenecks and inefficiencies. Simplifying these processes significantly reduces the time required to produce accurate reports. Cultivate a culture that values punctuality in data submission and reporting. Encourage teams and individuals to prioritize timely delivery, and recognize their efforts to meet reporting deadlines. This fosters a proactive environment where the organization operates with efficiency and reliability in its reporting practices.

Overcoming Challenges in Reporting

Establishing an effective reporting system often presents several challenges that organizations must navigate:

- **Dealing with data overload:** One common issue is dealing with data overload, where the sheer volume of available information can overwhelm decision-makers. To address this challenge, prioritize data according to its strategic relevance. Utilize advanced analytical tools to sift through large datasets and distill them into actionable insights that drive informed decision-making.

- **Training and capacity building:** Another significant hurdle is ensuring that staff possess the necessary skills and knowledge to effectively utilize advanced reporting systems. To tackle this challenge, organizations should develop comprehensive training programs. These programs should encompass training on reporting tools, data analysis techniques, and best practices for data management. By investing in staff training and capacity building, organizations can empower their teams to leverage reporting systems effectively, enhancing overall operational efficiency and decision-making capabilities.

Building a robust reporting system is essential for leaders of any organization size to effectively oversee operations and drive performance. Now that we've examined this critical second pillar, let's move on to the third component of the discipline of drive: Consequence management.

Understanding and Mastering Consequence Management

Consequence management refers to the systems and processes established to reward achievements and address shortcomings within an organization. It involves creating a clear link between performance and outcomes, ensuring that employees understand the impact of their actions and are motivated to perform optimally.

Effective consequence management is critical for making the principles of drive not just theoretical but practical, actively influencing organizational behavior and outcomes. Public sector leaders must develop and implement a robust consequence management system to enhance their organization's performance and accountability. This involves rewarding high performers to encourage continued excellence and addressing underperformance to foster improvement and accountability.

Key Objectives of Effective Consequence Management

Effective consequence management serves several critical objectives within an organization, shaping its culture and driving performance.

- **Building a culture of accountability:** By clearly defining expectations and the repercussions of actions, employees understand their roles and responsibilities better, fostering a sense of ownership and commitment to maintaining organizational standards. This framework not only clarifies boundaries but also ensures that every team member contributes positively towards collective goals.

- **Reinforcing positive behaviors:** Beyond addressing shortcomings, a well-executed consequence management system actively recognizes and rewards high performance. Whether through promotions, bonuses, or public acknowledgments, these incentives encourage employees to sustain or enhance their contributions. By celebrating achievements, organizations cultivate a culture that values excellence and continuous growth, inspiring teams to strive for even greater success.

- **Facilitating corrective actions for underperformance:** When employees fail to meet expectations, the system offers structured interventions such as coaching, mentoring, or skills development. These measures are designed not only to support individuals in improving their performance but also to align their skills with organizational needs. By nurturing talent and addressing gaps, organizations enhance overall productivity and effectiveness.

- **Promoting open communication:** A key aspect of effective consequence management is open communication. Clear and constructive feedback plays a crucial role in guiding employees towards improvement. Equally important is fostering an environment where employees feel safe to voice concerns about potential consequences. Transparent communication channels ensure that feedback is received openly and acted upon promptly, promoting mutual understanding and trust within the team.

Ultimately, the goal of effective consequence management is to prevent future issues from arising. By identifying and addressing root causes of performance gaps, organizations can proactively mitigate risks. This may involve refining training programs, optimizing workflows, or allocating additional resources where needed. By continuously improving processes and anticipating challenges, organizations strengthen their resilience and sustain long-term success.

Steps to Implement an Effective Consequence Management System

To successfully implement an effective consequence management system, organizations must follow structured steps that align performance expectations with strategic goals, promote transparency, and support continuous improvement.

Step 1: Define Clear Performance Standards

Establishing clear and measurable performance standards forms the foundation of an effective consequence management system. These standards should be SMART (specific, measurable, attainable, relevant, and time-bound) and communicated clearly across all levels of the organization. By aligning these standards with strategic objectives, employees gain a clear understanding of their roles and how their contributions impact organizational success.

Step 2: Develop a Transparent Rewards System

Designing a rewards system that ties rewards directly to performance metrics motivates employees to strive for excellence. Whether through financial incentives, promotions, public recognition, or professional development opportunities, transparency in how rewards are earned fosters fairness and encourages employees to meet or exceed expectations. Regular reviews ensure the rewards system remains relevant and effective.

Step 3: Structure Constructive Corrective Measures

Implementing corrective measures focused on improvement rather than punitive actions is crucial. These measures might include additional training, mentorship programs, or temporary reassignments aimed at developing employee skills and capabilities. Consistently applying these measures across the organization promotes fairness and underscores the organization's commitment to supporting employee growth.

Step 4: Implement Regular Performance Reviews

Scheduled performance reviews provide opportunities to assess progress, offer feedback, and make necessary adjustments. These reviews not only help in tracking performance but also facilitate a two-way feedback process where employees can contribute insights on their experiences and challenges. This feedback loop is essential for refining performance standards and corrective measures.

Step 5: Monitor and Evaluate the System

Continuously monitoring and evaluating the consequence management system will ensure its effectiveness in driving performance improvements. Analyzing data and gathering feedback helps identify areas for refinement and adjustment. Being responsive to evaluation findings allows organizations to adapt the system to evolving needs and maintain its relevance over time.

By following these steps, organizations can establish a robust consequence management system that promotes accountability, supports employee development, and enhances overall organizational performance.

The discipline of drive is built upon three core components: Execution rhythm, reporting systems, and consequence management. We have thoroughly explored each of these. A leader's ability to effectively integrate these components within their organization directly impacts their ability to drive performance sustainably. Only after mastering these components can leaders effectively implement the stage-by-stage guide below to apply the discipline of drive within their organizations.

Executing Drive: A Stage-by-Stage Guide

After gaining a thorough understanding of the three key components that define a robust culture of drive within organizations, the following is a comprehensive, end-to-end guide that leaders can use to implement the discipline of drive in their organizations.

By carefully following the stages below, leaders will significantly enhance organizational effectiveness by aligning daily operations with strategic goals, ensuring accountability, and achieving sustained performance improvement.

Figure 19. The Three Stages of Performance Drive

Stage 1: Establish an Execution Rhythm

Establishing an execution rhythm is vital to cultivating and sustaining drive in an organization. The following practices will ensure consistency, clarity, and standardization during execution, empowering teams to meet their and the organization's goals.

- **Define strategic objectives:** Clearly articulate the long-term goals and objectives of the organization, breaking them down into actionable tasks.

- **Develop operational calendars:** Create detailed calendars outlining daily, weekly, monthly, and quarterly activities aligned with strategic objectives, including key performance indicators (KPIs).

- **Establish review rhythms:** Schedule regular review meetings to assess reports, discuss operational strategy implications, and foster collaborative feedback.

- **Foster Team Alignment and Commitment:** Continuously emphasize the significance of each team's role in advancing organizational goals to maintain motivation and focus. Keep lines of communication open and encourage teamwork among departments to ensure a unified and integrated execution rhythm.

Stage 2: Set up Advanced Reporting Mechanisms

Robust reporting systems are essential for tracking progress, making informed decisions, and adjusting strategies in real time. Strategies to enhance reporting systems are:

1. **Implement integrated reporting tools:** Deploy advanced data management systems to collect and analyze performance data in standardized reporting formats, ensuring compatibility with existing IT infrastructure.

2. **Customize reporting dashboards:** Design dashboards providing real-time insights into KPIs and metrics, and train staff on their use for informed decision-making.

Stage 3: Implement an Effective Consequence Management System

Linking performance outcomes to appropriate rewards and consequences is crucial for maintaining motivation and accountability. Develop a consequence framework to standardize the criteria by which performance is judged and how the resulting consequences are handled.

- **Define performance thresholds:** Establish clear, measurable criteria that trigger rewards or corrective actions, ensuring transparency and alignment with organizational values.

- **Develop reward systems:** Create comprehensive systems including financial bonuses, promotions, and recognition opportunities, and communicate these clearly to all employees.

- **Set up corrective measures:** Outline constructive actions for underperformance, focusing on improvement through training, reassignment, or other interventions.

The successful implementation of the discipline of drive hinges on the meticulous execution of these three foundational stages: Establishing an execution rhythm, setting up advanced reporting mechanisms, and implementing an effective consequence management system.

By defining clear strategic objectives, developing operational calendars, standardizing procedures, and aligning teams, organizations can foster a cohesive and goal-oriented environment.

Robust reporting systems, integrated tools, and customized dashboards enable leaders to monitor progress and make informed decisions swiftly. Finally, linking performance outcomes to appropriate rewards and corrective measures ensures accountability and motivates continuous improvement.

Together, these stages form a comprehensive framework that aligns daily operations with strategic goals, driving sustained organizational performance and growth.

To ensure that leaders maximize the effectiveness of their drive intervention, it is crucial to address common challenges that frequently arise during the process and the strategies for overcoming them.

Navigating Challenges in Implementing Drive: Overcoming Common Obstacles

1. Overcoming resistance to change: This is particularly challenging in environments like the public sector where traditional practices are deeply entrenched. Employees may resist new initiatives due to concerns about increased workloads or disruptions to familiar routines. Addressing this challenge requires patience and clear communication from leaders. They must effectively articulate the benefits of drive and demonstrate how it aligns with the organization's overarching goals. Transparency about the implementation process and its expected outcomes can help alleviate fears and build trust among team members. Additionally, providing robust support systems such as comprehensive training and mentoring programs is crucial. These initiatives equip employees with the necessary skills and knowledge to adapt to new practices, thereby reducing anxiety and resistance. Mentorship programs, in particular, offer valuable guidance and support from experienced colleagues, smoothing the transition to new ways of working.

2. Balancing performance expectations with compassion and understanding: While drive emphasizes achieving results, leaders must recognize and address the human side of operations. This involves understanding and empathizing with the limitations and personal circumstances of employees. Leaders should be attuned to the professional and personal challenges their team members face, fostering a more empathetic leadership approach.

By maintaining awareness of these factors, leaders can adopt strategies that support employee well-being while driving performance. This compassionate leadership approach is essential for maintaining morale and motivation within the organization. By demonstrating empathy and providing support, leaders create a positive work environment where employees feel valued and understood. This balance between driving performance and supporting employee welfare enhances overall productivity and strengthens commitment to achieving the organization's goals.

While the framework for executing drive described above holds significant potential for enhancing performance within organizations, achieving outstanding results hinges on leaders' unwavering commitment to the process.

In the following sections, we will explore the critical role of leadership in the drive process and provide additional resources to ensure that leaders always remain on top of interventions.

The Role of Leadership in Fostering Drive

The success of implementing drive within an organization largely depends on the effectiveness and commitment of its leadership. Leaders play a pivotal role in setting the tone, creating a vision, and inspiring action. They are the catalysts for change and the driving force behind the adoption and sustainability of the principles fundamental to drive.

Energy Management

Breakthrough leadership hinges on a powerful, yet often overlooked, factor: Energy management. Leadership must take charge of their energy management. Neuroscience tells us that a leader's ability to self-regulate emotions and maintain optimal energy levels directly impacts their decision-making, team dynamics, and the overall success of the organization.

A leader's first and foremost responsibility, therefore, is to take charge of their energy. This involves self-awareness, self-regulation, and a commitment to personal excellence.

Self-aware leaders understand their personal strengths, weaknesses, and emotional triggers. This awareness helps them manage their energy and stay grounded. Similarly, their ability to control impulses and stay calm under pressure ensures consistent and rational decision-making. Ultimately, a leader's commitment to excellence will filter down to the entire organization. Leaders who relentlessly pursue personal and professional growth set a positive example for their entire team.

Orchestrate the Energy of the Team

Once leaders have harnessed their own energy, their next crucial task is to orchestrate the energy of those around them. This entails motivating, inspiring, and guiding team members toward achieving the organization's goals. Effective leaders excel at channeling their team's energy into productive and aligned actions. Below, we discuss strategies that empower leaders to cultivate and sustain drive within their teams:

- **Leading by example:** Leaders must embody the behaviors they wish to see in their employees, such as adhering meticulously to the Execution Rhythm, actively engaging in reporting processes, and openly discussing performance consequences. By demonstrating a commitment to these practices, leaders inspire their teams to embrace them as well, fostering a culture of Drive throughout the organization.

- **Creating alignment and unity across all levels of management:** Ensuring that every manager understands and commits to the objectives of drive facilitates the cascading of these principles throughout the organization. Regular alignment sessions, workshops, and clear communication play a vital role in maintaining focus and unity, ensuring that everyone works towards common organizational goals with shared dedication.

- **Empowering employees:** Providing team members with the necessary tools, resources, and autonomy empowers them to excel in their roles. Additionally, encouraging employees to contribute ideas for process improvement fosters a culture of innovation and engagement. This empowerment not only enhances individual performance but also strengthens the collective drive of the team, leading to greater organizational success.

To ensure that drive initiatives are progressing effectively, leaders must continuously measure and evaluate their leadership effectiveness.

Measuring the Impact of Leadership on Drive

The following are key strategies to assess and enhance the impact of leadership on drive.

- **Feedback and evaluation:** Leaders are encouraged to actively solicit feedback from employees to gauge the effectiveness of drive initiatives and their leadership approach. This feedback can be obtained through various channels such as surveys, suggestion boxes, or direct communication. It is essential for feedback mechanisms to ensure anonymity to foster candid and constructive input from employees, enabling leaders to pinpoint areas needing improvement. Additionally, leaders can consider implementing 360-degree review processes, where feedback is gathered from peers, subordinates, and superiors alike. This comprehensive feedback offers valuable insights into a leader's strengths and areas for further development.

- **Continuous leadership development:** Leadership development should be viewed as an ongoing journey. Leaders must commit to continuous learning and improvement to effectively navigate new challenges and organizational changes. Structured programs such as workshops, seminars, and online courses should be regularly offered to support leaders in acquiring new skills and honing existing ones.

These initiatives not only enhance leadership capabilities but also ensure that leaders remain adaptable and resilient in guiding their teams toward achieving organizational goals.

Equally important to measuring the impact of leadership is assessing how well the organization is aligning with drive initiatives. This evaluation is crucial for tracking progress, identifying areas for improvement, and ultimately demonstrating the impact of drive on organizational performance.

We will now explore the key metrics and performance evaluation strategies that public sector leaders can employ to track the success of drive implementation.

Drive Metrics and Performance Evaluation

To assess how effectively the organization aligns with the drive initiative, it is essential to utilize specific key performance indicators (KPIs) designed to measure the initiative's effectiveness:

- **Goal achievement rate:** This metric offers insights into how well drive initiatives contribute to driving performance and achieving results. Leaders should consistently measure the percentage of established goals and targets that are successfully accomplished within predefined time frames.

- **Execution rhythm adherence:** Evaluating execution rhythm adherence provides a measure of the organization's discipline and commitment to maintaining consistent performance levels.

Leaders should assess adherence to established execution rhythms, encompassing daily operational tasks through to annual strategic objectives.

- **Reporting accuracy and timeliness:** Monitoring the accuracy and timeliness of reporting processes is crucial. This involves ensuring that performance dashboards and reports are generated and disseminated promptly, providing decision-makers with current information to drive informed actions.

- **Consequence management effectiveness**: Assessing the effectiveness of consequences management systems is vital for shaping desired behaviors and outcomes. Leaders should gauge how rewards and consequences impact employee motivation, engagement, and overall performance alignment with organizational goals.

By integrating these metrics, public sector leaders not only assess the success of drive implementation but also cultivate a culture of performance excellence and adaptive leadership. Each metric serves as a guiding beacon, informing strategic decisions and reinforcing the organization's commitment to achieving sustained success and meaningful societal impact in an ever-evolving landscape.

Strategies for Evaluating Drive

In addition to the metrics discussed above, leaders must also carefully select and employ strategies to evaluate drive. The following strategies outline how leaders can effectively evaluate their drive initiatives:

1. **Regular performance reviews:** Conduct regular performance reviews to meticulously assess progress against established goals and objectives. Offer constructive feedback to employees, acknowledging achievements and addressing areas needing improvement.

2. **360-Degree feedback mechanisms:** Implement 360-degree feedback mechanisms to gather comprehensive insights from various stakeholders, including peers, supervisors, and subordinates. Utilize

this feedback to pinpoint individual strengths, identify development areas, and uncover opportunities for enhancing overall performance.

3. **Continuous improvement initiatives:** Cultivate a culture of continuous improvement by empowering employees to propose and implement process enhancements and innovations. Regularly review and refine drive initiatives based on ongoing feedback and performance data to enhance effectiveness and adaptability.

4. **Outcome-based evaluation:** Focus on outcome-based evaluation to gauge the tangible results and overall impact of drive initiatives on organizational performance. Align evaluation metrics closely with strategic objectives and prioritize initiatives that deliver substantial value to the organization's mission and goals.

These strategies ensure that evaluation efforts are comprehensive, responsive to feedback, and aligned with the organization's overarching strategic priorities.

In the next section, we will explore how leaders can effectively evaluate the impact of their drive initiative on the organization's overall performance.

Evaluating the Impact of Drive on Organizational Performance

Assessing the impact of drive initiatives is pivotal for leaders seeking to gauge the effectiveness of their efforts in enhancing performance and achieving strategic goals. Regular evaluation provides actionable insights that guide public sector leaders in making informed decisions on resource allocation, process refinement, and future planning. This process not only fosters transparency and accountability but also ensures alignment across all levels of the organization with the overarching goals and standards set by the drive framework.

Within this framework, metrics and methodologies play a crucial role in assessing the outcomes of drive initiatives, enabling organizations to continuously refine and optimize their strategies for maximal benefit.

Performance Metrics

The following metrics are instrumental in this evaluation process, offering a comprehensive view of performance across various dimensions.

Operational Metrics

- **Efficiency gains:** Measure improvements in operational efficiency, such as reduced processing times or increased throughput in service delivery. These metrics provide tangible evidence of operational enhancements and resource utilization efficiencies driven by drive initiatives.

- **Quality metrics:** Evaluate advancements in service quality through metrics like customer feedback and compliance rates. This data offers insights into how drive initiatives impact service standards and customer satisfaction, essential for maintaining high organizational performance standards.

Employee Metrics

- **Engagement levels:** Track changes in employee engagement and satisfaction before and after implementing drive initiatives. Surveys and interviews provide qualitative and quantitative data on workforce sentiment, reflecting the initiative's influence on organizational culture and employee morale.

- **Turnover rates:** Monitor turnover rates to gauge organizational health and employee retention under the framework of new drive policies. These metrics illuminate workforce stability and the effectiveness of strategies aimed at enhancing employee commitment and retention.

Financial Metrics

- **Cost savings:** Quantify cost reductions achieved through streamlined processes and optimized resource allocation facilitated by drive initiatives. These metrics quantify financial efficiencies and resource savings, contributing to overall organizational effectiveness.

- **Return on investment (ROI):** Calculate the ROI of drive initiatives to assess their financial impact relative to the initial investment. This metric provides a clear financial perspective on the effectiveness and profitability of drive strategies, guiding future investment decisions and strategic priorities.

Integrating these metrics into their evaluation framework allows public sector leaders to effectively measure the success of drive initiatives. Next, we will explore the methodologies leaders can use to assess their drive interventions.

Methodologies for Effective Evaluation

Robust evaluation methodologies are critical for assessing the effectiveness of drive initiatives. They provide leaders with the insights needed to make informed decisions, optimize strategies, and foster a culture of continuous improvement. The following methodologies are essential for effective evaluation:

- **Comparative analysis:** Conducting a before-and-after analysis allows leaders to compare organizational performance before and after implementing drive initiatives. This method provides a clear picture of the impact of specific changes introduced by drive. Additionally, using control groups within the organization, where applicable, can help isolate the effects of these changes, offering a more precise assessment of their effectiveness.

- **Stakeholder feedback:** Gathering feedback from both internal and external stakeholders is crucial for gaining diverse perspectives on the effectiveness of drive initiatives. Structured surveys, focus groups, and one-on-one interviews provide comprehensive feedback, highlighting strengths and areas for improvement. This feedback is invaluable for understanding the broader impact of drive initiatives and for making informed adjustments.

- **Case studies:** Developing detailed case studies of successful projects showcases the role of drive strategies in achieving these successes.

These case studies not only document best practices and successful outcomes but also serve as learning tools. Analyzing failures or less successful initiatives is equally important, as it helps identify areas for improvement and prevents future missteps. These case studies provide concrete examples and lessons learned, contributing to the continuous improvement of drive initiatives.

By integrating these methodologies, public sector leaders can effectively evaluate the success of their drive initiatives. Comparative analysis, stakeholder feedback, and case studies provide a comprehensive framework for understanding the impact of drive strategies on organizational performance. These methodologies ensure that evaluation efforts are thorough, data-driven, and aligned with the organization's strategic objectives.

After thoroughly examining the principles and mechanics of an effective drive intervention, we will now illustrate how drive works through practical examples using two case studies: One showcasing a successful drive and the other highlighting failures in the execution of the drive process.

Case Study 1
Drive Done Right

Background

The Public Education Department (PED) faced significant challenges in achieving academic excellence and operational efficiency across its schools due to outdated procedures and inconsistent execution of educational programs. Dr. Amina Chukwuma, the Director of PED and a visionary leader, recognized the need for a systematic approach to improve educational outcomes and ensure the department's goals were not only met but exceeded.

Key Players

- **Dr. Amina Chukwuma (director of PED):** Visionary leader who initiated the drive initiative.

- **Mr. Joseph Adekunle (operations manager):** Responsible for the day-to-day implementation of the drive strategies.

- **Mrs. Maryam Abubakar (data and IT specialist):** Tasked with developing and managing the new reporting dashboards.

- **Ms. Asma'u Mohammed (HR director):** Overseeing structural changes, consequences management, and other HR-related aspects of the drive initiative.

- **PED staff and local community (audience):** Direct beneficiaries of improved educational services due to enhanced operational efficiency.

The Drive Process

Stage 1: Establish an Execution Rhythm

Objective setting: Dr. Chukwuma, supported by Mr. Joseph Adekunle and Ms. Asma'u Mohammed, led sessions to define PED's strategic objectives: "To provide high-quality and inclusive education that fosters academic excellence and prepares students for future success."

Operational calendars: Detailed calendars were created outlining daily, weekly, and monthly activities aligned with strategic objectives, including key performance indicators (KPIs) related to student achievement and teacher performance.

Review rhythms: Regular review meetings were scheduled to track the implementation of designed educational programs, discuss deliverables and milestones, discuss strategic implications based on data analysis, address bottlenecks, and provide collaborative feedback to improve teaching and learning practices.

Team alignment: During these review meetings, Dr. Chukwuma continuously emphasized the significance of each team's role in advancing the organization's goals. This helped to maintain motivation and focus among staff. She also ensured open lines of communication to encourage teamwork among departments, fostering unity throughout the process.

Stage 2: Set up Advanced Reporting Mechanisms

Integrated reporting tools: Mrs. Maryam Abubakar implemented advanced data management systems to collect and analyze performance data in standardized formats, ensuring compatibility with existing IT infrastructure and educational reporting requirements.

Customized reporting dashboards: Dashboards were designed to provide real-time insights into student progress, teacher effectiveness, and school performance metrics. Training sessions were conducted to empower staff to use these dashboards for informed decision-making.

Stage 3: Implement an Effective Consequence Management System

Performance thresholds: Clear, measurable criteria were established to evaluate student achievement, teacher performance, and overall school effectiveness, ensuring transparency and alignment with PED's educational values.

Reward systems: A comprehensive system of rewards, including recognition programs and professional development opportunities, was developed to incentivize high performance and acknowledge educational excellence.

Corrective measures: Asma'u Mohammed outlined constructive interventions for underperformance, focusing on targeted training, mentorship programs, and resource allocation adjustments to support struggling teachers and schools.

Outcomes

- **Improved educational performance:** The structured execution and enhanced reporting mechanisms led to a 30% increase in academic performance indicators, with notable improvements in standardized test scores and student graduation rates.

- **Enhanced employee engagement:** The transparent performance management system and supportive HR practices contributed to a 25% increase in staff satisfaction and retention rates, fostering a culture of continuous improvement and professional growth.

- **Community impact:** The initiatives resulted in better educational outcomes for students, as evidenced by improved school rankings and positive feedback from parents and community stakeholders.

Key Success Factors

- **Strong leadership commitment:** Dr. Chukwuma's visionary leadership and decisive actions were instrumental in driving educational transformation and fostering a positive work culture.

- **Effective stakeholder engagement:** Engaging teachers, parents, and community leaders ensured broad support and alignment with PED's educational goals.

- **Transparent communication:** Regular updates and transparent communication facilitated effective change management and maintained stakeholder trust throughout the initiative.

Conclusion and Lessons Learned

This case study illustrates the transformative power of a structured performance drive process in improving educational outcomes within public sector organizations. By aligning with strategic objectives, establishing an effective execution rhythm, prioritizing reporting and consequence management systems, collaboration was fostered among key stakeholders, and PED successfully enhanced educational quality and operational efficiency. The initiative not only achieved its goals but also laid a foundation for sustained educational excellence and community impact.

Case Study 2
Drive Gone Wrong

Background

The City Social Welfare Department (CSWD) embarked on an ambitious initiative aimed at delivering an intervention in response to economic shocks adversely affecting the nation's citizens. Spearheaded by Prof.

Karimi Ibiso, the Director of CSWD, the initiative sought to expand service delivery and optimize resource allocation to support vulnerable populations. However, from its inception, the initiative faced significant challenges that undermined its intended outcomes.

Key Players

- **Prof. Karimi Ibiso (Director of CSWD):** Advocated for the implementation of the initiative without sufficient groundwork.

- **Ms. Ella Williams (Chief Operations Officer):** Tasked with overseeing the execution of the intervention components but struggled with resistance and unclear directives.

- **Mr. Ahmed Bello (HR Director):** Responsible for managing structural changes and staff deployment but was not adequately consulted during the process.

- **Mr. Tony Oto (IT Manager):** In charge of implementing the new performance reporting software and data systems.

- **CSWD staff and beneficiaries (audience):** Directly affected by heightened tensions within the department leading to inefficiency and low beneficiary coverage.

The Drive Process

Stage 1: Establish an Execution Rhythm

Objective setting: Led by Prof. Karimi Ibiso, sessions were held to define CSWD's strategic objectives, emphasizing efficient and reliable service delivery to support citizens affected by economic shocks.

Operational calendars: Ms. Ella Williams attempted to introduce new operational schedules and procedures without adequately assessing staff readiness or aligning them with operational needs. Essential tasks were overlooked or duplicated, causing significant delays in services and project timelines. The new schedules and task assignments were not adequately communicated, further complicating operations.

Review rhythms: Regular review meetings were scheduled, but they failed to effectively use data to track daily and weekly coverage of welfare interventions, address bottlenecks, drive improvements or engage staff constructively.

Team alignment: During these review meetings, Prof. Ibiso did not emphasize the significance of each team's role in advancing organizational goals, resulting in a lack of motivation and focus among staff. Communication lines were not adequately kept open, leading to poor teamwork and disunity among departments.

Stage 2: Set up Advanced Reporting Mechanisms

Integrated reporting tools: Mr. Tony Oto introduced new reporting systems with complex software that staff were not adequately trained to use. The system did not include features to support real-time data reporting by field staff. Data inaccuracies proliferated due to user errors and a lack of understanding of the new system.

Customized reporting dashboards: Dashboards were designed without alignment to operational needs or providing meaningful insights, rendering decision-making processes ineffective. Training sessions on data interpretation and system usage were insufficient, hindering effective implementation.

Stage 3: Implement an Effective Consequence Management System

Performance thresholds: Prof. Ibiso established performance thresholds without clear, measurable criteria that would trigger rewards or corrective actions, causing confusion and a lack of transparency. The criteria did not align with CSWD's organizational values, further exacerbating staff dissatisfaction.

Reward systems: A comprehensive reward system, including recognition and bonuses for exceptional performance, was not effectively developed or communicated to employees. Mr. Ahmed Bello's input was not sought in designing these systems, leading to inconsistencies and a lack of motivation among staff.

Corrective measures: Corrective measures focused more on punitive actions than constructive feedback, further demoralizing the staff. The approach neglected developmental interventions such as targeted training, reassignment, or other supportive measures.

Outcomes

- **Operational efficiency decline:** The initiative resulted in increased inefficiencies and unreliability of data relating to the intervention, adversely affecting service delivery standards.

- **Morale and turnover crisis:** Dissatisfaction and lack of motivation among staff resulted in slow execution, location boycotts, and reduced beneficiary reach.

- **Public confidence erosion:** Visible failures eroded public trust in the department's ability to manage social services effectively.

Key Failures

- **Leadership oversight:** Prof. Ibiso's push for implementation without sufficient groundwork overlooked critical readiness and training needs, exacerbating operational challenges.

- **Stakeholder engagement:** Insufficient communication and alignment with staff needs by Ms. Ella Williams led to widespread resistance and operational disruptions.

- **Misaligned strategy:** The emphasis on punitive measures rather than constructive support undermined employee morale and hindered program implementation and operational improvement efforts.

- **Failure to leverage HR expertise:** The lack of consultation with Mr. Ahmed Bello, the HR director, compounded issues by failing to align consequence management with organizational values and employee development goals.

Conclusion and Lessons Learned

The social welfare intervention initiative at the City Social Welfare Department serves as a cautionary tale about the risks of poorly planned and executed performance drive strategies. Failure to maintain an effective execution rhythm, optimize integrated reporting and balance the focus on rewards and punitive measures for constructive development can lead to poor performance and disastrous results.

Call to Action
Master Drive for Breakthrough Results

The single most significant difference between a leader renowned for consistently delivering strong results and those who fall short lies in the ability to drive performance. The Oxford Dictionary defines drive as: "The ability to propel or carry along by force in a specified direction." This definition encapsulates why drive is such a vital discipline for performance. A public leader's ability to pull their organization in the right direction, in line with carefully crafted strategies and objectives, is the key that makes all the difference in the world of leadership. Drive is essential for converting plans into actions and ambitions into realities. It ensures that initiatives are not only launched but also sustained and driven to their intended conclusions.

By mastering the discipline of drive, leaders can transform strategic blueprints into real-world successes. Embedding a culture of execution, enhancing reporting systems, and implementing robust consequence management are key actions that enable public sector leaders to ensure their organizations operate at peak performance. The principles outlined in this chapter provide a comprehensive roadmap for leaders to navigate the complexities of public service, driving sustained success and making a meaningful impact on the communities they serve.

Finally, drive is not just about pushing forward; it is about steering the organization in the right direction, ensuring that every effort contributes to the broader mission. By mastering this discipline, public sector leaders can turn strategic goals into tangible achievements, ensuring that their organizations not only meet but exceed their objectives.

Embark on the continuous journey of drive with unwavering commitment and adaptability, the rewards—enhanced efficiency, effectiveness, measurable results and public trust—are well worth the effort.

The Discipline of Drive at a Glance

Figure 20. Framework for Mastering DRIVE: ERC

⚡ WHY IS DRIVE IMPORTANT FOR PUBLIC LEADERS?

- **Drive delivers results:** It helps public leaders achieve goals, optimize performance, and make the most of resources.

- **Drive fosters agility:** The adaptable nature of drive allows leaders to address evolving community needs and challenges.

- **Drive motivates employees:** Clear expectations and recognition within the drive process lead to a more engaged and productive public workforce.

- **Drive builds trust:** Transparency and accountability within the framework ensure results and foster public confidence in leadership.

💡 WHAT ARE THE BIG IDEAS?

- **Structured execution for results:** Drive goes beyond setting goals. It provides a structured execution rhythm with consistent processes and routines, ensuring smooth operations and on-time goal achievement.

- **Leadership as the energy source:** Leaders set the tone. Their positive energy inspires and motivates teams, leading to a productive and engaged workforce.

- **Consequence management for growth:** Drive's approach to consequence management focuses on fostering a culture of continuous improvement, utilizing corrective actions for development alongside acknowledgment of achievements.

- **Balancing performance with empathy:** Drive recognizes the importance of a supportive work environment, balancing performance expectations with empathy for employee well-being.

🔧 HOW DO I MAKE IT HAPPEN?

Follow a three-stage process to sustainably drive performance within your organization:

Stage 1: Establish an Execution Rhythm

Stage 2: Set up Advanced Reporting Mechanisms

Stage 3: Implement an Effective Consequence Management System

PART 4
EXCEL

Chapter 8
Discipline 7 - Deliver

Public sector leadership is plagued by a damaging trend: "Reset culture." This occurs when new leaders, driven by the desire to make a distinct mark or to react against the perceived shortcomings of their predecessors, dismiss existing systems and initiatives regardless of their value. This obsession with novelty can have severe consequences, as it overlooks a crucial truth: significant progress builds on past successes.

Consider some notable achievers in history. Marie Curie, the first person to win a Nobel Prize twice, did not invent radioactivity from scratch. She built on Henri Becquerel's discovery, leading to groundbreaking advancements in our understanding of the atom. Steve Jobs and Steve Wozniak did not create the first personal computer from nothing; they improved upon earlier models from pioneers like Altair and Commodore, revolutionizing the industry with user-friendly designs. Nelson Mandela did not single-handedly dismantle Apartheid; he stood on the shoulders of countless activists, achieving victory through negotiation and reconciliation.

These leaders understood a simple principle: Previous successes create momentum and a foundation for further progress. Discarding them is like starting over, wasting time and resources. The best leaders analyze what works and what does not to inform their strategies. They rarely fix what is not broken.

Reset culture, on the other hand, creates a cyclical disruption that can devastate institutional momentum and morale. Each leadership transition potentially unravels years of progress, squandering resources and eroding public trust. This ongoing instability not only stifles innovation but also engenders a chaotic environment where strategic objectives become subservient to personal or political agendas. The cost of this disruption is enormous, not just in financial terms but in the lost potential of public institutions to effectively serve the citizenry. Unfortunately, for many African countries, reset culture is a major obstacle for public institutions.

Amidst the frequent changes in political appointments and the instability they bring, **DELIVERY**, the seventh discipline of breakthrough results, is the solution to this devastating pattern.

The Criticality of Delivery in the Public Sector

Delivery is not merely about administrative diligence, it is a cornerstone of enduring institutional success. It embodies the profound responsibility of implementing and sustaining practices that transcend the tenure of transient leaders and continue to serve the public effectively. At its core, delivery is about ensuring continuity by establishing resilient and robust frameworks that enable public institutions not only to survive but also to thrive amidst the complexities and challenges of government operations.

Consider the impact on public institutions when a new leader builds upon existing effective systems, initiatives, and infrastructures established by their predecessor rather than discarding them regardless of their value. Such a disciplined approach would not only withstand the ebb and flow of leadership changes but would also elevate the institution's ability to consistently and efficiently fulfill its long-term missions. This is the essence of the seventh discipline of breakthrough results. Delivery is about creating a legacy of systems and practices that outlast any single leader and continue to drive the institution forward.

Why does this matter? Because public institutions are the pillars upon which the welfare of society rests—they are not the personal fiefdoms of transient leaders. They require a steadfast approach to leadership that focuses on long-term goals and sustainable practices. The benefits of a well-structured delivery system are clear: It provides stability, encourages rational and measured progress, and fundamentally changes the way public institutions operate by embedding a culture of accountability and effectiveness.

Adopting a delivery mindset means leaders commit to a value-creation process that is not disrupted by leadership transitions. Instead, it champions the continuity of effective policies, practices, and strategies that are designed to achieve and exceed the institution's goals. Leaders, both new and existing, must engage with this delivery value creation process, not as a choice but as an imperative. By doing so, they not only safeguard the institution's legacy but also enhance its capacity to serve future generations.

This approach to delivery is not just about maintaining the status quo but about advancing a dynamic and robust agenda that adapts to changing needs while preserving the core mission of the institution. It is a call to action for all leaders to rise above the fray of political expediency and to anchor their leadership in practices that build, rather than erode, the foundations of their institutions.

Thus, the call for a disciplined approach to delivery is both a challenge and an opportunity—an opportunity to redefine public sector leadership and to ensure that these institutions not only survive but thrive, irrespective of who is at the helm. It is a commitment to excellence, stability, and, most importantly, to the relentless pursuit of the public good.

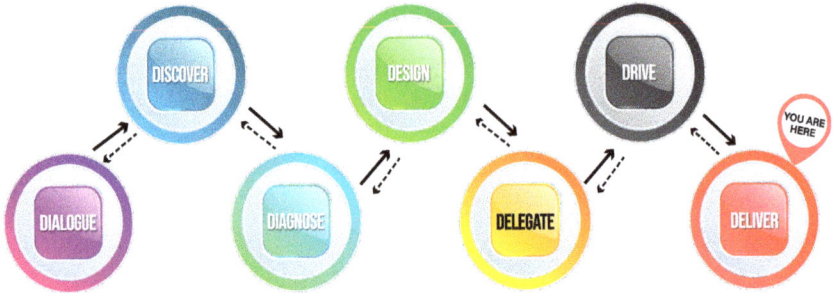

Figure 21. The Seven Disciplines of Breakthrough Results: Deliver

Introduction to Delivery: Institutionalizing High-Performance Systems in the Public Sector

To fully appreciate the discipline of delivery, it is crucial to understand the devastation left in the wake of reset culture. History is littered with the wreckage of well-designed organizational structures, policies, and visions abandoned by leaders blinded by ideology or arrogance. They discard the hard-won progress of their predecessors, resulting in stalled advancement, wasted resources, and, in some cases, even societal collapse. Every time a new leader hits the reset button, years of hard-earned progress can be undone, setting back public service initiatives.

Many African nations have struggled and continue to struggle with leadership changes that disregard existing development plans. New regimes often dismantle the previous administration's projects, leading to instability and hampering progress. This pattern has created a cycle of disruption and inefficiency that significantly hinders development.

A Full View of the Detrimental Consequences of Reset Culture

The prevalence of reset culture demands urgent attention, akin to a full-blown emergency. African countries and their governments must awaken to the profound implications of this destructive phenomenon. Below are the consequences of reset culture for public and government institutions, and the people they serve:

- **Disruption of institutional momentum:** Reset culture disrupts the continuity of projects and initiatives, causing frequent starts and stops that impede the momentum needed for effective governance. This leads to inefficiency and wasted resources as efforts are repeatedly redirected.

- **Erosion of public trust:** Constant changes in direction can erode public trust in government institutions, as citizens may perceive inconsistency and lack of commitment to addressing pressing issues. This can damage the credibility of the government and undermine its ability to effectively serve the public.

- **Loss of institutional knowledge:** With each reset, valuable institutional knowledge and expertise are lost as initiatives and strategies are discarded. This loss of continuity can hinder organizational learning and impede the development of effective policies and programs.

- **Stifled innovation:** The focus on starting anew with each leadership change can stifle innovation, as leaders may be hesitant to propose bold ideas or experiment with new approaches, knowing that they may be discarded in the next reset. This can prevent government agencies from adapting to changing circumstances and finding creative solutions to complex problems.

- **Fragmented governance:** The lack of continuity resulting from reset culture can lead to fragmented governance, with different administrations pursuing conflicting priorities and agendas. This can create confusion and inefficiency, making it difficult to effectively coordinate and implement government policies and programs.

- **Undermined employee morale:** The constant churn associated with reset culture can undermine employee morale, as staff may become disillusioned with the lack of stability and direction. This can lead to decreased engagement, productivity, and job satisfaction, ultimately impacting the government's ability to attract and retain talented employees.

- **Wasted resources:** The frequent changes in direction can result in wasted resources as efforts and investments are redirected or abandoned. This can have significant financial implications for government agencies, particularly in terms of budgetary constraints and missed opportunities for more strategic investment.

- **Long-term damage:** Most importantly, reset culture can inflict long-term damage on government institutions, as the cumulative effects of frequent changes in direction can undermine their ability to effectively fulfill their mandates and serve the public interest. This can have far-reaching consequences for governance, democracy, and society as a whole.

Without a doubt, reset culture in government is a costly game that derails organizations and ultimately nations. While political winds may shift, the needs of the public remain constant. The discipline of delivery ensures that public institutions can weather change and continue to serve effectively.

Transformative Impact of Delivery on Public Sector Organizations

In one word, the power of delivery lies in its ability to ensure one vital principle: Continuity. Why is continuity in public sector leadership important? It serves as the bedrock upon which effective governance and sustainable development are built. Imagine an organization trapped in a cycle of perpetual restarts, where every change in leadership brings about the abandonment of carefully laid development plans. This scenario is all too common in many public institutions across Africa, severely impeding progress and frustrating efforts to address pressing societal needs. Structured delivery emerges as the antidote to this destructive cycle, embodying the wisdom of mathematician and philosopher Alfred North Whitehead: "Progress is rarely a matter of throwing away the old, but of putting the new in its proper place." In essence, structured delivery ensures continuity and optimizes public service delivery amidst inevitable leadership transitions.

A key benefit of this approach is its ability to maintain continuity across different administrations. By embedding effective policies and practices that transcend individual leadership tenures, it cultivates a culture of long-term vision. Critical infrastructure projects such as hospitals and schools can advance steadily without the disruptions caused by abrupt policy changes. This continuity allows African nations to build sustainable momentum and achieve lasting progress in crucial areas of development, enhancing stability and fostering growth.

Furthermore, delivery promotes fiscal responsibility by optimizing the use of resources for sustainable development. Through clear project management processes, it minimizes waste and maximizes the impact of public funds. This ensures that projects are completed on time and within budget, freeing up resources for additional initiatives that benefit communities. Healthcare facilities properly equipped to serve populations and educational programs consistently receiving necessary funding are achievements made possible through efficient resource management facilitated by structured delivery.

Beyond operational efficiency, delivery enhances public trust and credibility as essential pillars of institutional stability. When citizens experience consistent and reliable service delivery, their confidence in public institutions grows. Structured delivery fosters transparency and accountability, empowering citizens to monitor progress and hold institutions accountable for their actions. This transparency not only builds legitimacy but also strengthens social cohesion by fostering a sense of shared responsibility in national development efforts.

In conclusion, the discipline of delivery emerges as a transformative force in public sector organizations, providing a clear pathway to sustainable development and institutional resilience. Through its focus on continuity, resource optimization, and bolstering public trust, delivery empowers African nations to navigate challenges and achieve enduring progress that positively impacts all citizens.

With this foundation laid, let's now delve into how public leaders can effectively master the discipline of delivery.

Mastering the Discipline of Delivery in Public Sector Leadership

Representing a significant departure from reset culture, the discipline of delivery establishes a stable and predictable environment where proven systems endure, facilitating the uninterrupted pursuit of long-term goals across different administrations and societal shifts. This transition is not just beneficial; it is imperative for public institutions to fulfill their mandates effectively, especially given the transient nature of political appointments and leadership. Delivery ensures stability despite this inherent impermanence.

When public leaders master delivery and embed a culture of excellence, they lay a solid foundation for future leaders to effectively serve citizens. Inheriting organizations where high-performance systems are institutionalized allows leaders to implement policies and programs more efficiently, respond swiftly to crises, and adapt nimbly to evolving needs. This fosters enhanced public trust, strengthens social cohesion, and promotes the general good of society.

By embracing the principles of delivery, public leaders can cultivate a more efficient, effective, and responsive public sector that delivers real value to the communities it serves. Therefore, leaders who champion the discipline of delivery are, and will continue to be, the true heroes of society.

To master the art of delivery, leaders must focus on several foundational elements that support the development and implementation of effective practices. With these foundational elements firmly established, leaders can execute delivery with true effectiveness.

The Foundations of an Effective Delivery System

Effective delivery relies on the following key elements:

1. Institutionalization of Practices

The first step in mastering delivery is the institutionalization of practices that are not only effective but are also resilient to changes in leadership. This involves:

- **Developing standard operating procedures (SOPs):** SOPs are detailed, written instructions designed to achieve uniformity in the performance of specific functions. They are essential in public institutions where tasks need to be performed consistently regardless of personnel changes. SOPs provide a framework that guides staff actions, ensures continuity, and maintains service quality.

- **Creating robust monitoring systems:** To ensure that practices are being followed and objectives are being met, robust monitoring systems are crucial. These systems should provide real-time data on performance and facilitate timely corrections where necessary. Effective monitoring allows for proactive management, helping to identify issues early and implement solutions swiftly.

- **Preserving institutional memory:** Institutional memory involves retaining and utilizing the accumulated knowledge and experiences of an organization. This can be achieved through comprehensive documentation, knowledge management systems, and mentorship programs. Preserving institutional memory ensures that valuable insights and proven practices are not lost over time, particularly during transitions in leadership or staffing.

2. Scalability and Flexibility

As public needs and technologies evolve, so too must the practices within public institutions. Scalability and flexibility are critical to adapting to changing demands without compromising service quality. This can be achieved by:

- **Adopting modular approaches:** Modular approaches involve breaking down complex systems or processes into smaller, interconnected components that can be easily modified or expanded. This flexibility in policy development and service delivery allows institutions to adjust and expand services without overhauling the entire system.

- **Leveraging technology:** Advanced technologies support scalable solutions, such as digital services that accommodate increasing numbers of users or automated systems that reduce manual workload. From cloud computing to data analytics, technology solutions empower public institutions to streamline processes, enhance productivity, and respond rapidly to emerging challenges.

3. Predictability through Standardization

Predictability is essential for public confidence and operational reliability. Standardization of processes ensures that no matter who is in charge, outcomes are not left to chance. This involves:

- **Clear guidelines and criteria**: Public institutions should develop and enforce clear, well-documented guidelines and criteria for decision-making and service delivery. These guidelines ensure consistency and fairness, reducing the risk of arbitrary or ad-hoc practices. For example, in procurement, standardized procedures ensure transparency and integrity in the selection of vendors and contractors.

- **Training and development:** Continuous training ensures that all staff members are up to date with the latest procedures and technologies, further supporting standardized delivery.

Mastering these foundational elements of delivery sets the stage for public institutions to achieve operational excellence and adaptability. With these foundations in place, we can now explore the stage-by-stage process by which leaders can execute the discipline of delivery effectively.

Executing Delivery: A Stage-by-Stage Guide

In the opening chapter of this book, "The Call to Public Leadership," we established the core responsibility of public service: leaving a lasting positive impact. We emphasized that a public leader's call to serve is a summons to relentlessly pursue progress and commit to leaving their organization, constituents, state, and nation in a better state than they found it. This commitment demands selfless service, often at the expense of personal ambition.

This guide is designed for leaders who share this commitment and are dedicated not only to building high-performing organizations but also to ensuring the sustainability of effective leadership and operational practices beyond their terms. By following the guidelines below, you will ensure that your public sector institution not only meets current mandates but also continues to operate efficiently and effectively, even during leadership transitions.

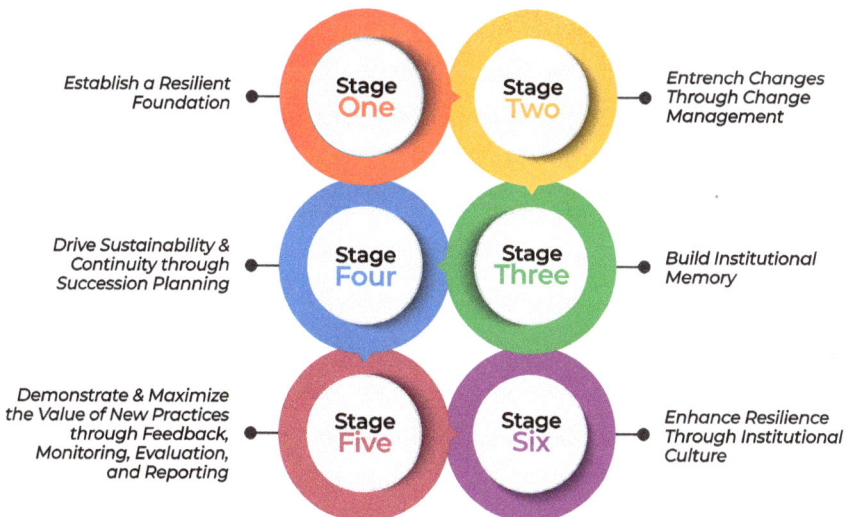

Figure 22: The Six Stages of Delivery

Stage 1: Establish a Resilient Foundation through Systematic Documentation

Establishing a solid foundation is paramount to successful delivery. Begin by documenting key changes systematically and ensuring that they are supported by robust policy frameworks.

Document and Review Key Changes Made to Existing Systems

- Create a centralized digital change register to document all key changes introduced from dialogue to drive. This register should be accessible to all relevant stakeholders and updated regularly.

- Review the change register to identify items that require policy support for sustainability and institutionalization.

Authorize Changes through Policy Frameworks

- Develop new policies or review, update, and revise existing policies to provide corporate or institutional backing for the introduced changes as applicable.

- Secure approvals from relevant authorities (executive management committee, board, governing council, etc.) according to specified approval responsibilities, scopes, and thresholds.

Embed Changes into Daily Operations

- Embed new practices into standard routines to ensure consistency and reliability.

- Update employees' job descriptions and workflows to reflect the changes, ensuring everyone understands their new roles and responsibilities.

- Develop supportive resources by creating comprehensive toolkits, frameworks, and templates to codify and promote the adoption of new methodologies, principles, and practices in a teachable, replicable, and scalable manner.

Formalize New Processes and Procedures

- **Develop clear, concise documentation:** Create comprehensive standard operating procedures (SOPs) and guidance manuals for all relevant functions. Include step-by-step instructions and define roles and responsibilities for critical tasks.

- **Ensure accessibility and understanding:** Make sure these documents are easily accessible and understandable to all relevant stakeholders.

- **Train staff on SOPs:** Conduct thorough training sessions for staff on new or revised SOPs to ensure proper understanding and implementation.

Stage 2: Entrench Changes through Effective and Inclusive Change Management

Building on the foundation established during the previous stage, effective change management is essential for embedding new practices across the organization.

Identify and Manage Stakeholders

- Identify all stakeholders and manage them to build and sustain consensus and commitment to key changes.

- Regularly engage with stakeholders to ensure new updates meet their needs and corporate requirements. Hold meetings and workshops to keep stakeholders informed and involved in the change process.

- Maintain open lines of communication to build trust and ensure stakeholders are aware of the benefits and progress of the changes.

Build a Change Coalition

- Identify and empower individuals at various levels of the organization who can champion the changes and influence their peers. These "change champions" will be instrumental in managing change.

- Involve senior leaders, managers, and influential employees from various departments in the change coalition to create a sense of ownership and accountability.

- Provide continuous capacity building for staff on the skills and competencies needed to implement and sustain change.

- Socialize the change journey by displaying change communications, celebrating successes, highlighting success stories, and recognizing achievements.

Establish Robust Governance Frameworks

- **Create oversight committees:** Form committees or councils to oversee the implementation and adherence to new policies and processes.

- **Embed accountability:** Assign clear roles and responsibilities to ensure accountability at all levels. Regular audits and reviews can help maintain adherence.

Stage 3: Build Institutional Memory through Knowledge Management and Capacity Building

Create and execute strategies for knowledge management and capacity building to preserve institutional knowledge and promote continuous learning.

Create and Execute a Knowledge Management Strategy

- Develop a knowledge management strategy with clearly defined objectives and processes for knowledge creation, sharing, storage, and retention.

- Define stakeholder roles and responsibilities for knowledge management.

- Create a knowledge-friendly culture that values knowledge sharing, collaboration, open communication, and continuous learning.

- Establish user-friendly, accessible, and secure knowledge management infrastructure, such as a centralized knowledge repository (intranet, digital library, or knowledge portal).

- Implement systems and standardized formats for capturing, documenting, storing, cataloging, and retrieving insights, best practices, lessons, models, frameworks, real-life case studies, toolkits, templates, and tacit knowledge for institutional memory.

Establish Infrastructure for Continuous Learning and Development

- Establish regular knowledge-sharing sessions, communities of practice, and cross-departmental collaboration through joint projects and task forces.

- Implement training and development programs in areas of change to equip employees with the requisite skills.

- Create backup systems to ensure knowledge is preserved and accessible in case of leadership changes or emergencies.

Stage 4: Drive Sustainability and Continuity through Succession Planning and Leadership Development

Ensure continuity of high-performance practices by preparing future leaders and fostering a culture of succession planning.

Create a Succession Planning Strategy

- Identify critical roles and potential successors regularly within the organization.

- Develop a succession planning strategy to ensure continuity of key changes and positions.

- Train and mentor future leaders to manage the delivery system, drive improvements, and sustain change.

Empower Future Leaders

- Encourage delegation and sharing of responsibilities to prepare potential future leaders.

- Ensure that critical knowledge is transferred when employees or leaders leave or retire to maintain long-term success.

- Create structures and processes that outlast individual leaders and ensure the longevity of changes regardless of leadership changes. One effective way to do this is by using technology to automate and streamline processes where possible. This reduces dependency on individual leaders.

Stage 5: Demonstrate and Maximize the Value of New Practices through Feedback, Monitoring, Evaluation, and Reporting

Validate organizational effectiveness by establishing feedback loops and evaluation mechanisms to measure the impact of new practices.

Create Mechanisms for Feedback, Review, Adaptation, and Flexibility

- Establish regular feedback loops for employees to provide input on new practices and suggest improvements.

- Demonstrate responsive leadership by implementing feasible suggestions and keeping feedback providers informed.

- Conduct regular reviews of practices and encourage small group reviews and innovation recommendations. Share the feedback with leadership.

Build Lasting Change through Effective Monitoring & Evaluation and Learning Systems

- Conduct objective routine monitoring and periodic evaluation to assess the overall success of implemented changes.

- Maintain an updated catalog of changes and records of measurable, verifiable, and progressive successes and impacts achieved by new initiatives, projects, programs, policies, and processes to prevent uncontested reversals and resets.

- Support experimentation with new approaches and encourage learning from both successes and failures.

- Document successes and challenges to build a repository of lessons learned and promote a culture of success and continuity.

- Implement a transparent reporting system to keep all stakeholders informed about the progress and impact of changes.

- Share evaluation reports and success records with relevant internal and external stakeholders as references for future change initiatives and to support continuity.

Stage 6: Enhance Resilience through Institutional Culture

Cultivate a resilient institutional culture—a shared belief system and set of values—that embraces change and fosters commitment to sustained high-performance practices regardless of leadership changes.

Demonstrate Leadership Commitment

- Leaders must not only advocate for effective delivery but also demonstrate this commitment through their actions. They must set an example by modeling the behaviors and attitudes they wish to see in their teams, such as demonstrating a commitment to accountability and a willingness to adapt and improve.

- Leaders must participate in planning sessions, monitor progress, and make data-driven decisions to guide the institution.

- Leaders should empower their teams by providing the autonomy and resources needed to implement effective delivery practices, which includes removing obstacles, securing necessary funding, and fostering a supportive environment.

Promote a Culture of Adaptability

- Embed the idea that change is inevitable and should be seen as an opportunity for learning, improvement, and growth. Reiterate this message through leadership communication and team discussions.

- Encourage open dialogue and risk-taking. Create a safe space for employees to share ideas and concerns about new practices. This fosters open communication and a willingness to take calculated risks in pursuit of improvement.

Establish a System of Recognition and Rewards

- Recognize change champions. Publicly acknowledge and reward employees who actively champion and contribute to the success of new practices. Celebrate their leadership and dedication.

- Institute teamwork and collaboration awards. Recognize and reward teams that demonstrate effective collaboration in implementing and improving new systems. This reinforces the importance of teamwork for successful change.

- Align performance metrics and incentives with the successful implementation and ongoing use of new practices. This encourages individual and team accountability for sustaining change.

- Ensure leaders who demonstrate commitment to sustaining high-performance systems are recognized. This reinforces the importance of leadership buy-in for long-term success.

This comprehensive guide to effective delivery across stages provides a structured pathway for public sector leaders to institute high-performance practices. By embedding these principles into daily operations and fostering a culture of continuous improvement, organizations can achieve sustained success even amidst leadership transitions. Embracing these strategies ensures not only current mandate fulfillment but also future readiness and resilience.

Navigating Challenges in the Delivery Process: Overcoming Common Obstacles

Successfully executing a delivery system in public sector institutions requires a keen understanding of potential challenges at each stage of the process. The following are common obstacles that leaders can encounter during the process and the strategies to address them, ensuring a smoother transition and sustainable implementation of changes.

1. **Resistance to change:** Employees may hesitate to alter their routines and workflows. Mitigating this requires clear communication, involving employees in the change process, and providing necessary training.

2. **Inadequate documentation:** Poor documentation of key changes can lead to confusion and inconsistency. This underscores the importance of rigorous documentation practices and regular reviews of the change register.

3. **Approval delays:** Securing approvals for new policies from relevant authorities can be time-consuming. Early stakeholder engagement and providing clear justifications for policy changes can expedite the process.

4. **Stakeholder engagement:** Ensuring that all stakeholders are on board with the changes is crucial. Regular communication, meetings, and workshops are essential to keep stakeholders informed and involved, thereby building trust and consensus.

5. **Building a change coalition:** Empowering change champions and involving senior leaders, managers, and influential employees from various departments can create a sense of ownership and accountability. Continuous capacity building is also necessary to equip staff with the skills needed to implement and sustain change.

6. **Knowledge management strategy:** Developing a strategy for knowledge creation, sharing, storage, and retention is crucial but can be challenging. The key to navigating this challenge includes defining stakeholder roles, fostering a knowledge-friendly culture, and establishing a secure knowledge management infrastructure.

7. **Succession planning strategy:** Regularly identifying critical roles and potential successors is demanding yet vital. Developing a strategy to ensure continuity in key positions, managing transitions effectively,

and providing training and mentorship for future leaders are essential steps in this process.

8. **Leadership commitment:** Leaders must not only advocate for effective delivery but also demonstrate this commitment through their actions. Participating in planning sessions, monitoring progress, and making data-driven decisions to guide the institution are essential steps.

9. **Culture of adaptability:** Encouraging open dialogue, risk-taking, and viewing change as an opportunity for learning and growth can foster a culture of adaptability. Recognizing and rewarding employees who champion and contribute to the success of new practices can also reinforce the importance of sustaining high-performance systems.

To effectively navigate the common obstacles in the delivery stages, leaders will require strategic planning, effective communication, and committed leadership. By understanding these challenges and implementing the outlined strategies, public sector institutions can achieve smoother, more sustainable changes. Leaders who anticipate and address these obstacles proactively will be better equipped to build high-performing, resilient organizations capable of adapting to future challenges and opportunities.

Now that we have thoroughly examined the principles and mechanics of an effective delivery intervention, we will illustrate how delivery works through practical examples using two case studies: one showcasing a successful delivery and the other highlighting failures in the execution of the delivery process.

Case Study 1
Delivery Done Right

Background

This case study details the comprehensive transformation of the Urban Development Authority (UDA) under the visionary leadership of DG

Idawari Esei. Facing the end of her tenure and aiming to institutionalize all the effective practices and systems that had proven to deliver results, Ms. Idawari Esei led a strategic initiative to execute the discipline of delivery and institutionalize the high-performing practices and systems within the organization.

Key Players

- **Ms. Idawari Esei (DG):** A visionary leader dedicated to transforming UDA's approach to urban development.

- **Mr. John Ebokpo /Ibrahim Abdullahi (COO):** Led operational strategy and change implementation.

- **Ms. Aisha Maidawa (chief policy officer):** Formulated and implemented sustainable urban policies.

- **Mr. Happiness Lukas /Chinedu Okafor (HR director):** Ensured workforce alignment and capacity building.

- **UDA Staff and Local Community:** Beneficiaries of improved urban development services.

The Delivery Process

Stage 1: Establish a resilient foundation through systematic documentation

Centralized digital change register: Mr. John Ebokpo implemented a digital register to document all changes introduced from dialogue to drive. He also made them accessible to all relevant stakeholders.

Policy support: Ms. Aisha Maidawa reviewed the change register to identify items requiring policy support for sustainability and institutionalization. Updated policies were developed to provide institutional backing for the introduced changes. Approvals from relevant authorities were obtained according to specified approval responsibilities, scopes, and thresholds.

Standard routines: New practices were embedded into standard routines. Employees' job descriptions and workflows were updated to reflect changes. Comprehensive toolkits, frameworks, and templates were created to promote new methodologies, principles, and practices.

Clear documentation: Comprehensive standard operating procedures (SOPs) and guidance manuals were developed. Documents were made easily accessible and understandable and thorough training sessions for staff ensured proper understanding and implementation.

Stage 2: Entrench changes through effective and inclusive change management

Identify and manage stakeholders: Ms. Idawari Esei identified all relevant stakeholders and ensured regular engagement with stakeholders to ensure that new updates met their needs and corporate requirements. Lines of communication were opened to build trust and ensure stakeholders were aware of the benefits of the initiative and its progress.

Empower change champions: Individuals at various levels of the organization were empowered to champion the changes. Mr. John Ebokpo identified and trained these champions. Senior leaders and influential employees were involved in the change coalition to create ownership and accountability. Ms. Aisha Maidawa and Mr. Happiness Lukas supported John Ebokpo in these efforts.

Continuous capacity building: Mr. Happiness Lukas spearheaded training sessions to provide staff with the skills and competencies needed to implement and sustain change.

Socialize the change journey: The DG actively communicated and recognized achievements throughout the change journey, displaying change communications, celebrating successes, highlighting success stories, and publicly recognizing efforts.

Establish robust governance frameworks: Oversight committees were formed to oversee the implementation and adherence to new policies and processes. Ms. Aisha Maidawa chaired these committees.

Embed accountability: Assigned clear roles and responsibilities to ensure accountability at all levels. Mr. John Ebokpo ensured each department had clear deliverables.

Stage 3: Build institutional memory through knowledge management and capacity building

Create and execute a knowledge management strategy: Mr. Happiness Lukas and his team developed a strategy with defined objectives for knowledge creation, sharing, storage, and retention. They also established a centralized knowledge repository. Mr. John Ebokpo advocated for the creation of routine knowledge sharing sessions to promote a culture of collaboration and continuous learning. Together, they implemented systems for capturing, documenting, storing, and retrieving insights, best practices, and lessons.

Establish infrastructure for continuous learning and development: Happiness Lukas organized regular sessions, communities of practice, and cross-departmental collaborations. Ms. Aisha Maidawa implemented programs to equip employees with requisite skills, ensuring alignment with policy changes. They ensured knowledge preservation and accessibility.

Stage 4: Drive sustainability and continuity through succession planning and leadership development

Create a succession planning strategy: Mr. Happiness Lukas led the task of identifying critical roles and potential successors, with support from the DG. Together with Mr. John Ebokpo, they conducted mentoring programs to prepare future leaders for managing the delivery system and sustaining change.

Stage 5: Demonstrate and maximize the value of new practices through feedback, monitoring, evaluation, and reporting

Create mechanisms for feedback, review, adaptation, and flexibility: Under the guidance of Mr. John Ebokpo, the team set up feedback loops for employees to provide input on new practices.

Implement responsive leadership: Small group reviews and innovation recommendations were encouraged, and the DG ensured feasible suggestions were implemented and kept feedback providers informed.

Build lasting change through effective monitoring and evaluation and learning systems: Ms. Aisha Maidawa led assessments of the success of implemented changes. Records of measurable successes and impacts were maintained. The DG also promoted a culture of learning from successes and failures.

Ensure transparent reporting: Mr. John Ebokpo ensured that stakeholders were informed about progress and impact.

Stage 6: Enhance resilience through institutional culture

Demonstrate leadership commitment: The DG actively participated in all planning sessions and engaged actively with staff. All the leaders in the organization demonstrated commitment to accountability and adaptability.

Empower teams: The COO ensured teams had the autonomy and resources for effective delivery practices.

Promote a culture of adaptability: DG Idawari Esei and Aisha Maidawa frequently communicated that change is an opportunity for learning and growth. Mr. John Ebokpo encouraged a safe space for sharing ideas and concerns.

Establish a system of recognition and rewards: Mr. Happiness Lukas managed the recognition program for employees contributing to success. Ms. Aisha Maidawa supported initiatives to recognize teams demonstrating effective collaboration.

Recognize leadership: Leaders committed to sustaining high-performance systems were publicly recognized.

Final Outcomes

The Urban Development Authority (UDA) achieved its goal of setting up delivery structures to institutionalize reforms for sustainable urban development.

- UDA maintained inclusive and continuous stakeholder engagement for effective change management.

- The organization promoted continuous learning, enhancing institutional knowledge and operational efficiency.

- UDA developed a resilient leadership pipeline, ensuring operational continuity and effective project management.

- Teams were encouraged to innovate, fostering a culture of flexibility and accountability.

- UDA cultivated an institutional culture that embraced change and high-performance practices, reinforced through recognition and teamwork rewards.

Key Success Factors

- **Visionary leadership:** The DG's proactive approach and unwavering commitment set a clear direction for sustainable urban development and operational excellence.

- **Effective stakeholder engagement:** Regular, transparent communication fostered trust and alignment with stakeholder expectations, integrating their needs into strategic initiatives.

- **Comprehensive change management:** Inclusive stakeholder involvement, empowerment of change champions, and robust governance frameworks ensured smooth adoption of new policies and practices.

- **Knowledge management:** The HR director's structured strategy facilitated effective knowledge creation, sharing, and retention, enhancing operational efficiency and decision-making.

- **Continuous learning and development:** Ongoing capacity building initiatives spearheaded by the HR director equipped employees with skills to foster a culture of continuous improvement and adaptability.

- **Sustainability and succession planning:** The COO and HR director's efforts in succession planning ensured a resilient leadership pipeline and maintained operational continuity for long-term stability.

These factors were pivotal in institutionalizing a high-performance system at the Urban Development Authority, driving innovation, adaptability, and sustainable urban development outcomes.

Conclusion and Lessons Learned

The transformation of the Urban Development Authority under DG Idawari Esei's leadership serves as a testament to the power of strategic delivery in driving organizational change. By establishing a resilient foundation, fostering stakeholder engagement, building institutional memory, ensuring succession planning, evaluating to showcase the value of new practices, and enhancing institutional culture, the UDA not only improved operational efficiency but also set a new standard for future leaders and urban development agencies nationwide. Ms. Idawari Esei's proactive approach and unwavering commitment have positioned the UDA as a leader in sustainable urban development, prepared to tackle future challenges and opportunities with confidence.

....

Case Study 2
Delivery Gone Wrong

Background

This case study explores the ambitious but ultimately unsuccessful attempt by the National Media and Communications Authority (NMCA) to implement the delivery discipline under the leadership of Director Ms. Oluwatosin Okoro. With the goal of achieving comprehensive digital transformation to revolutionize media and communications operations nationwide, the NMCA embarked on a mission to institutionalize introduced changes. However, the mission faced significant challenges based on critical errors that impeded its success.

Key Players

- **Ms. Oluwatosin Okoro (Director)**: Visionary leader committed to transforming media and communication operations nationwide.

- **Mr. Emem Okon (Deputy Director)**: Responsible for operational strategies and overseeing the institutionalization process.

- **Mr. Osato Iboro (Chief Technology Officer)**: Provided essential expertise in digital media technologies and communication systems.

- **Mrs. Obong Ekpai (HR Director)**: Tasked with aligning workforce capabilities and managing human resources.

The Delivery Process

Stage 1: Establish a Resilient Foundation through Systematic Documentation

Centralized Digital Change Register: Initially, Ms. Oluwatosin Okoro commissioned a digital change register to track digital transformation reforms, but the team struggled to maintain consistency in updates. This inconsistency led to significant gaps in data, resulting in the loss of details on completed quick-win initiatives and short-term reforms implemented in previous years. Consequently, there was a loss of valuable lessons and institutional memory, impacting the organization's ability to build on past successes and effectively manage ongoing digital improvements.

Neglected Policy Frameworks: Despite recommendations from Mr. Osato Iboro, the NMCA failed to update existing policies or establish new ones to support digital transformation. This lack of policy alignment created confusion amongst stakeholders and inconsistency in adoption of new approaches, hampering effective project management and technology integration.

Integration Challenges: Mr. Emem Okon's efforts to integrate new digital tools and practices into daily operations were hindered by the failure of departmental heads to update job descriptions, standard operating procedures and workflows. This oversight meant that existing staff lacked documentation to support revised work patterns, while new hires had no clear reference points.

Stage 2: Entrench Changes through Effective and Inclusive Change Management

Inadequate Stakeholder Engagement: Despite efforts led by Ms. Oluwatosin Okoro and Mr. Emem Okon, engagement with stakeholders across various levels, including media partners and communication professionals, remained inadequate. Communication channels were sporadic, leading to misinformation and resistance among key stakeholders.

Weak Change Coalition: Mr. Emem Okon identified champions for the digital transformation effort but failed to empower and support them effectively. Senior leadership did not advocate strongly for the reforms or provide necessary resources, resulting in a lack of ownership and commitment among key influencers.

Lack of Governance Oversight: Despite efforts to establish oversight committees, these lacked defined mandates and accountability structures. This oversight gap contributed to ineffective monitoring of policy adherence and implementation progress.

Stage 3: Build Institutional Memory through Knowledge Management and Capacity Building

Absence of Knowledge Strategy: The NMCA underutilized Mr. Emem Okon's expertise in developing a comprehensive knowledge management strategy. Valuable insights and best practices in digital media and communications were not systematically captured or shared, limiting learning and improvement opportunities.

Limited Learning Initiatives: Training and development efforts led by Mrs. Obong Ekpai were sporadic and insufficiently targeted. There was no cohesive approach to building staff capacity aligned with new digital tools and reforms, leading to skill gaps and resistance among employees.

Stage 4: Drive Sustainability and Continuity through Succession Planning and Leadership Development

Neglected Succession Planning: Critical roles were identified, but the NMCA lacked a formal succession planning strategy. This oversight resulted in leadership gaps during transitions, disrupting continuity and jeopardizing the ongoing digital transformation efforts.

Leadership Instability: The NMCA experienced frequent leadership changes, complicating the sustained implementation of reforms. New leaders were not adequately briefed or prepared to uphold ongoing initiatives, leading to setbacks and regression.

Stage 5: Demonstrate and Maximize the Value of New Practices through Feedback, Monitoring, Evaluation, and Reporting

Inadequate Monitoring and Evaluation: The NMCA lacked robust mechanisms to monitor and evaluate the impact of digital transformation reforms. Without clear metrics or benchmarks, there was no systematic assessment of progress or strategy adjustment based on feedback.

Resistance to Feedback: Although feedback loops were established, they were underutilized. Leadership did not effectively act on feedback or integrate suggestions, contributing to disillusionment and decreased morale among staff.

Stage 6: Enhance Resilience through Institutional Culture

Lack of Leadership Commitment: While the Director advocated for change, her actions did not consistently align with stated commitments. This gap eroded trust and commitment among employees.

Resistance to Adaptability: The NMCA struggled to foster a culture of adaptability and innovation. Risk-taking was discouraged, and there was reluctance to experiment with new approaches, stifling creativity and growth.

Ineffective Recognition and Rewards: Efforts to recognize and reward employees for championing change were sporadic and inconsistent. There were no formal incentives tied to successful reform implementation, leading to a lack of motivation and recognition.

Final Outcomes

Despite initial enthusiasm and efforts, the NMCA under Ms. Oluwatosin Okoro's leadership risks failing to sustain the impactful digital transformation reforms if a reset occurs. Key factors contributing to this risk include gaps in policy alignment, insufficient stakeholder engagement, failure to build a robust change coalition, limited stakeholder buy-in, inadequate succession planning, weak evaluation systems, and a fragile organizational culture.

Key Leadership Failures

- **Inconsistent Leadership Commitment**: The Director's actions did not consistently support reform efforts, leading to skepticism and mistrust among stakeholders.

- **Lack of Strategic Policy Development**: Failure to update policies and align them with reforms led to confusion and hindered effective implementation.

- **Poor Stakeholder Engagement**: Insufficient efforts to engage and empower stakeholders resulted in resistance and limited support.

- **Weak Governance Oversight**: Ineffective oversight committees and governance structures failed to ensure accountability and monitor progress.

- **Absence of Knowledge Management Strategy**: Missed opportunities to capture and share critical insights limited organizational learning.

- **Neglected Succession Planning**: Lack of formal succession planning resulted in leadership gaps and disrupted continuity.

Conclusion and Lessons Learned

The experience of the National Media and Communications Authority serves as a powerful reminder of the complexities and challenges in implementing sustainable organizational change. By highlighting critical mistakes at each stage—ranging from inadequate documentation and policy alignment to weak stakeholder engagement and leadership instability—this case study underscores the importance of careful planning, clear communication, and supportive leadership in achieving scalable and institutionalized transformation.

A Call to Action

Master the Discipline of Delivery for the Good of Society

For far too long, many public organizations have fallen victim to the devastating phenomenon of reset culture. While leadership transitions are inevitable, progress must remain uninterrupted. The frequent overhaul of initiatives with each new administration leads to wasted resources, eroded public trust, and stifled innovation, undermining the very foundations of effective governance. This cycle of disruption triggered by leaders tapping the reset button when they take the reins must come to an end.

Leadership in the public sector must transcend political agendas and fundamentally focus on delivering real value to citizens. For this to happen, leaders must demonstrate a steadfast commitment to structured delivery, which will ultimately transform good intentions into tangible benefits. By building on the successes of their predecessors, public leaders can create resilient frameworks that withstand political changes.

When executed effectively, structured delivery offers many benefits. It ensures continuity across leadership transitions, optimizes resources, and enhances transparency and accountability. It also fosters a culture of innovation and adaptability, enabling public organizations to respond effectively to evolving challenges. Structured delivery establishes a legacy of systems and practices that continue to drive institutional progress and prosperity.

For public institutions to truly serve the public interest, leaders must adopt a delivery mindset. This means committing to a process that prioritizes long-term goals and sustainable practices over short-term gains. It's a call to action for public leaders to rise above the allure of immediate recognition and instead focus on creating enduring value for society.

The future of public service depends on leaders dedicated to excellence, stability, and the relentless pursuit of the public good. By institutionalizing structured delivery practices, public sector leaders can transform their organizations into engines of sustained progress. Commit to disciplined strategies for sustainable delivery to transform your public institution into a beacon of operational excellence and a legacy of enduring impact, resilient in the face of change.

The Discipline of Delivery at a Glance

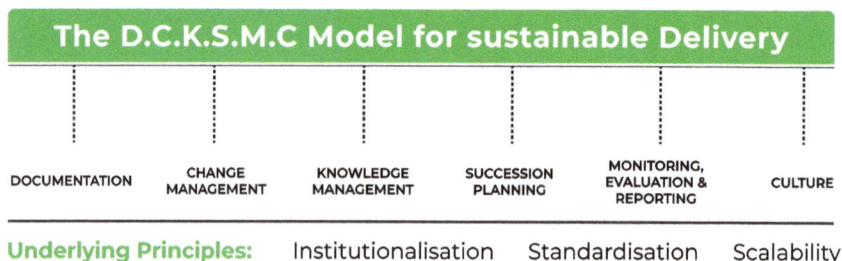

The D.C.K.S.M.C Model for sustainable Delivery					
DOCUMENTATION	CHANGE MANAGEMENT	KNOWLEDGE MANAGEMENT	SUCCESSION PLANNING	MONITORING, EVALUATION & REPORTING	CULTURE

Underlying Principles: Institutionalisation   Standardisation   Scalability

Figure 23. Framework for mastering DELIVERY: The DCKSM-C Model for sustainable DELIVERY

⚡ WHY IS DELIVERY IMPORTANT FOR PUBLIC LEADERS?

- **Stability amidst change:** Delivery ensures practices and systems keep functioning even when leadership changes. This continuity is crucial for effective governance.

- **Public trust and credibility:** Consistent service delivery builds trust with the public. Delivery promotes transparency and accountability, strengthening the government's legitimacy.

- **Efficiency and resource management:** Delivery avoids wasted efforts and redirects resources towards achieving goals. It optimizes project management and ensures public funds are used effectively.

- **Sustainable development:** Delivery allows public institutions to focus on long-term goals and avoid setbacks caused by leadership changes. This fosters lasting progress in crucial areas.

💡 WHAT ARE THE BIG IDEAS?

- The reset culture, where new leaders discard existing systems and practices established by their predecessors, hinders progress and wastes resources.

- The solution to the reset culture is the discipline of delivery. This emphasizes building on past successes and institutionalizing effective practices for long-term impact.

- Delivery promotes stability, public trust, efficiency, and institutional memory during leadership transitions.

- To master the discipline of delivery, leaders must adhere to the principles of institutionalization, standardization, and scalability.

🔧 HOW DO I MAKE IT HAPPEN?

Follow a six-stage process to institutionalize effective practices and systems within your organization:

Stage 1: Establish a resilient foundation through systematic documentation

Stage 2: Entrench changes through effective and inclusive change management

Stage 3: Build institutional memory through knowledge management and capacity building

Stage 4: Drive sustainability and continuity through succession planning and leadership development

Stage 5: Demonstrate and maximize the value of new practices through feedback, monitoring, evaluation, and reporting

Stage 6: Enhance resilience through institutional culture

Chapter 9
Conclusion

Putting It All Together

"The best leaders are the ones who get everyone to the place they want to be but never knew was possible."

– Simon Sinek

In the world of government and public leadership, there have been many promising beginnings but few good endings. Term after term, numerous leaders arrive with clear, burning visions of what they aim to achieve, only to struggle to turn those visions into reality. They start brimming with ambitious goals and a compelling blueprint for transformation. They understand the desired outcomes and the kind of impact they want their organizations to make.

However, for most, the harsh realities of the public sector soon take hold. Political pressures, budgetary constraints, and the sheer complexity of navigating public bureaucracy dim even the most passionate vision, and what began as a clear and unwavering path soon becomes shrouded in doubt and frustration.

This is the reality of what it means to lead in the public sector.

Leadership in all domains and sectors will test one's mettle, but leading in the public sector is often a severe test of leadership capabilities. This is because it requires leaders to navigate obstacles, adapt strategies, and inspire others to persevere toward a better future, even when the path seems obscured.

Yet, the most effective public leaders possess not only vision but also grit, determination, and, most importantly, a proven roadmap to navigate these obstacles. This book was written to provide that roadmap.

The overriding question addressed by this volume is how public leaders can predictably achieve high performance as they navigate a difficult terrain filled with old and new challenges. It offers a trusted roadmap for patriotic and determined leaders to systematically plan, execute, and achieve the bold and ambitious visions they hold to better the lives of the people they serve through the public institutions they lead.

Amid today's worldwide financial turmoil and severe economic crisis, **the demand for effective leadership is more urgent than ever.** Public leaders can no longer afford to be crippled by a lack of effective decision-making capacity, the strength to act, and the in-depth insight needed to deliver transformative results.

Many books have been written on effective public leadership and performance management. This one is distinctive because it is not a theoretical stream of advice. It was built on decades of careful study of how leaders have systematically navigated and led organizations facing significant challenges, following a stage-by-stage blueprint and systematic, step-by-step guide to clear waters.

It is based on the premise that amidst the cacophony of conflicting voices and interests characteristic of the public sector environment, leaders must have a model or framework for staying grounded, organizing their organizations for high performance, and ensuring the delivery of desperately needed breakthrough results. The book was written with the fundamental expectation that new and returning public leaders will approach their decision to serve the public with a firm determination to succeed. This commitment will drive them to ask the following fundamental questions:

1. How do we hit the ground running?

2. How do we achieve full buy-in and sustained support from the entire organization?

3. How do we quickly and deeply understand the organization to recognize its strengths, weaknesses, threats, and opportunities?

4. How do we create a strategy/agenda that will truly deliver results for the people?

5. How do we structure the organization to execute that strategy?

6. How do we select and assign the right people to execute that strategy?

7. How do we set up a supportive infrastructure to drive and sustain the performance of the strategy?

8. And after we leave office, how do we ensure that the organization remains effective and continues to deliver results?

These complex and compelling questions form the foundation of high-performing organizations. They are essential and relevant for all public leaders today. The effectiveness with which leaders answer and execute these questions will determine whether they succeed or struggle.

The entire goal of *The Seven Disciplines of Breakthrough Results* has been to help leaders effectively answer these questions for their organizations. It has provided fact-based insights into the nitty-gritty of what it takes to steer a public organization to deliver on its mandate even in the face of heightened complexity. The book has not taken the position of a wishy-washy manual on current performance management issues; instead, it has deconstructed the anatomy of what it takes to achieve breakthrough results in a public organization. It offers clear and actionable details on how leaders can get into the trenches, roll up their sleeves, and get the job done effectively.

In this final chapter, we pull together all seven disciplines of breakthrough results and demonstrate concisely what this book has set out to do: To lay bare before leaders the anatomy of breakthrough results and provide them with a clear understanding of the pathway to achieve high performance.

The Seven Disciplines: The Steps that Lead to Breakthrough Results

"Discipline is the soul of an army. It makes small numbers formidable; procures success to the weak, and esteem to all."

– George Washington

It has long been established that without the right set of disciplines, a leader can only hope for mediocre performance.

This book opens the doors to a transformative journey, providing public leaders with a powerful framework to propel their organizations from mediocrity to extraordinary achievement.

By following the seven disciplines outlined in this book, public leaders can turn their vision into reality, ensuring their efforts lead to tangible, meaningful improvements for the communities they serve.

The disciplines are not just nice to have, they are necessities for breakthrough results.

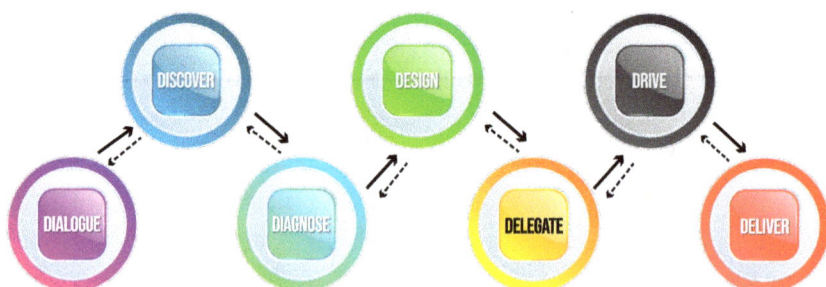

Figure 24. The Seven Disciplines of Breakthrough Results

The Necessity of Discipline 1: Dialogue

How do you become the kind of leader people want to follow? How do you inspire others, by their own volition, to move forward together in pursuit of a common vision? How do you mobilize them to embrace shared aspirations?

As a public leader, it's crucial to acknowledge the challenges of managing government institutions. Without the support of your organization, the path to failure becomes all too likely. Leading public institutions requires more than just vision and policy; it hinges on harnessing the collective wisdom and dedication of your team and the communities you serve.

This is where the discipline of dialogue comes into play. Dialogue goes beyond routine communication; it establishes a platform for open, honest conversations that bridge divides and align aspirations. It must be approached from both internal and external perspectives. Internally, leaders must demonstrate competence and passion while fostering an inclusive environment where every voice matters. Externally, dialogue involves deep engagement with the external stakeholders that the organization serves. Done effectively, this provides insights into community needs and expectations, enabling you to deliver impactful results.

Strategic dialogue serves several essential purposes:

- **Setting new directions**: It allows leaders to introduce fresh ideas, assess readiness for change, and chart a course for organizational transformation.

- **Alignment and buy-in:** Through dialogue, consensus is built and stakeholders commit to shared goals, ensuring unified efforts toward success.

- **Issue detection and resolution**: Regular dialogue sessions uncover underlying issues early, enabling proactive solutions and preventing escalation.

- **Observation and insight gathering**: Leaders gain valuable insights into team dynamics and sentiments, guiding informed decision-making.

- **Renewing hope and commitment:** Open dialogue provides a safe space for team members to express concerns and rejuvenate their dedication to collective objectives.

- **Identifying change agents:** Dialogue identifies influential individuals who can champion change within the organization, fostering innovation and progress.

Engaging in meaningful dialogue is not optional for public leaders; it is fundamental to effective governance. It builds trust, enhances transparency, and fosters a collaborative culture essential for navigating complex challenges. By embracing dialogue, leaders affirm their commitment to inclusivity and responsiveness, transforming skepticism into support and plans into actions.

As a public sector leader, your proficiency in dialogue will define your legacy. It is only through effective dialogue sessions that you can guide your organization toward resilience, adaptation, and achievement.

The Necessity of Discipline 2: Discover

How do you gain a profound understanding of your organization's past and current state to effectively chart its future course? This compelling question highlights the importance of the second discipline: Discover.

After concluding dialogue sessions with both internal teams and external stakeholders of your public institution, an avalanche of feedback is anticipated. This comprehensive feedback serves as a compelling call to action. As a leader tasked with navigating these complexities, your next critical step is to embark on the discovery phase.

The discovery phase is crucial for leaders to gain a comprehensive understanding of their organization's current state and historical context. Its goal is to thoroughly examine every facet of the organization, ensuring leaders are fully informed about the next strategic steps. When executed adeptly, discovery reveals a wealth of often surprising information.

These insights are pivotal in crafting a compelling vision for the future. Effective discovery hinges on leaders obtaining accurate and detailed information across all departments. It involves delving deep into the organization's inner workings—from HR and procurement to financial integrity and stakeholder relationships. By meticulously uncovering these realities, you pave the way for informed decision-making and transformative change.

Discovery is not merely about gathering data. The process sheds light on organizational strengths and weaknesses and sets the stage for strategic initiatives that align with both internal capabilities and external expectations. The discovery phase is indispensable for leaders, equipping them with the in-depth insights necessary to formulate effective decisions, policies, strategies, and actions. It serves as the foundation from which leaders derive clear pathways and robust ideas to fulfill the commitments made to the public.

Engaging in the discipline of discovery not only deepens your understanding of your organization but also instills confidence in your ability to drive significant change within your organization as a leader.

The Necessity of Discipline 3: Diagnose

As a leader, how do you ensure that the information presented to you in the discovery phase is accurate, comprehensive, and not misleading? How do you uncover the underlying causes that hinder your organization from achieving its full potential? What proactive steps can you take to ensure that the strategies and solutions you eventually design effectively address core issues rather than merely alleviating symptoms?

These questions underscore the criticality of the third discipline of breakthrough results: Diagnosis. While the discovery phase relies on self-reported information from department heads, the diagnosis phase requires leaders to engage in forensic audits, verify facts against presented data, and drill down to uncover the true state of the organization and its root problems.

Frequently, in my work with public leaders during this phase, we have found that much information presented by unit and departmental heads during the discovery phase was inaccurate and misleading, especially in the areas of finances and data about employees. We've discovered undisclosed accounts, unexecuted contracts that were paid for, and ghost workers, among other inconsistencies.

When executed effectively, the diagnosis phase will uncover both the pleasant and unpleasant truths about an organization. Where systemic rot exists, it will track it down to the root. Where there is potential, it will reveal it and help leaders identify the best path forward. Diagnosis also provides leaders with insights into the character and capabilities of their teams, aiding in the organizational redesign process.

Transitioning from discovery to diagnosis is pivotal. Diagnosis involves delving deep into findings to identify the root causes behind organizational challenges. This meticulous process ensures that solutions address core issues, not just symptoms, fostering sustainable change and enhancing stakeholder confidence. By engaging stakeholders in the diagnosis phase, leaders harness collective knowledge to prioritize issues and develop tailored interventions.

Strategic diagnosis empowers leaders with a clear roadmap for effective solutions. It moves beyond surface-level observations to uncover interdependencies and external influences that impact organizational health. This comprehensive understanding strengthens decision-making and builds trust among stakeholders, ensuring alignment and support for proposed initiatives.

Embracing discovery and diagnosis as ongoing practices equips public sector leaders to navigate complexity with confidence. It transforms leadership from being reactive to being proactive, paving the way for resilient organizations capable of anticipating and mitigating challenges. By leveraging these disciplines, leaders can propel their institutions toward sustained effectiveness and impactful change. The discipline of diagnosis is therefore critical for leaders who seek to deliver meaningful results for their organizations.

The Necessity of Discipline 4: Design

After a thorough diagnosis reveals the root causes hindering performance, the critical question for leaders becomes: **How do we design an organization that delivers impactful results?**

This is where the discipline of design comes into play.

In the design phase, leaders leverage the Four-Step Organizational Design Model outlined in this book. This model empowers them to systematically establish the organization's purpose in conjunction with senior leaders. After confirming the organization's purpose, the next step is to decide on the strategy and strategic objectives that will enable its execution. Once the agenda has been set, leaders design an organizational structure optimized for executing these strategies and objectives. Finally, the model guides them in identifying the mission-critical roles and capabilities needed to fulfill the agenda. Leaders then source and develop the talent necessary to fill these roles.

An organization's performance is inextricably linked to its design, mirroring the way a building's blueprint dictates its strength and functionality. This fundamental principle underscores the critical role of design in leadership strategy: without a strong design, achieving desired results becomes significantly more challenging. Effective design acts as the foundation upon which all strategies are built. It seamlessly integrates an organization's core elements – mission, vision, and purpose – with its strategic goals and daily operations, ensuring a clear and aligned path toward success.

The discipline of design is therefore critical for leaders who seek to deliver meaningful results for their organizations.

The Necessity of Discipline 5: Delegate

A well-crafted design process meticulously addresses two crucial questions: what initiatives are essential to propel the organization toward its goals, and how should these initiatives be executed for optimal outcomes? However, the true differentiator between success and failure often lies not just in the strategic "what" or the tactical "how," but rather in the "who." This refers to the organization's human capital – the talented individuals whose skills and dedication breathe life into strategic plans.

The discipline that ensures the right people are sourced and assigned to execute the organization's strategic objectives is delegation. Effective delegation involves the strategic alignment of people not just with tasks, but with the mission, vision, and core values of the organization. It demands a profound understanding of individual capabilities and a commitment to develop these capabilities in alignment with organizational needs.

In the delegation phase, leaders must identify the key people with the skills and capabilities necessary to deliver on the roles and strategic objectives. This stage requires leaders to identify job requirements, set key performance indicators (KPIs), key result areas (KRAs), metrics and measures, and detailed performance contracts that everyone critical to achieving the organization's goals will sign.

The discipline of delegation is the wise deployment of human resources. It is how leaders transform potential into performance, aspirations into achievements, and challenges into victories. By focusing on the "Who," leaders ensure that the right people are empowered to drive the organization's strategic initiatives, creating a synergistic effect that leads to exponential growth and success.

The Necessity of Discipline 6: Drive

Following successful delegation, the next critical step is to establish a rhythm of execution where assigned strategic objectives are consistently and effectively implemented. It is often a serious mistake for leaders to assume that delegation alone will guarantee flawless execution. This assumption, as time has shown, can be costly.

Just as a car requires consistent acceleration to maintain speed, organizations need a sustained effort to achieve strategic objectives. The primary reason many organizations underperform is often not due to inadequate strategic plans or personnel capabilities but rather a failure of implementation—a lack of a consistent, well-orchestrated rhythm to drive performance. The discipline of drive addresses this by ensuring that strategies and intentions are transformed into measurable, meaningful results. Drive establishes a performance rhythm that sustains initiatives and ensures they reach their intended conclusions, enabling leaders to translate plans into actions and aspirations into realities.

To drive people effectively, leaders must establish transparent systems for tracking progress, such as key performance indicators (KPIs) and visible scoreboards, align incentives with organizational performance, and manage performance consequences effectively. This embodies the essence of drive, which is indispensable for producing breakthrough results.

The Necessity of Discipline 7: Deliver

A hallmark of truly successful public leaders is their ability not only to deliver impactful results that enhance lives but also to institutionalize high-performing systems and infrastructure. These enduring frameworks ensure continued delivery of results long after their tenure ends, irrespective of subsequent leadership changes.

Implementing delivery presents a formidable challenge, especially amidst the persistent threat of reset culture. However, this book has provided a practical framework that dedicated leaders can employ to establish and sustain these critical systems. Delivery advocates for a disciplined approach where proven systems persist across administrations, fostering stability and optimizing public service delivery. By embracing delivery, leaders commit to a framework that withstands political shifts, promotes fiscal responsibility, and enhances public trust through transparent and accountable governance.

Structured delivery is particularly vital for African nations grappling with governance instability. It guarantees the steady progress of essential infrastructure projects and social programs, shielding them from the disruptions caused by successive resets. This methodical approach also ensures efficient resource allocation, maximizing the impact of development initiatives and promoting sustainable growth.

Advocating for structured delivery is a call to uphold stability and effectiveness within public institutions. It necessitates a steadfast commitment to continuity and responsible resource management, ensuring that each leadership transition builds upon existing progress rather than resetting it. By embedding this discipline, leaders safeguard institutional legacies and lay the groundwork for sustained societal advancement and prosperity.

A Final Call to Action

The Seven Disciplines of Breakthrough Results: How to Predictably Achieve High Performance for Director-Generals, CEOs, ESs, PSs, Directors, and Senior Leadership Teams in the Public Sector, has offered a comprehensive and practical roadmap for public sector leaders striving to achieve high performance and deliver exceptional results.

Through the disciplines of Dialogue, Discovery, Diagnosis, Design, Delegation, Drive, and Delivery, leaders can effectively navigate the complexities of the public sector, surmount challenges, and propel their organizations to unprecedented levels of success.

While the path to breakthrough results is demanding, perseverance, strategic planning, and a steadfast commitment to excellence pave the way for achieving the extraordinary and leaving a lasting impact on the lives of those we serve.

A Call to Embrace the Challenge: Lead with Breakthrough Results

Public service offers a unique opportunity to make a real difference in the lives of others. By embracing the Seven Disciplines of Breakthrough Results, leaders can transform their organizations into powerful forces for positive change.

I encourage you to step forward, take up the challenge, and use this framework to guide you on your journey towards extraordinary leadership and lasting societal impact.

Appendix

Resources

Discipline 1 - Dialogue

Facilitator's Manual for Executing a Dialogue Session

This manual serves as your comprehensive and handy resource for navigating the complexities of dialogue.

Stage 1: Preparing for Dialogue

1. Define objectives:

- Clearly articulate what you aim to achieve with the dialogue session. Objectives may include introducing new policies, gathering feedback on existing programs, or resolving specific organizational issues.

2. Identify stakeholders:

- Compile a list of participants who need to be involved in the dialogue. Consider including a diverse group that represents different levels and functions within the organization, as well as relevant external stakeholders.

3. Develop the agenda:

- Create a detailed agenda that outlines the topics to be discussed, the goals for each topic, and the time allotted for each segment.

- Include welcome remarks, a brief overview of the session's objectives, main discussion points, and a closing summary.

4. Choose the venue and setup:

- Select a neutral, comfortable, and accessible location to conduct the session.
- Arrange the seating to facilitate open discussion, such as a round table or U-shaped setup.

5. Communicate with participants:

- Send out invitations well in advance, including the agenda, objectives, and logistical details.
- Encourage participants to come prepared to discuss the agenda topics.

Stage 2: Conducting the Dialogue

1. Opening the session:

- Start by clearly stating the objectives and agenda.
- Establish ground rules for the discussion (e.g., respect for different opinions, no interruptions).

2. Facilitate the discussion:

- Use open-ended questions to encourage participation.
- Actively listen to participants' responses and summarize their points to ensure clarity and understanding.
- Manage time effectively to cover all agenda items.

3. Handle conflicts:

- Address conflicts constructively and impartially.
- Steer the discussion back to the agenda if deviations occur.

4. Documentation:

- Assign a team member to take detailed notes during the session or record the discussions for accuracy.
- Capture key points, decisions made, and action items.

5. Closing the session:

- Summarize the discussion, reiterate key outcomes, and outline the next steps.

- Thank participants for their contributions.

Stage 3: Post-dialogue Actions

1. Distribute meeting notes:

- Share the documented notes with all participants and stakeholders who need to be informed.

- Include a feedback form to gather participants' impressions of the dialogue session.

2. Follow-up:

- Ensure that action items identified during the session are assigned and timelines are established.

- Schedule follow-up meetings to review progress.

3. Evaluate the session:

- Analyze feedback received to assess the effectiveness of the dialogue.

- Identify areas for improvement in future sessions.

Facilitator's Checklist for Executing Dialogue

This checklist can be used to ensure that all necessary steps are covered before, during, and after the dialogue session. Adjust as needed to fit specific project requirements and organizational contexts.

Stage 1: Preparing for Dialogue

☐ Define the session's objectives.

☐ Identify and list all relevant stakeholders.

☐ Develop a detailed agenda.

☐ Choose an appropriate venue and setup.

☐ Send out invitations and session materials in advance.

Stage 2: Conducting the Dialogue

☐ Start with clear opening remarks.

☐ Facilitate the discussion according to the agenda.

☐ Employ active listening and summarize key points.

☐ Manage conflicts and stay on track with the agenda.

☐ Assign a note-taker or record the session.

Stage 3: Post-dialogue Actions

☐ Distribute meeting notes and action items.

☐ Follow up on assigned tasks.

☐ Evaluate the session based on participant feedback.

☐ Plan for subsequent dialogue sessions if necessary.

Discipline 2 – Discover

Facilitator's Manual for Executing the Discovery Process

This manual provides a detailed, stage-by-stage guide for helping leaders discover their organizations.

Stage 1: Planning and Preparation

1. Define clear objectives:

- Define precise goals for the discovery phase, such as understanding organizational challenges, identifying opportunities, or evaluating past decisions.

- Conduct stakeholder meetings to align on objectives.

- Document objectives clearly and in an actionable format.

2. Identify key stakeholders:

- Compile a comprehensive list of internal and external stakeholders crucial for the Discovery process.

- Create a stakeholder map identifying roles and responsibilities.

- Determine engagement strategies for different stakeholder groups.

3. Develop a detailed timeline:

- Establish a realistic timeline outlining milestones and deadlines for each phase of the discovery process.

- Break down the discovery process into manageable phases (e.g., planning, data collection, and analysis).

- Allocate sufficient time for data gathering and analysis.

Stage 2: Data Collection

1. Data collection strategies:

- Gather comprehensive data from internal and external sources to provide a holistic view of the organization.

- Conduct thorough reviews of internal documents (e.g., financial statements, HR reports).

- Deploy surveys and questionnaires to capture anonymous employee feedback.

- Schedule interviews with key personnel and external stakeholders for nuanced insights.

Stage 3: Analysis

1. Data analysis:

- Analyze collected data to identify trends, anomalies, and correlations informing strategic decision-making.

- Utilize statistical tools and methods for quantitative data analysis.

- Perform a SWOT analysis to assess internal strengths, weaknesses, and external opportunities and threats.

- Conduct a gap analysis to identify areas needing immediate attention.

Stage 4: Synthesis and Reporting

1. Compilation of findings:

- Synthesize data and insights to get a comprehensive overview of the organization's current state and future opportunities.

- Compile findings into a structured report format.

- Ensure clarity and conciseness in presenting findings.

2. Stakeholder feedback sessions:

- Present findings to senior management and stakeholders for validation and additional insights.

- Schedule feedback sessions to discuss findings and gather input.

- Document feedback and insights to refine recommendations.

3. Developing actionable Insights:

- Translate data-driven insights into actionable strategies and initiatives enhancing organizational effectiveness.

- Develop a roadmap of strategic initiatives based on discovery findings.

- Align recommendations with organizational goals and stakeholder expectations.

Checklist for Executing the Discovery Process

With this comprehensive checklist, you can confidently navigate the discovery process. As you complete each step, tick it off to ensure nothing is missed. This approach helps you avoid mistakes and oversights.

Stage 1: Planning and Preparation

Define Clear Objectives

☐ Specify goals and objectives for the discovery phase.

☐ Ensure objectives are aligned with organizational priorities and strategic initiatives.

Identify Key Stakeholders

☐ Compile a list of internal and external stakeholders.

☐ Define roles and responsibilities for each stakeholder.

☐ Plan engagement strategies to involve stakeholders effectively.

Develop a Detailed Project Plan

☐ Create a timeline with milestones and deadlines for each discovery stage.

☐ Allocate resources (budget, personnel, tools) necessary for data collection and analysis.

☐ Assign responsibilities to team members and stakeholders.

Stage 2: Data Collection

Establish Data Collection Methods

☐ Identify sources of data (internal documents, surveys, interviews, etc.).

☐ Select appropriate data collection tools and methodologies.

☐ Ensure compliance with data privacy regulations and ethical guidelines.

Conduct Data Collection

☐ Gather data from identified sources as per the project plan.

☐ Review internal documents (financial statements, operational reports, etc.).

☐ Administer surveys and questionnaires to capture diverse perspectives.

☐ Conduct interviews with key personnel and external stakeholders.

Stage 3: Analysis

Analyze Collected Data

☐ Utilize statistical tools and methods to analyze quantitative data.

☐ Perform qualitative analysis to identify trends, patterns, and insights.

☐ Conduct SWOT analysis to assess organizational strengths, weaknesses, opportunities, and threats.

☐ Perform gap analysis to identify areas needing immediate attention.

Stage 4: Synthesis and Reporting

Synthesize Findings

☐ Compile data and analysis into a structured report format.

☐ Ensure clarity, accuracy, and relevance of synthesized findings.

☐ Present findings in a format suitable for stakeholders and decision-makers.

Validate Findings

☐ Review findings with key stakeholders and subject matter experts.

☐ Gather feedback to validate the accuracy and relevance of findings.

☐ Document feedback and incorporate necessary revisions into the final report.

Develop Actionable Recommendations

☐ Translate insights and findings into actionable recommendations.

☐ Prioritize recommendations based on strategic importance and feasibility.

☐ Align recommendations with organizational goals and stakeholder expectations.

Discipline 3 – Diagnose

Facilitator's Manual for Executing the Diagnosis Process

This manual provides a detailed, stage-by-stage guide for helping leaders diagnose their organizations.

Stage 1: Preparing for Diagnosis

1. Objective setting:

- Define clear goals aligned with organizational objectives.
- Articulate expected outcomes to guide the diagnostic intervention.

2. Stakeholder identification:

- Compile a comprehensive list of stakeholders involved or affected by the issues.
- Include employees, management, board members, and external partners.

3. Resource allocation:

- Determine necessary resources (personnel, technology, budget).
- Assign roles and responsibilities for accountability.

Stage 2: Data Collection

1. Data collection planning:

- Select appropriate methods (surveys, interviews, document analysis, observation).
- Align methods with objectives established in Stage 1.

2. Tool development:

- Develop tailored tools (surveys, interview guides, focus group questions).
- Ensure tools capture relevant data to inform the diagnosis.

3. Data collection execution:

- Implement the data collection plan rigorously.
- Verify data accuracy, relevance, and comprehensiveness.

Stage 3: Analysis

1. Data analysis:

- Utilize qualitative and quantitative methods for thorough analysis.
- Apply statistical tools for quantitative data and content analysis for qualitative insights.

2. Synthesis of findings:

- Integrate findings from various data sources.
- Identify key themes and patterns to understand diagnosed issues.

Stage 4: Reporting and Feedback

1. Drafting the diagnosis report:

- Compile findings into a comprehensive report.
- Include an executive summary, detailed findings, and actionable recommendations.

2. Stakeholder feedback:

- Present findings to stakeholders for validation and feedback.
- Ensure accuracy and relevance of the report.

Stage 5: Action Planning and Implementation

1. Development of action plans:

- Based on findings, create detailed action plans.
- Specify steps, timelines, and responsible parties for each action.

2. Implementation:

- Execute action plans with close monitoring.
- Adjust plans based on ongoing feedback and evaluation.

Checklist for Executing the Diagnosis Process

This checklist allows for easy tracking and management of each stage in the diagnosis process, ensuring thoroughness and accountability in achieving organizational improvements.

Stage 1: Preparation

☐ Define clear objectives for the diagnosis.

☐ Identify and categorize stakeholders.

☐ Allocate necessary resources and assign roles.

☐ Schedule the diagnosis activities.

Stage 2: Data Collection

☐ Select and design appropriate data collection methods.

☐ Develop and test data collection tools.

☐ Conduct data collection according to the plan.

☐ Ensure high-quality and comprehensive data gathering.

Stage 3: Analysis

☐ Perform detailed data analysis.

☐ Synthesize findings from different data sources.

☐ Identify key themes and insights.

☐ Prepare an initial analysis report for review.

Stage 4: Reporting and Feedback

☐ Draft the comprehensive diagnosis report.

☐ Present findings to stakeholders for feedback.

☐ Incorporate feedback and finalize the report.

Stage 5: Action Planning and Implementation

☐ Develop detailed action plans.

☐ Begin implementation of the plans.

☐ Monitor and adjust the plans as needed.

Discipline 4 – Design

Facilitator's Manual for Executing the Design Process

This manual provides a detailed, stage-by-stage guide for helping leaders design their organizations.

Stage 1: Purpose Definition

1. Workshops and discussions:

- Engage the design team and stakeholders to define a clear purpose collaboratively.

2. Communication:

- Ensure widespread understanding by disseminating the purpose through internal channels.

3. Reorientation programs:

- Implement ongoing sessions to maintain alignment and commitment across all levels.

Stage 2: Strategy Development

4. Stakeholder engagement:

- Conduct town halls and focus groups to gather input and ensure strategic alignment.
- Utilize data-driven approaches to balance stakeholder expectations.

5. Action planning:

- Break down high-level goals into actionable steps with clear deliverables and timelines.
- Create detailed action plans to ensure practical implementation.

Stage 3: Structural Alignment

1. Deliverable-based structure:

- Adopt a deliverable-centric approach to encourage collaboration

- Design an organizational structure that supports efficient execution of the strategy.

- Focus departments on key outcomes aligned with organizational goals.

2. Role clarity:

- Define responsibilities, accountabilities, and decision-making authority clearly for each role.

- Avoid overwhelming roles with conflicting responsibilities to enhance focus.

Stage 4: Role Clarity

1. Role definition:

- Define mission-critical roles with clear responsibilities and success metrics.

- Clearly articulate role expectations, including performance indicators and metrics.

- Develop objective metrics aligned with strategic goals for fair evaluation.

2. Talent management:

- Attract and retain skilled individuals with career development opportunities.

- Emphasize impact potential and career development within the organization.

Checklist for Executing the Design Process

This checklist serves as a guide for ensuring thorough execution of each stage of the Four-Stage Organizational Design Model in the public sector context.

Stage 1: Purpose Definition

☐ Conduct workshops and discussions to define organization's mission, vision, and values.

☐ Communicate purpose through internal channels (e.g., emails, town halls).

☐ Implement ongoing reorientation programs for stakeholders and employees.

Stage 2: Strategy Development

☐ Engage stakeholders through town halls and focus groups.

☐ Break down high-level goals into actionable steps with clear deliverables.

☐ Develop detailed action plans with specific timelines.

Stage 3: Structure

☐ Design deliverable-based structure focused on key outcomes.

☐ Define roles clearly with responsibilities, accountability, and authority.

☐ Avoid role overload by ensuring roles have clear, manageable responsibilities.

Stage 4: Roles

☐ Clearly articulate success metrics and performance indicators for each role.

☐ Implement talent management strategies to attract and retain skilled individuals.

☐ Develop objective performance metrics aligned with strategic goals.

General

☐ Ensure collaboration and inclusivity in decision-making processes.

☐ Utilize data-driven approaches to prioritize strategies and actions.

☐ Maintain transparency and communication throughout the design process.

Discipline 5 – Delegate

Facilitator's Manual for Executing Delegation

This manual provides a structured approach to delegation using the SIMPLE Framework, ensuring clarity, support, and accountability throughout the process.

Stage 1: Select What to Delegate

- Clarify tasks with specific, measurable goals.
- Differentiate between tasks requiring personal attention and those suitable for delegation.

Stage 2: Identify the Right Delegate

- Assess skills, interests, and workload of potential delegates.
- Align tasks with the career growth goals of delegates.

Stage 3: Map out the Task Clearly

- Define task scope, limitations, and authority clearly.
- Set measurable milestones and deadlines for progress tracking.

Stage 4: Provide Adequate Support and Resources

- Equip delegates with necessary tools, data, and access to expertise.
- Offer ongoing mentorship and create a supportive environment.

Stage 5: Lead through Monitoring Progress

- Conduct regular check-ins to monitor progress and offer guidance.
- Provide positive reinforcement and constructive feedback.

Stage 6: Evaluate and Reflect

- Assess outcomes against goals and expectations.
- Reflect on the process to identify improvements for future delegations.

Checklist for Executing Effective Delegation

This checklist is structured to guide leaders through each stage of the delegation process, ensuring comprehensive and effective delegation within organizational settings.

Stage 1: Select What to Delegate

☐ Clearly define tasks with specific goals.

☐ Determine tasks that can be effectively delegated.

Stage 2: Identify the Right Delegate

☐ Evaluate skills, interests, and workload of potential delegates.

☐ Match tasks with career development goals of delegates.

Stage 3: Map out the Task Clearly

☐ Provide detailed explanations of task scope, limitations, and authority.

☐ Set clear milestones and deadlines for progress tracking.

Stage 4: Provide Adequate Support and Resources

☐ Equip delegates with necessary tools, data, and access to expertise.

☐ Offer ongoing mentorship and create a supportive environment.

Stage 5: Lead through Monitoring Progress

☐ Schedule regular check-ins to monitor task progress.

☐ Provide timely feedback and guidance to delegates.

Stage 6: Evaluate and Reflect

☐ Assess task outcomes against established goals.

☐ Reflect on the delegation process to identify areas for improvement.

Discipline 6 – Drive

Facilitator's Manual for Executing Drive

This manual outlines a comprehensive approach to executing the discipline of drive.

Stage 1: Establish an Execution Rhythm

1. Define Strategic Objectives:

- Clearly articulate the long-term goals and objectives of the organization.
- Break down these goals into actionable tasks.

2. Develop Operational Calendars:

- Create detailed calendars outlining daily, weekly, monthly, and quarterly activities.
- Ensure these activities align with strategic objectives.
- Include key performance indicators (KPIs).

3. Establish Review Rhythms:

- Schedule regular review meetings.
- Assess reports, discuss operational strategy implications, and foster collaborative feedback.

4. Foster Team Alignment and Commitment:

- Continuously emphasize the significance of each team's role in advancing organizational goals.
- Maintain motivation and focus by keeping lines of communication open.
- Encourage teamwork among departments to ensure a unified and integrated execution rhythm.

Stage 2: Set Up Advanced Reporting Mechanisms

1. Implement Integrated Reporting Tools:

- Deploy advanced data management systems to collect, analyze and standardize performance data.

- Ensure compatibility with existing IT infrastructure.

2. Customize Reporting Dashboards:

- Design dashboards to provide real-time insights into KPIs and metrics.

- Train staff on the use of these dashboards for informed decision-making.

Stage 3: Implement an Effective Consequence Management System

1. Define Performance Thresholds:

- Establish clear, measurable criteria that trigger rewards or corrective actions.

- Ensure transparency and alignment with organizational values.

2. Develop Reward Systems:

- Create comprehensive systems including financial bonuses, promotions, and recognition opportunities.

- Communicate these clearly to all employees.

3. Set Up Corrective Measures:

- Outline constructive actions for underperformance.

- Focus on improvement through training, reassignment, or other interventions.

📋 *Checklist for Executing Drive*

This checklist serves as a guide to ensure each stage of implementing the discipline of drive is executed effectively, fostering organizational effectiveness and sustained performance improvement.

Stage 1: Establish an Execution Rhythm

☐ Define clear and SMART strategic objectives.

☐ Develop operational calendars with detailed activities and KPIs.

☐ Schedule regular review meetings

☐ Foster team alignment and commitment

Stage 2: Set up Advanced Reporting Mechanisms

☐ Implement integrated reporting tools for data collection, analysis and standardization.

☐ Customize reporting dashboards to provide real-time insights.

☐ Schedule regular review meetings to assess reports and provide feedback.

Stage 3: Implement an Effective Consequence Management System

☐ Define measurable performance thresholds.

☐ Develop a comprehensive reward system and communicate it clearly.

☐ Outline constructive corrective measures for underperformance.

General

☐ Ensure alignment of daily operations with strategic goals.

☐ Foster a culture of accountability and continuous improvement.

☐ Monitor progress and adjust strategies as needed.

Discipline 7 – Deliver

Facilitator's Manual for Executing Delivery

This manual serves as a detailed guide to navigate through each stage of the delivery process, emphasizing best practices and strategies for institutionalizing high-performance practices.

Stage 1: Establish a Resilient Foundation through Systematic Documentation

- Lay the groundwork for sustainable change.
- Document key changes in authorized policy frameworks, embed changes into daily operations, and formalize new processes and procedures.

Stage 2: Entrench Changes through Effective and Inclusive Change Management

- Build stakeholder consensus and commitment.
- Identify and manage stakeholders, build a change coalition, and establish robust governance frameworks.

Stage 3: Build Institutional Memory through Knowledge Management and Capacity Building

- Ensure knowledge retention and continuous learning.
- Create a knowledge management strategy and infrastructure.
- Establish continuous learning and development programs.

Stage 4: Drive Sustainability through Succession Planning and Leadership Development

- Ensure continuity of high-performance practices.
- Develop a succession planning strategy and empower future leaders.

Stage 5: Demonstrate and Maximize the Value of New Practices through Feedback, Monitoring, Evaluation, and Reporting

- Demonstrate and enhance the impact of implemented changes.

- Create mechanisms for feedback and adaptation.

- Implement effective monitoring, evaluation, and learning systems.

Stage 6: Enhance Resilience through Institutional Culture

- Foster a resilient and adaptive organizational culture.

- Promote adaptability, establish a system of recognition and rewards, and reinforce high-performance values.

Facilitator's Checklist for Executing Effective Delivery

This checklist is designed to guide facilitators and leaders through each stage of the delivery process, ensuring systematic implementation of high-performance practices and sustained organizational success.

Stage 1: Establish a Resilient Foundation through Systematic Documentation

☐ Create a centralized change register.

☐ Review changes for policy support.

☐ Develop/update policies.

☐ Embed new practices into routines.

☐ Update job descriptions and workflows.

☐ Develop toolkits, frameworks, and templates.

☐ Create SOPs and guidance manuals.

☐ Train staff on SOPs.

Stage 2: Entrench Changes through Effective and Inclusive Change Management

☐ Identify stakeholders.

☐ Regularly engage stakeholders.

☐ Maintain open communication.

☐ Empower change champions.

☐ Involve senior leaders and managers.

☐ Provide continuous capacity building.

☐ Form oversight committees.

☐ Embed accountability mechanisms.

Stage 3: Build Institutional Memory through Knowledge Management and Capacity Building

☐ Develop a knowledge management strategy.

☐ Define roles for knowledge management.

☐ Foster a knowledge-sharing culture.

☐ Establish a knowledge management infrastructure.

☐ Implement systems for capturing and documenting insights.

Stage 4: Drive Sustainability and Continuity through Succession Planning and Leadership Development

☐ Identify critical roles.

☐ Develop a succession planning strategy.

☐ Train and mentor future leaders.

☐ Encourage delegation and knowledge transfer.

Stage 5: Demonstrate and Maximize the Value of New Practices through Feedback, Monitoring, Evaluation, and Reporting

☐ Establish feedback mechanisms.

☐ Implement responsive leadership.

☐ Conduct regular reviews and adaptations.

☐ Monitor and evaluate implemented changes.

☐ Document successes and challenges.

Stage 6: Enhance Resilience through Institutional Culture

☐ Promote adaptability and learning.

☐ Foster open dialogue and risk-taking.

☐ Recognize change champions.

☐ Institute teamwork awards.

☐ Align performance metrics with new practices.

☐ Recognize leaders supporting high-performance systems.

Online Support Resources

To access supplementary materials, such as video tutorials, webinars, and upcoming workshops, visit us at https://nlonigeria.org/breakthroughresults/workshop

About the Workshop

The Seven Disciplines of Breakthrough Results Workshop for Public Leaders is a holistic developmental experience designed for new, aspiring, and established public sector leaders committed to delivering transformative and sustainable outcomes for their institutions and stakeholders.

The workshop offers an in-depth exploration of the seven disciplines, emphasizing their importance, applications, and real-life success stories. Participants get the chance to gain exclusive insights from the author and a distinguished faculty of researchers and facilitators, beyond the content of the book. Additionally, attendees connect with a network of like-minded leaders and experts dedicated to pioneering positive change in the public sector.

Immersing learners in a rich environment of knowledge and inspiration, the program equips participants with strategic tools, workbooks, practical frameworks, and a notable certification credential. The workshop delivers a transformative experience that challenges learners to embrace public leadership with a difference, empowers them to overcome challenges and capacitates them to deliver high-performance results for societal upliftment and increased public trust.

Glossary

1. **360-degree feedback**: Comprehensive performance feedback from various sources.

2. **Adult contract**: An implicit agreement in organizational performance signifying mutual accountability and respect between employers and employees, emphasizing the treatment of employees as responsible, autonomous adults.

3. **Breakthrough results**: Substantial and transformative changes achieved through high-performance leadership practices that significantly enhance the efficiency, effectiveness, and impact of public services.

4. **Catalog of changes**: A documented list of all changes made within an organization.

5. **Change champions**: Individuals within the organization who actively promote and facilitate the change process.

6. **Change coalition**: A group of leaders and employees who support and drive the change process.

7. **Change management**: The process of guiding and managing organizational change to achieve desired outcomes.

8. **Change register**: A centralized digital record where all key changes introduced within an organization are documented.

9. **Collaboration**: Working together cooperatively with others to achieve a common goal, often involving cross-functional teams and stakeholder engagement.

10. **Communities of practice**: Groups of individuals who share a concern or passion for something they do and learn how to do it better through regular interaction.

11. **Competence mapping**: A systematic process used to identify, assess, and document the skills, knowledge, abilities, and behaviors required for individuals to perform their roles effectively within an organization.

12. **Consequence management**: Systems and processes to reward achievements and address shortcomings within an organization.

13. **Constructive corrective measures**: Actions aimed at improving performance without being punitive.

14. **Constructive feedback**: Feedback that is specific, objective, and relevant, focusing on outcomes and behaviors to avoid defensiveness and encourage a positive response.

15. **Continuous improvement**: Ongoing efforts to improve products, services, or processes.

16. **Control groups**: Groups used for comparison in evaluations.

17. **Course correction**: Making timely adjustments to a task based on early identification of roadblocks to keep the project aligned with its goals.

18. **Cross-departmental collaboration**: Cooperation between different departments within an organization.

19. **Culture of accountability**: An environment where individuals are responsible for their actions and outcomes.

20. **Culture of earning**: An environment where rewards are based on contributions.

21. **Data integrity checks**: Processes to ensure accuracy and reliability of data.

22. **Data triangulation**: A method of validating findings by comparing information from multiple sources or methods to reduce bias and enhance reliability.

23. **Data-driven decisions**: Decisions based on data and evidence rather than intuition or guesswork.

24. **Delegate**: The discipline of empowering teams to implement strategies and achieve peak performance.

25. **Deliver**: The discipline of setting up systems and infrastructures to institutionalize high performance within organizations. This involves creating sustainable processes and frameworks to ensure ongoing success amidst leadership transitions.

26. **Design**: The discipline of translating insights from discovery and diagnosis into actionable strategies and creating structures and processes within an organization to improve performance and better align with strategic goals.

27. **Developmental potential**: A comprehensive assessment of team members' potential for future growth, identifying individuals who possess necessary skills and demonstrate a strong potential for development.

28. **Dialogue**: The discipline of effective communication that builds trust and engages both internal team members and external stakeholders.

29. **Diagnose**: The discipline of identifying root causes of organizational issues to facilitate data-driven decisions for maximum impact.

30. **Discover**: The discipline of gathering and analyzing information to inform leadership decisions, including stakeholder analysis and environmental scanning.

31. **Drive**: The discipline of establishing processes and systems to maintain momentum and ensure the execution of strategies and the achievement of tangible results.

32. **Energy management**: Regulating personal energy to maintain optimal performance.

33. **Entitlement mentality**: An attitude where individuals expect benefits based on status rather than contribution.

34. **Environmental scanning**: The process of systematically analyzing external and internal environments to identify opportunities and threats.

35. **Execution rhythm**: The discipline of managing and completing tasks using structured cycles of planning, execution, and review.

36. **Execution rhythm adherence**: Consistency in following structured performance processes.

37. **External discovery**: Systematically gathering insights and data from sources outside the organization, including stakeholders, market trends, and competitive landscapes, to inform strategic decision-making and enhance organizational responsiveness.

38. **Feedback fatigue**: Overwhelming delegates with too frequent or overly detailed feedback sessions, which can diminish the effectiveness of feedback.

39. **Financial incentives**: Monetary rewards for achieving performance targets.

40. **Goal achievement rate**: The percentage of goals successfully accomplished.

41. **High performers**: Employees who consistently exceed performance expectations.

42. **High-performance leadership**: Leadership practices that consistently achieve exceptional results and high standards of performance.

43. **High-performance systems**: Efficient and effective operational frameworks that enable public institutions to achieve their goals.

44. **Incentive plans**: Programs designed to motivate and reward employees.

45. **Information overload**: Excessive data that complicates decision-making and analysis.

46. **Inertia**: Resistance to change within an organization, often due to established habits, structures, or processes.

47. **Institutional culture**: The set of shared beliefs, values, and practices that characterize an organization.

48. **Institutional knowledge**: The collective expertise and experience accumulated within an organization over time.

49. **Institutional momentum**: The sustained progress and continuity in governance and organizational operations.

50. **Institutional resilience**: The ability of public institutions to withstand and adapt to changes and challenges.

51. **Institutionalization of practices**: The embedding of effective practices and systems within an organization to ensure continuity and consistency.

52. **Internal discovery**: Exploring and understanding the organization's internal processes, culture, and stakeholder perceptions.

53. **Iterative feedback loops**: Continuous cycles of presenting findings, gathering feedback, and refining insights to enhance accuracy and completeness.

54. **Key performance indicators (KPIs)**: Metrics used to evaluate the success of an organization or its employees.

55. **Knowledge management strategy**: A systematic approach to capturing, organizing, sharing, and evaluating knowledge within an organization. It ensures that valuable information is accessible and preserved for future use.

56. **Leadership competencies**: The skills, knowledge, and abilities required to be an effective leader.

57. **Legacy systems**: Established systems and practices that continue to drive an institution forward.

58. **Matrix**: An organizational structure that combines multiple lines of reporting, typically by function and by project, allowing for more flexibility and collaboration.

59. **Misalignment**: A state where organizational elements (such as structure, strategy, and operations) are not properly coordinated or aligned, leading to inefficiencies and obstacles in achieving goals.

60. **Modular approaches**: Breaking down complex systems or processes into smaller, interconnected components that can be easily modified or expanded.

61. **Motivational techniques**: Strategies used to inspire and encourage individuals and teams to achieve their best performance.

62. **Nimble**: The ability of an organization to respond quickly and effectively to changes or challenges in the environment.

63. **Organizational behavior**: Actions and attitudes of individuals and groups within an organization.

64. **Performance history**: Insights gained from past performance evaluations and project reports regarding a team member's reliability, work ethic, and ability to meet deadlines.

65. **Performance standards**: Benchmarks for evaluating employee performance.

66. **Positive behaviors**: Actions that contribute to organizational success.

67. **Predictability through standardization**: Ensuring consistent and reliable outcomes through standardized processes and guidelines.

68. **Process mapping**: Visual representation and analysis of workflow processes to identify inefficiencies and areas for improvement.

69. **Project management tools**: Software used to plan, organize, and manage tasks.

70. **Purpose**: The fundamental reason for the existence of an organization, often expressed in its mission and vision statements.

71. **Real-time data collection**: Gathering and analyzing data instantly as it is generated.

72. **Redesign**: The process of altering the structure, processes, or elements of an organization to improve performance and better align with strategic goals.

73. **Reporting systems**: Mechanisms for tracking progress and outcomes.

74. **Reset culture**: The tendency of new leaders to dismiss existing systems and initiatives in favor of introducing their own.

75. **Resilience**: The ability of an organization to withstand and recover quickly from challenges, disruptions, or adversity.

76. **Resistance to change**: The opposition or reluctance of individuals or groups within organizations to adopt new ideas, processes, or behaviors.

77. **Reward systems**: Mechanisms for providing incentives based on performance.

78. **Root causes**: Fundamental reasons for performance gaps.

79. **Scalability**: The capability of an organization to expand or adapt its services to meet changing demands.

80. **Self-regulation**: Controlling one's emotions and behaviors.

81. **Siloed mindsets**: Departmental barriers that hinder information sharing and collaboration.

82. **Skill gaps**: Lack of expertise or training in conducting effective discovery and analysis.

83. **Skill inventory**: A systematic record of the skills, qualifications, and experience of all the employees within an organization.

84. **Soft skills**: Personality traits and interpersonal skills that can be crucial for task success and team dynamics.

85. **Stakeholder analysis**: The process of identifying and understanding the needs and expectations of all stakeholders involved in or affected by leadership decisions.

86. **Stakeholder mapping and engagement**: Identifying and categorizing key stakeholders based on their influence and interests, and actively involving them in the discovery process.

87. **Standard operating procedures (SOPs)**: Detailed, written instructions designed to achieve uniformity in the performance of specific functions.

88. **Standardized reporting formats**: Consistent methods for collecting and presenting data.

89. **Strategic alignment**: The arrangement of organizational elements (such as structure, processes, and culture) to ensure they work together harmoniously toward achieving strategic goals.

90. **Strategic priorities**: Key focus areas that align with organizational goals.

91. **Structures**: The formal arrangement of roles, responsibilities, and relationships within an organization.

92. **Succession planning strategy**: A plan for identifying and developing future leaders to ensure continuity.

93. **Sustainable success**: Long-term achievement and impact that can be maintained and built upon over time.

94. **Sustainability**: The ability to maintain or improve organizational performance over the long term without depleting resources or causing negative impacts.

95. **Tailored reporting dashboards**: Customized tools for displaying relevant performance data.

96. **Team dynamics**: Interactions and relationships within a team.

97. **Transformative leadership**: Leadership that brings about significant change and improvement within an organization or community.

98. **Transparency in selection**: Clearly communicating why an individual was chosen for a task, highlighting their strengths and the trust the organization has in their capabilities.

99. **Turnover rates**: The rate at which employees leave an organization.

100. **Underperformance**: Failure to meet performance expectations.

101. **Value-creation process**: The continuous improvement and enhancement of organizational practices to achieve and exceed goals.

102. **Visible scoreboards:** Tools that display progress towards goals.

About the Author

Dr. Bolaji Olagunju is a seasoned High-Performance Leadership and Organisational Development Expert, Strategic Advisor, Coach, and Mentor to prominent leaders and some of the most notable public and private institutions in Africa, with a track record of major accomplishments across several industries and sectors.

He is the Founder & Executive Chairman of Workforce Group, an indigenous firm that has helped Public Leaders, Heads of Government Institutions, CEOs, Senior HR Executives, Chief Learning Officers, and Heads of Strategy across Africa improve their performance effectiveness and achieve strategic results over the last 20 years.

Prior to assuming the role of Executive Chairman, he played a pivotal role in the company's accelerated growth and transformation over his 15-year tenure as CEO. During this period, Workforce Group evolved from a startup with a single line of business operating out of a 10-square-meter borrowed office to become a leading player with operations in 30 African countries, a 10,000-square-meter headquarters, and over 10,000 employees under management.

His extensive experience in advising leaders across the private and public sectors, helping them achieve distinctive advantages, coupled with his passion and commitment to building high-performance leadership capability in the nation, singled him out for his current appointment as the Director-General of the National Leadership Organisation, a social enterprise dedicated to transforming the nation by fostering effective leadership, enhancing institutional capacity, promoting a culture of collective contribution, and empowering citizens with essential skills and opportunities for growth. Under his leadership, the National Leadership Organisation champions initiatives for National Public Leadership Excellence, National Capacity Building Excellence, National Philanthropy Activation, and National Empowerment with clear and compelling impact targets.

Dr. Bolaji has always been at the forefront, exemplifying and advocating for tangible and intangible collective contributions and societal generosity to empower future generations. In the last 20 years, he has contributed significantly to building human capacity, increasing employability, and facilitating employment creation in Nigeria. He has left indelible footprints on the sands of time through several impact projects and initiatives, coaching and mentoring of strategic leaders & impact makers, and facilitation of local job opportunities through offshoring. His approach has always been centered on the redefinition of sustainability—meeting the needs of the present without compromising, but rather strengthening, the ability of future generations to meet their own needs.

Dr. Olagunju is a renowned author of several bestselling books and insightful publications that provide practical guidance and valuable lessons. Some of his books include *The 7 Disciplines of Breakthrough Results for Public Sector Leaders, Hiring Right, You Must Become a Trainer,* and *Own, Don't Owe Your Future.*

He holds a Doctorate degree in Human Resource Management and Leadership. He is an alumnus of Harvard Kennedy School of Government, London Business School, and has attended several programs in leading universities all over the world, including Berkeley Haas School of Business, Columbia Business School, Michigan Ross Business School, Kellogg School of Management, and UNC Kenan-Flagler Business School.

www.ingramcontent.com/pod-product-compliance
Lightning Source LLC
Chambersburg PA
CBHW041207220326
41597CB00030BA/5073